From Nothing

From Nothing

A Theology of Creation

IAN A. MCFARLAND

WESTMINSTER
JOHN KNOX PRESS
LOUISVILLE · KENTUCKY

© 2014 Ian A. McFarland

First edition
Published by Westminster John Knox Press
Louisville, Kentucky

14 15 16 17 18 19 20 21 22 23—10 9 8 7 6 5 4 3 2 1

Except as otherwise indicated, Scripture quotations are from the New Revised Standard Version of the Bible, copyright © 1989 by the Division of Christian Education of the National Council of the Churches of Christ in the U.S.A., and are used by permission.

Book design by Sharon Adams
Cover design by Dilu Nicholas
Urban Jungle © KC Fonts Desktop License for Pubication

Library of Congress Cataloging-in-Publication Data

McFarland, Ian A. (Ian Alexander), 1963–
    From nothing : a theology of creation / Ian A. McFarland.
       pages cm
    Includes bibliographical references and indexes.
    ISBN 978-0-664-23819-3 (alk. paper)
    1. Creation. I. Title.
    BT695.M44 2014
    231.7'65—dc23
                                        2013049525

♾ The paper used in this publication meets the minimum requirements
of the American National Standard for Information Sciences—
Permanence of Paper for Printed Library Materials, ANSI Z39.48-1992.

Conlegis meis in schola divinitatis
collegii regii
universitatis Aberdonensis
MCMXCVIII–MMV
cum gratia in memoria et remuneratione honoris et amicitiarum

Contents

Preface

Most of my previous writing has focused on theological anthropology, or the Christian doctrine of human being. I was drawn to this topic by what seemed to me a persistent problem in the tradition: how to affirm the fundamental equality of all human beings under God (including the very practice of speaking of "humanity" as a single reality) while ascribing genuine theological significance to the differences that mark human beings as distinct individuals before God and one another. Over against approaches that either dismiss differences as irrelevant to our humanity or, worse, interpret them as indices of human inequality, I have argued that difference is central to human life before God, because God calls each human being to a different place within the body of Christ. Human beings are therefore equal in that they are all called by God to be persons in Christ (so that their equality is grounded extrinsically in God rather than in any intrinsic attribute or property they possess); but they differ in that they are called to enact that personhood in distinct and unsubstitutable ways. All are called to live under Christ, the one head, but no two people occupy the same place in the body.

I continue to view this account of God's relationship to humanity as fundamentally sound; yet in isolation from a broader theology of creation, it runs the risk of reducing Christ's significance to purely human terms and thus of failing to take into account the cosmic scope of redemption. In Romans 8, for example, Paul certainly ascribes a distinctive role to human beings as those who have been called to be children of God (vv. 15–17; cf. John 1:11–13), but he also declares that the eschatological revelation of God's (human) children will have redemptive significance for the whole (nonhuman) creation, which "will be set free from its bondage to decay and will obtain the freedom of the glory of the children of God" (v. 21). An equally remarkable statement of the cosmic scope of God's concern is found in the Psalms:

> Your steadfast love, O LORD, extends to the heavens,
>   your faithfulness to the clouds.
> Your righteousness is like the mighty mountains,
>   your judgments are like the great deep;
>   you save humans and animals alike, O LORD.
>   (Ps. 36:5–6)

Here God's care encompasses the whole of the created order, with animals mentioned explicitly as the focus of God's saving activity alongside human beings. So elsewhere in Scripture the promise of "a new heaven and a new earth" (Rev. 21:1; cf. Isa. 65:17; 66:22; 2 Pet. 3:13), in which renewal extends to the nonhuman realm (Isa. 11:6; 65:25), warns against an anthropocentrism that restricts the scope of God's love—and the promise of glory—to humanity. Indeed, even from a purely anthropological perspective, the promise of bodily resurrection suggests some enduring relationship between human beings and the nonhuman creation, since it is precisely our bodies that link us human beings ontologically to the rest of the terrestrial creation—air, water, plants, and animals—from which we draw sustenance and apart from which we can neither flourish nor survive. The Lutheran theologian Joseph Sittler made this point eloquently:

> Because men exist and are as relational entities, only a redemption *among* can be a real redemption. Only, that is to say, when the meaning and act of redemption is within the web of creation can a salvable identity be "saved" in any sense that makes sense. . . . In a bluntly human sense *my* redemption must include the possibility of redemption of everything.[1]

To be sure, the fate of the nonhuman creatures remains a marginal theme in the Bible. It is, after all, a book addressed to human beings and, as such, maintains a natural focus on human affairs and humanity's own peculiar predicaments. When sustained attention is given to the nonhuman realm, the overall effect is to suggest humanity's incapacity to do much more than gesture toward its mysterious character. For example, in speaking to Job out of the whirlwind, God stresses the deep incomprehensibility of the ways of other animals; and Scripture is still more reticent when it comes to spiritual beings, whose role in creation is even less subject to human reckoning. These features of the biblical witness suggest that to a very large extent the nature and destiny of the nonhuman creation is simply none of our business. And yet not entirely, for it is the task of human beings not only to care for the land in which God has placed them (Gen. 2:15; cf. Deut. 26:1–11), but also to exercise dominion over the whole of the animal kingdom (Gen. 1:26, 28; Ps. 8:6–8)—even if human beings' evident

---

1. Joseph Sittler, *Evocations of Grace: The Writings of Joseph Sittler on Ecology, Theology, and Ethics*, ed. Steven Bouma-Prediger and Peter Bakken (Grand Rapids: Wm. B. Eerdmans Publishing Co., 2000), 178–79. Cf. Allan D. Galloway, *The Cosmic Christ* (New York: Harper & Brothers, 1951), 205.

equality in difference.

confusion and incapacity in the face of the bewildering complexity of the created order casts doubt on their ability to fulfill that mandate. Here, too, humanity's destiny seems bound up in some way with that of all other creatures—heavenly and earthly, living and nonliving, vegetable and animal—that together with humanity constitute a whole that God judges "very good" (Gen. 1:31).

In what follows I address the issue of the connection of the human and the nonhuman by arguing that the emphasis on God's action that I have used as the theological basis for affirming human equality-in-difference can be applied, mutatis mutandis, to creation as a whole. In making this argument, I do not seek to show that all creatures are equal in the same way that all human beings are. Even apart from passages like 1 Corinthians 9:9,[2] Scripture's talk of human dominion over other animals and of humanity's seemingly unique call to the status of God's children raises difficult questions for a strong assertion of creaturely equality across species (though possibly no more difficult than those raised for the idea of human equality by passages like 1 Corinthians 11:3–7 and 1 Timothy 2:11–15). I will, however, want to insist quite pedantically on the point that there is one, absolutely fundamental respect in which all creatures are equal: in the fact that they are *created.* Within traditional Christian discourse this claim is significant because to be created is to have been brought into being by God "from nothing" (*ex nihilo* in Latin), and therefore to be absolutely distinct from God, who is uncreated. This means that the creation is not properly conceived as a great chain of being, in which angels, humans, animals, plants, minerals, and so forth constitute a scale in which the former members are ontologically closer to God and the latter farther removed. On the contrary, the classical Christian doctrine of creation suggests that the most theologically significant thing that can be said about any creature is simply that it is not God and, as such, no closer to or farther from God than any other creature. Since all creatures have God as their sole source and condition of existence, all of them—from the angel in heaven to the slime at the bottom of the septic tank—are equally near to (or far from) God. It follows that a crucial measure of our commitment to love God as Creator of all things is our willingness to honor God's commitment to the flourishing of all creatures by "our readiness . . . to challenge and resist the making or remaking of exclusions or inequalities in creation."[3]

This fundamental equality of all creatures, as derived from the doctrine of creation from nothing, is the ground for what will emerge as one of this book's themes: that Christian teaching about creation is more idiosyncratic than is generally recognized. It is not my experience (at least within my own North Atlantic context) that people—whether or not they identify themselves as Christian—think that the doctrine of creation from nothing is especially striking or odd in its implications for how we view the world. On the contrary, in the realms of apologetics and interreligious dialogue alike, the doctrine of creation is often

2. "For it is written in the law of Moses, 'You shall not muzzle an ox when it is treading out the grain.' Is it for oxen that God is concerned?"

3. Rowan Williams, *On Christian Theology* (Oxford: Blackwell, 2000), 76.

treated as something of a "forecourt of the Gentiles," a means by which Christians can find common theological ground with non-Christians at a generous remove from the more knotty questions associated with topics like atonement, original sin, or the Trinity. Even among Christianity's atheist critics, the doctrine of creation tends not to be regarded as unusual. It may be rejected as irrational or incredible, but it tends to be viewed as very much part of the standard furniture of "religious" discourse—not least, I suspect, because Christians, too, often treat it that way.

Religious traditions the world over and extending as far back in time as written records extend have "creation stories," accounts of how the present world order came to be. Their content is quite varied. In some cases the central theme is violence, in which the world and its denizens are manufactured by the gods from the corpse of some primeval monster (e.g., the Babylonian epic *Enuma Elish*, which may also lie behind the Greek myth of humanity made from the remains of the Titans). In others, the stories have a more naturalistic cast, in which the world is birthed from a cosmic egg (e.g., certain Hindu and Taoist traditions, the Finnish *Kalevala*), or is understood as an emanation from the divine (Plotinus's *Enneads*, Jewish kabbalistic thought). Notwithstanding these significant differences, however, all these cosmogonies share the presupposition of a fundamental ontological continuity between Creator and creature: the world and its inhabitants derive from divinity in such a way that the visible cosmos includes traces of divinity, however obscure or deformed these may be.[4]

The Christian Bible, arising as it did in the midst of a religiously diverse region over a long period of time, retains something of this range of imagery. The Old Testament contains a number of references to Israel's God as the one who defeated the ancient sea serpent, much as the Babylonian god Marduk slew the dragon Tiamat (Job 26:12; Ps. 89:10; Isa. 51:9). Less explicitly but no less significantly, the image of the wind or spirit of God moving over the primordial waters may echo the imagery of the mother bird brooding over its eggs (Gen. 1:2; cf. Deut. 32:11–12; Matt. 23:37 and par.; cf. *4 Ezra* = 2 Esd. 1:30). And descriptions of God's own Spirit as the source of created life (Gen. 2:7; Ps. 104:30) are at least suggestive of emanationist ontologies in which the visible world is in some sense continuous with the divine. Nevertheless, with extraordinary rapidity the early church rejected the claim that such language had anything other than purely metaphorical significance, insisting instead on

---

4. What Kathryn Tanner says of Greek and Roman religion can to this extent be applied more generally: "Divinity refers to a kind of being distinct from others within the matrix of the same cosmos. . . . As a distinct sort of being differentiated from others, like any other kind, within the same spectrum of being making up the cosmos, divinity is a predicate determined by commonality and susceptible of difference: it is the sort of thing which can be said to be shared generically with specifying differences of degree." Kathryn Tanner, *God and Creation in Christian Theology: Tyranny or Empowerment?* (Oxford: Basil Blackwell, 1988), 39.

the radical ontological discontinuity between Creator and creature encapsulated in the doctrine of creation from nothing.[5]

Of course, Christianity is not the only tradition to affirm creation from nothing, which is also upheld by Jews and Muslims. While creation from nothing seems to have been less settled in Judaism in particular than it was in Christianity prior to the modern period, the doctrine remains a significant point of agreement among the three Abrahamic faiths—to the extent that it was singled out by the great medieval Jewish thinker Moses Maimonides as the only doctrine the three held in common.[6] And although each tradition followed its own distinctive path in arriving at the doctrine, there was in the medieval period significant cross-fertilization among Jewish, Christian, and Muslim thinkers on the metaphysics of creation and its implications for human freedom in particular.[7] Be that as it may, I argue that the church's doctrine of creation from nothing is best understood in the context of the specifically Christian doctrine of the Trinity and, still more specifically, as a corollary of the belief that Christ is the one in whom all things were created (Col. 1:16) and apart from whom nothing was made that was made (John 1:3).

The argument I make in support of this position begins in chapter 1 with a basic orientation to the Christian doctrine of creation from nothing. This survey includes reflection on the lack of explicit biblical support for this teaching, its emergence in the latter half of the second century CE, and contemporary challenges to its coherence. The rest of the book is divided into two parts that together constitute a more detailed exposition of the doctrine. Part 1 focuses on the claim that the world originates in God, undertaken through a sequential exegesis of the statement "God creates from nothing," over the course of three chapters that explore, respectively, the meaning of "God," "creates," and "from nothing." Part 2 explores the ways in which God is also the world's goal and end through an examination of evil (that which runs counter to God's will for the world), providence (God's interaction with creation), and glory (the consummation of God's creative work). Because the conceptual territory covered by these two parts corresponds more or less to the Christian vision of the world as both emerging from and moving toward God, I have given the two parts the classic Latin superscriptions *exitus* (outflow) and *reditus* (return). In line with this distinction, part 1 focuses on creation's rootedness in God's life, while part

5. Although Thomas Aquinas characterizes creation as emanation in *Summa theologiae* 1.45, he uses the word as a neutral term for "emergence," and not to describe an automatic process whereby God produces a world that is in any way ontologically continuous with the divine.

6. For Maimonides, see Janet M. Soskice, "*Creatio ex Nihilo*: Its Jewish and Christian foundations," in *Creation and the God of Abraham*, ed. David B, Burrell et al. (Cambridge: Cambridge University Press, 2011), 24. For the debates within Judaism on the "ex nihilo," see Seymour Feldman, "'In the Beginning God Created': A Philosophical Midrash," in *God and Creation: An Ecumenical Symposium*, ed. David B. Burrell and Bernard McGinn (Notre Dame, IN: University of Notre Dame Press, 1990), 3–26; and more extensively, Norbert M. Samuelson, *Judaism and the Doctrine of Creation* (Cambridge: Cambridge University Press, 1994).

7. See David B. Burrell's two books, *Faith and Freedom: An Interfaith Perspective* (Oxford: Blackwell, 2004) and *Towards a Jewish-Christian-Muslim Theology* (Oxford: Wiley-Blackwell, 2011).

2 regards creation from the perspective of its existence over against God. The Trinitarian and christological dimensions of the doctrine are, correspondingly, more evident in the first part of the book. They are less prominent in the second half, not because God's creative work becomes any less triune when considered in light of creation's "return" to God, but rather because the classical principle that the external works of the Trinity are undivided (*opera Trinitatis ad extra indivisa sunt*) means that the distinct roles of the divine persons in preserving, empowering, and directing creation to its divinely intended end are not immediately open to creaturely perception.

This thematic shift from creation's rootedness *in* God to the contours of its existence *under* God is further reflected in the way that the chapters that make up part 2 take up in inverse order the topics introduced in part 1. Thus the reality of evil examined in chapter 5 is a paradox inseparable from the analysis of the phrase "from nothing" in chapter 4; likewise chapter 6's discussion of providence takes up the implications of divine "creating" as laid out in chapter 3; and the reflections on glory in chapter 7 bring the discussion back to the character of the Creator, which is the subject of chapter 2. This chiastic structure should not, however, be understood as charting a historical narrative, as though the chapters of part 1 cast the world's emergence from God as a sequential process, and those of part 2 a parallel (if inverse) process of return. Even the shift from providence to glory in the book's final two chapters does not correspond in a straightforward way to a movement in time from present to future, and the succession of topics in the earlier chapters is even less a matter of temporal sequence. For while it is true, according to the doctrine of creation from nothing, that evil is logically subsequent to creation even as God is logically prior to creation, the movement from God to creation to the topics of nothing and evil in chapters 2 through 5 is better understood as the successive examination of a single idea from different perspectives—the exploration of various facets or aspects of the Christian belief in creation as a reality that is distinct-from-yet-originating-in God—than as a historical narrative of how the world came to assume its current form.

This nontemporal structure points to a fundamental theological presupposition that shapes my analysis of creation. Although it is true that throughout the history of the church the overwhelming majority of Christians have understood "creation" as referring to a historical event (equivalent to what contemporary cosmologists identify as $t = 0$), and that most current discussion of "creation" in the public sphere turns on the dating of this putative event, it seems to me that the Christian doctrine of creation is only marginally concerned with the question of the world's temporal origin. Far more fundamentally, the doctrine of creation from nothing is a proposal about the character of God's relationship to the world. As David Kelsey observed more than thirty years ago, the doctrinal claim that the world had a temporal beginning is at bottom a question about biblical interpretation that, while certainly significant in its own right, has no bearing on the issues of God's transcendence, immanence, and sovereignty that lie at the heart of the doctrine of creation from nothing.[8] To put it in a nutshell, it is my contention that while the Christian confession of the lordship of Christ is inseparable from the doctrine of creation from nothing, it is completely unaffected by the scientific question of whether or not (let alone when) the world had a temporal beginning.[9] I will thus have very little to say about the question of beginnings, not because I find it uninteresting, but because I do not believe that it is of decisive significance for the Christian belief that God created the world from nothing.

A second way in which theologies of creation sometimes intersect with contemporary scientific discourse has to do with ecological questions. Here there is more overlap with this project, which shares with contemporary ecological theologies the concern that Christian reflection on creation has been so overwhelmingly anthropocentric in character that it has failed to take seriously God's love for and commitment to the well-being of all creatures, with disastrous consequences for the natural environment. In contrast to many others motivated by this concern, however, in what follows I do not offer a theology of nature and,

8. Kelsey reports that in the medieval period "the claim about an absolute origination of the world was included in the doctrine of creation . . . solely on the grounds that . . . it is taught by Scripture. Debates about the validity of the contrary view, that the world is eternal, were conducted as philosophical arguments. Nobody argued that any other part of the doctrine, or any other Christian doctrine, would be undercut were Aristotle's view [that the world is eternal] to be validated." David H. Kelsey, "The Doctrine of Creation from Nothing," in *Evolution and Creation*, ed. Ernan McMullin (Notre Dame, IN: University of Notre Dame Press, 1985), 184. For a still more extensive evaluation of the question of the logical relationship between belief in creation from nothing and belief in t = 0, see Donald D. Evans, *The Logic of Self-Involvement: A Philosophical Study of Everyday Language with Special Reference to the Christian Use of Language about God as Creator* (London: SCM Press, 1963), 242–49.

9. Those who affirm the doctrinal importance of t = 0 tend to do so on the grounds that the admission of any error in the Bible undermines its authority (i.e., if Scripture cannot be relied upon in matters of cosmology, neither can its claims about Jesus be trusted). Leaving aside the (to me very doubtful) exegetical claim that the opening chapters of Genesis are properly understood as history along the lines of the books of Samuel, Thucydides, or Macaulay, the claim that the trustworthiness of the gospel is predicated on biblical inerrancy only follows if one confuses Scripture with God. Scripture itself is the best antidote to such bibliolatry, since though it has to do with nothing less than the "gospel of God" (Rom. 1:1), it gives us that "treasure in earthen vessels" (2 Cor. 4:7 KJV), so that we find in it no "Gospel according to God," but rather the Gospel according to Matthew, Mark, Luke, and John; no "Prophecy of God," but of Amos, Isaiah, and Jeremiah; no "Acts of God," but the Acts of the Apostles; no "Letters of God," but those of Paul and Peter and James and Jude. That such writers, though "inspired by God," might have made some incorrect statements with respect to matters of history, astronomy, mathematics, and the like should no more undermine confidence that their works are "useful for teaching, for reproof, for correction, and for training in righteousness" (2 Tim. 3:16) than my surgeon's ascribing a painting of Raphael's to Da Vinci or claiming that the sun's surface temperature is 50,000 degrees Celsius makes me doubt her competence to remove my appendix. The idea that biblical authority is (as the authors of "The Chicago Statement on Biblical Inerrancy" argue) an all-or-nothing affair suggests a kind of epistemological neurosis far more indebted to Descartes than to the classical Christian tradition. My reliance on a gas station attendant to help me find an address in a strange town is not predicated on any sort of global confidence in his knowledge, but on the assumption that a resident will be a reliable guide to the local geography. Similarly, when I rely on Paul's Letters for my doctrine of justification, it is not because I view them as incapable of containing errors of any sort, but because in this matter their status as Scripture gives them authority.

in fact, do not make much use of the term "nature" in my analysis. This decision is based on two considerations. First, in colloquial English "nature" is often defined by contrast with "culture" in a way that tends to reenforce the anthropocentrism that I want to resist (as though "nature" referred to the nonhuman creation only, rather than encompassing all creatures, including human beings). Second, within the history of theology "nature" has sometimes been used to refer to the existence and operations of creatures in abstraction from God's grace (most notoriously, in the late Scholastic category of *natura pura*). Since it is a central feature of my argument that the created order is at every point sustained and empowered in its existence entirely and exclusively by God's grace, I try to avoid speaking of "nature" in order to forestall the inference that creation enjoys any degree of ontological autonomy vis-à-vis God.

A further, final caution has to do with clarifying the scope of a Christian doctrine of creation. The sheer range of material associated with the topic may, perhaps unavoidably, suggest to the reader that I am presenting a (or worse, *the*) "Christian worldview." This is emphatically not my intention. On the contrary, I operate under the presupposition that there is no such thing as a "Christian worldview," if by that is meant a particular way that all Christians, by virtue of their commitment to the gospel of Jesus Christ, understand the basic structure of the cosmos, history, and society. Even a cursory glance at the Christian tradition demonstrates that Christians have found it possible to preach the gospel while holding a wide array of worldviews, and moreover, that explicitly tying Christianity to a particular worldview (whether Aristotelian metaphysics and cosmology, or Romantic notions of cultural evolution and social progress) has often proved more a hindrance than a help in preserving the integrity of that confession over time. The point of the present volume is therefore not to generate a cosmological picture that Christians are supposed to keep in their heads as a framework within which to interpret reality. Part of the force of the argument will, indeed, be that any such comprehensive picture of things is likely to prove inadequate to the full range of Christian convictions about God's relationship to the world. Instead, the exposition of the belief in creation from nothing offered here serves the more modest function of suggesting some of the parameters governing the confession that Christians are called to make, whatever worldview may be in vogue at the time.

As is true of any book, this one has been shaped by conversation as much as research, and I am correspondingly grateful to the many people who have helped shape my thought. My approach to the subject finds its deepest roots in talks about creation with my former teachers, David Kelsey and Kathryn Tanner, and my former colleague, David Fergusson. More recently, Don McKim's invitation to produce the reader *Creation and Humanity* for Westminster John Knox's Sources of Christian Theology series provided the impetus for my undertaking this project, and I am grateful to him, David Dobson, and (especially) Bob

Ratcliff and Daniel Braden, who shepherded this manuscript through various stages of the publication process, for their support.

My colleagues in the Theological Studies program of Emory University's Graduate Division of Religion provided helpful feedback on several chapters. Mention must also be made of the members of my spring 2012 seminar, "Encountering God: Case Studies in the Material Mediation of Grace," who read an early draft of this text. I am thankful both for the grace with which they responded to the awkward task of being asked to comment on a professor's manuscript, and for their thoughtful comments on the substance of my argument. Finally, I owe a special debt of gratitude to my research assistant, Amaryah Armstrong, who undertook the supremely boring task of checking the footnotes, and to S. David Garber at Westminster John Knox for an extraordinarily meticulous job of copyediting. However many things may justly be said against what I have written here, their number would be far greater but for these contributions.

1

Introduction

In about the year 180 a Christian bishop, about whom we know very little, wrote the following to a pagan about whom we know even less: "God brought everything into being out of what does not exist, so that his greatness might be known and understood through his works."[1] To contemporary eyes, these words of Theophilus of Antioch may seem thoroughly unexceptional as a piece of Christian teaching, but at the time they represented something new: a doctrine of creation from nothing.

In the preface I recognized that while creation stories are found the world over, they typically describe the world's origins in terms of the reordering of already-existing material, whether through a process of birth, manipulation, emanation, conflict, or chance rearrangement. As the church moved into its second century, it was not self-evident that Christianity would break from this pattern. In the decades before Theophilus wrote, other Christians had been quite happy to endorse Plato's description of creation as God's ordering of unformed

---

1. Theophilus of Antioch, *To Autolycus* 1.4, in Patrologia graeca (hereafter PG), 6:1029B. An English translation is in vol. 2 of *The Ante-Nicene Fathers* (hereafter *ANF*), ed. Alexander Roberts and James Donaldson, 10 vols. (1867–73 [Edinburgh]; 1885–96 [American ed.]; repr., Grand Rapids: Wm. B. Eerdmans Publishing Co., 1975–; Peabody, MA: Hendrickson Publishers, 1994–).

matter.[2] Theophilus, however, did not find this position compatible with what he took to be basic Christian convictions regarding God's sovereignty: "But how is it great, if God made the universe out of pre-existing material? For a human craftsman, too, when he obtains material from someone, makes from it whatever he wishes. But the power of God is made manifest in this: that he makes whatever he wishes out of what does not exist."[3]

If God is to be confessed as Lord without qualification, then everything that is not God must depend on God for its existence without qualification. Otherwise, whatever realities existed independently of God would constitute a limit on God's ability to realize God's will in creation, in the same way that the properties of wood constrain the creative possibilities open to the carpenter. Because Theophilus refused to acknowledge any such limits, he concluded that creation cannot be thought of as God reshaping some preexisting material in the manner of a human artisan who, in making a pot from clay or bread from flour, creates *from something else*. Instead, God brings into being the very stuff of which the universe is made. In short, God creates *from nothing*.

EXEGETICAL DIFFICULTIES

That the doctrine of creation from nothing (*ex nihilo*) was something of a novelty in late second-century Christian circles may seem surprising. Much more than the Trinity or later teachings about the person of Christ, modern readers tend to take it for granted that creation from nothing is firmly grounded in Scripture. Certainly that was Theophilus's opinion:

> Therefore, in order that God might be known truly through [God's] works, and that [we should know that] God made the heaven and the earth and all that is in them by his Word, [Moses] says, "In the beginning God created heaven and earth." And then, after speaking of their creation, he explains to us, "The earth was invisible and unformed, and darkness was over the deep, and the Spirit of God moved over the waters." So Holy Scripture teaches this first of all: how the matter, from which God made and shaped the universe, itself came to be and was brought into being by God.[4]

Unfortunately, things are not so simple. Earlier in the second century, the Christian teacher Justin Martyr had commended Plato's description of creation as God's shaping of preexisting matter precisely on the grounds that it agreed with Genesis—and even argued that Plato had taken his account from Moses![5]

---

2. Plato's account is found in the dialogue *Timaeus*, esp. 27D–30C.

3. Theophilus, *To Autolycus* 2.4, in PG 6:1052B; cf. Irenaeus of Lyons, *Against Heresies* 2.10.4, in *ANF* 1:370.

4. Theophilus, *To Autolycus* 2.10, in PG 6:1065B. Like most early Christian writers, Theophilus quotes the Greek translation of the Jewish Scriptures known as the Septuagint (LXX).

5. Justin Martyr, *First Apology* 59, in *Early Christian Fathers*, ed. Cyril C. Richardson (New York: Collier, 1970), 280–81; cf. 270, which contains further discussion of Plato's dependence on Moses.

Perhaps still more significantly, although Theophilus's reading of the Bible's opening verses has carried the day among Christians for most of the last two millennia, many contemporary biblical scholars are more inclined to side with Justin.

Theophilus followed the grammar of the ancient Greek translation of the Hebrew Scriptures known as the Septuagint (as have most subsequent English translations) and so took the first verse of Genesis as a separate sentence, describing the opening phase of God's creative activity: the bringing into being of the basic substance of heaven and earth. The second verse, on this reading, offers a more detailed description of the state of the earth at this point in the creative process: a disordered mass surrounded by darkness. While this understanding of the Hebrew of Genesis 1:1–2 evidently commended itself to the Jewish translators who produced the Septuagint (as well as to the Masoretes who punctuated the modern Hebrew text[6]), many contemporary exegetes agree with the medieval Jewish commentator Rashi that the first verse of Genesis is better rendered as a dependent clause of a sentence that includes all of 1:1–3. According to this approach, the more accurate translation is: "When God began to create heaven and earth—the world being then a formless waste, with darkness over the deep and only an awesome wind sweeping over the face of the waters—God said, 'Let there be light'; and there was light."[7]

This reading implies that in creation God works on some sort of already-existing stuff: a watery deep enveloping a formless world. Though this swirling mass is not personified in the narrative, it is hard to avoid the impression that it is in some sense resistant to God's will; philologists have called attention to the etymological links between the Hebrew word for "deep," *těhôm*, and Tiamat, the chaos-dragon from whose corpse the world is constructed in the Babylonian creation epic, *Enuma Elish.* However envisioned, the idea of a "formless waste" already present to God as the raw material for God's creative activity is clearly more consistent with Justin's Platonic picture of creation as the shaping of pre-existing matter than with Theophilus's doctrine of creation from nothing.

While there remain many defenders of the more traditional rendering of Genesis 1:1 ("In the beginning God created the heaven and the earth" [KJV]), the unusual grammar of the Hebrew makes the prospect of a definitive judgment on the verse's meaning unlikely.[8] Nor do other passages from the Old

6. See Claus Westermann, *Genesis 1–11: A Commentary*, trans. John J. Scullion, SJ (1974; repr., Minneapolis: Augsburg Publishing House, 1984), 94.

7. Ephraim Avigdor Speiser, *Genesis* (Garden City, NY: Doubleday, 1964), 3, with trans. slightly alt.; cf. the commentary on 12. The Common English Bible is almost identical to Speiser; the translators of the NRSV follow his construal of the grammar in Gen. 1:1–2 but begin a new sentence with v. 3.

8. Terence Fretheim outlines four grammatically possible readings of the text in *God and the World in the Old Testament: A Relational Theology of Creation* (Nashville: Abingdon Press, 2005), 35. He himself concludes that v. 1 is best taken as an independent sentence, following Brevard Childs (*Myth and Reality in the Old Testament* [London: SCM Press, 1960], 30–42) and Westermann (*Genesis 1–11*, 93–101).

Testament provide a clear solution to the ambiguity of the Genesis text. On the one hand, there are passages (e.g., Job 26:12–13; Pss. 74:12–14; 89:10–11; Isa. 51:9) that seem to echo the *Enuma Elish*, with its story of God engaged in a primordial battle with a sea serpent. On the other, texts like Isaiah 45:7 and Psalm 148:4–6 suggest that even the watery powers of chaos were made by God.[9] The fact is that the work of creation is simply not the subject of much focused reflection in the Old Testament canon. The biblical writers, whether deploying the dramatic language of combat or the more sober imagery of God speaking the cosmos into existence (see Ps. 33:6–9 alongside Gen. 1), clearly wish to affirm God's sovereignty over the world, but show no particular interest in the metaphysical question of whether absolutely everything has its sole point of origin in God. It should therefore come as no surprise that when Greek thought began to influence Jewish thinking in the intertestamental period, the author of the Wisdom of Solomon had no problem affirming in good Platonist fashion that God had "created the world out of formless matter" (11:17).

There are, however, a small set of passages that appear at first glance to provide firmer biblical ground for the idea of creation from nothing. The oldest of these is found in another intertestamental book, which reports how a Jewish mother encouraged her son to remain faithful in the face of torture by appealing to God's power to bring even the dead to life: "I beg you, my child, to look at the heaven and the earth and see everything that is in them, and recognize that God did not make them out of things that existed [*ouk ex ontōn*]" (2 Macc. 7:28).[10] In the New Testament Paul draws a similar connection between God's power to bring the dead to life and the doctrine of creation, praising Abraham's faith in the God "who gives life to the dead and calls into existence the things that do not exist [*ta mē onta*]" (Rom. 4:17). And finally, the author of Hebrews teaches as a matter of faith that "the worlds were prepared by the word of God, so that what is seen was made from things that are not visible [*to mē ek phainomenōn*]" (11:3).

Although these three passages all seem to provide support for a biblical doctrine of creation out of nothing, closer examination suggests that such appearances are misleading. Like most of the references to God's creative work in the Old Testament, these later texts speak of creation only in passing, as part of a broader appeal to divine power and trustworthiness. None of them can be read as part of an explicit theology of creation. Beyond these contextual considerations, moreover, is the question of just what creation "from things that do not exist/are not visible" means in these passages. The grammar and vocabulary are indeed very close to Theophilus's claim that God creates "whatever he wishes

---

9. In *Genesis Rabbah* 1.9, Rabbi Gamaliel II cites these two texts, among others, in order to refute the contention that God made the world out of preexistent materials (viz., the darkness and waters of Gen. 1:2) not themselves made by God. Jacob Neusner, *Genesis Rabbah: The Judaic Commentary to the Book of Genesis; A New American Translation*, vol. 1 (Atlanta: Scholars Press, 1985), 13.

10. Here, as elsewhere, biblical translations are taken from the NRSV unless otherwise indicated. While 2 Maccabees and the Wisdom of Solomon are classed as Apocrypha by Protestants, both are part of the Septuagint and, as such, would have been treated as canonical Scripture by most Christians in the first centuries, as they still are in the Catholic and Orthodox churches.

out of what does not exist [*ex ouk ontōn*]."[11] Absent the kind of explicit contrast that Theophilus draws with the Platonist scheme of creation from preexisting matter, however, such language cannot be taken as evidence of belief in creation from nothing, because external evidence suggests that it is a Greek idiom used for the coming into being of anything new (e.g., children from their parents), without any implication for whether or not this new thing is derived from any preexisting substance.[12] Therefore, although these passages are certainly consistent with later language of creation from nothing, they cannot be taken as evidence that the doctrine is explicitly taught in Scripture. Its emergence in the work of Theophilus and others is a response to a set of theological challenges not confronted by the biblical writers.

THE ORIGINS OF THE DOCTRINE

In his detailed study of the emergence of the idea of creation from nothing in the early church, Gerhard May asserts that the "driving motive which underlies the Christian doctrine of *creatio ex nihilo* is the attempt to do justice to the absolute sovereignty and unlimited freedom of the biblical God."[13] As already noted, the various biblical references to God's creative activity are clearly shaped by the desire to affirm God's omnipotence, but this affirmation did not take the form of an explicit and unambiguous affirmation of creation from nothing. Moreover, when it is borne in mind that the early church was operating in a religious environment deeply shaped by Greek philosophy, for which the principle that "nothing comes from nothing" had long been axiomatic, it seems anything but obvious that Christians should have wanted to insist that the world was created "from nothing." What led them to make this move?

The evidence suggests that one factor behind the move toward the doctrine of creation from nothing was the emergence in Christian circles of theologies that called into question the goodness of material reality. These theologies are conventionally called "gnostic." Although they include a wide range of specific teachings, their common suspicion of the material order made the doctrine of creation a problem, and thus a focus of systematic reflection, in a way that it had not been for Christians up to that point. Quite simply, if God is good but the material world around us is not, then it becomes necessary to explain how this world came to be. The gnostic solution was to develop accounts of creation that

11. Theophilus, *To Autolycus* 2.4. See note 4 above.
12. Gerhard May summarizes the relevant evidence in *Creatio ex Nihilo: The Doctrine of "Creation out of Nothing" in Early Christian Thought* (1978; repr., Edinburgh: T&T Clark, 1994), 8. The language of children being made by their parents "from what does not exist" (*ek . . . ouk ontōn*) comes from Xenophon, *Memorabilia* 2.2–3. May also cites Plato, *Symposium* 205B; and Philo, *De specialis legibus* 2.2.225, 229.
13. May, *Creatio ex Nihilo*, viii. For an expansive study of patristic reflection on the doctrine of creation beyond the roots of *creatio ex nihilo*, see Paul M. Blowers, *Drama of the Divine Economy: Creator and Creation in Early Christian Theology and Piety* (Oxford: Oxford University Press, 2012).

put as much distance as possible between God and matter. The material world was viewed either as a kind of cosmic accident not directly caused by God or as the deliberate act of an inferior deity different from the true God. In either case the process of creation reflected a fundamental opposition between God and the world that cleared God of responsibility for the evil of material existence.

It would be convenient if it could be shown that the catholic doctrine of creation from nothing emerged as a straightforward vindication of the goodness of the material order in opposition to these world-denying strains of the early Christian movement.[14] Unfortunately, the history of the idea is more complicated. The example of Justin shows that it was possible to be firmly opposed to Gnosticism without feeling the need to argue for creation from nothing; and while Irenaeus of Lyons did direct his doctrine of creation from nothing against gnostic teaching, he seems to have been influenced by Theophilus, who wrote in opposition to pagan philosophy rather than Christian heresy.[15] But the most serious objection to any attempt to trace the doctrine of creation from nothing directly to Christian opposition to Gnosticism is the fact that the first Christian we know of to defend this teaching explicitly, the Alexandrian theologian Basilides, was himself a gnostic.

The details of Basilides' thought are difficult to ascertain with certainty since his works have survived only as quoted or explained by catholic writers who opposed him. It seems clear, however, that Basilides, writing half a century before Theophilus, developed an original cosmology that was different from that of gnostic writers who either downplayed or denied God's responsibility for bringing the material world into being.[16] The distinctiveness of Basilides' position lies in his insistence that the whole universe is derived directly and exclusively from God: "In this way the God who is nonexistent [*ouk ōn*] made the cosmos that is nonexistent [*ouk onta*] from those things that are nonexistent [*ex ouk ontōn*], having founded and established one particular seed [*sperma*] having in itself the entire universal seedbed of the cosmos [*tēn tou kosmou panspermian*]."[17]

14. I use the adjective "catholic" to refer to that majority of Christians in the second and third centuries who belonged to local churches associated with one another through mutual recognition of their bishops, but who did not identify themselves with a particular school or party. That this vision of "catholic Christianity" is not simply a polemical construct of self-proclaimed "orthodox" writers is shown by the fact that even the anti-Christian polemicist Celsus, writing at the end of the second century and eager to emphasize the factionalism of the Christian movement, acknowledged such a majority position, which he identified as the "great church." See Origen, *Contra Celsum* 5.59, trans. Henry Chadwick (Cambridge: Cambridge University Press, 1965).

15. Theophilus, *To Autolycus* 2.4, in PG 6:1052B. For an extraordinarily careful assessment of the evidence for Irenaeus's dependence on *To Autolycus*, see Anthony Briggman, "Dating Irenaeus' Acquisition of Theophilus' Correspondence *To Autolycus*: A Pneumatological Perspective," *Studia patristica* 45 (2010): 397–402; cf. May, *Creatio ex Nihilo*, 167–73.

16. My account of Basilides' thought follows the reconstruction offered in May, *Creatio ex Nihilo*, 67–76. May, in turn, bases his understanding of Basilides' system largely on the description found in the seventh and tenth books of *Refutation of All Heresies*, by the early third-century Roman writer Hippolytus. References to this work in what follows come from Hippolytus, *Refutatio omnium haeresium*, ed. Miroslav Marcovich (Berlin: Walter de Gruyter, 1986). A dated English translation is in vol. 5 of *ANF* (whose chapter numbers do not match the numbering in the Marcovich volume).

17. Hippolytus, *Refutatio* 7.21.4; cf. 10.14.1.

One difficulty immediately faced by the reader of this highly compressed passage is the frequency and variety of ways in which "nonexistent" is used. The affirmation of God's nonexistence appears to be Basilides' way of affirming divine transcendence: God is "nonexistent" (or "nonbeing") by virtue of surpassing all other beings as their Creator.[18] By contrast, the "nonexistence" of the cosmos seems to refer to its status as pure potentiality—a "seed" that has not yet been actualized (and thus does not yet truly "exist") as the sensible world of everyday experience. In short, both these types of "nonexistence" are metaphorical: the point is not that God and the cosmic seed are literally nothing, but that they cannot be described by using the conventional conceptual categories applied to objects in the everyday world of space and time.[19] But what about the "nonexistence" of that from which God forms the seed?

Basilides' talk of creation from nonexistent things parallels that of 2 Maccabees 7 and Romans 4, but unlike the case with these biblical passages, Basilides' use of the phrase is not incidental to a bit of pastoral encouragement, but part of a detailed theology of creation. At the heart of this theology is the insistence that originally there was "nothing" (which he defines as "not matter, neither being nor nonbeing, neither simple nor composite, neither intelligible nor sensible, neither human nor angel nor God"), and that this nothing is the context for God's work of creation.[20] It seems to follow that the "nonexistence" of this primordial state is, in contrast to that of God and the primordial seed that God creates, literally "nothing." The seed from which the world emerges is thus neither fashioned from a preexisting substance nor (as in other gnostic systems) an emanation from the divine being. It is brought into being out of nothing, by God's will alone.[21]

Even as transmitted through the unsympathetic eyes of later critics of his position, it is undeniable that Basilides taught a doctrine of creation from nothing. At the same time, the radical apophaticism of his theology gives his account of creation a very different feel from that of Theophilus and later catholic writers, none of whom appear to have been influenced by his thought.[22] On the one hand, with later proponents of creation from nothing, Basilides shares the idea that God's creative work is fundamentally disanalogous with human acts of creation: whereas humans always work from some already-existing material, God operates under no such constraints. This position naturally leads to an

18. See ibid., 7.21.1, where God's "nonexistence" is explicated in terms of a lengthy series of negations of finite qualities typical of later Christian apophaticism.

19. See ibid., 7.22.3, where in reference to the creation of light in Gen. 1:3 (which Basilides seems to have identified with the "seed" of creation), Basilides is reported to have affirmed, "The one speaking did not exist [ouk ēn], . . . neither did that which was spoken [oude . . . ēn]."

20. Hippolytus, Refutatio 7.21.1.

21. Although, in line with his emphasis on divine transcendence of all human categories, Basilides insisted that God could be said to have a "will" only in a loose and improper sense. See May, Creatio ex Nihilo, 70.

22. "So far as we know, the idiosyncratic creation doctrine of Basilides remained without historical effect" (ibid., 84).

affirmation of God's responsibility for the character of creation: unlike cosmologies that see God's will as deformed or constrained by the limits of material that is not subject to the divine will, the claim that God creates from nothing means that the character of the world reflects God's will. Basilides' understanding of creation from nothing follows this logic, and in this respect his cosmology is quite distinct from that of other gnostic thinkers; but his interpretation of the ontological distance between God and creation remains far more redolent of Gnosticism than of catholic thought. According to Basilides' understanding of creation from nothing, God does not, in fact, create the *existing* world at all. Rather, God creates a "seed" that is so far removed from actuality that it is properly characterized as "nonexistent." The actual (i.e., existing) world of objects in space and time unfolds from this seed of its own accord, without any divine stimulus or intervention.[23] In this way, the same emphasis on divine transcendence that leads Basilides to posit creation from nothing as a corollary of God's freedom from external constraint also leads him to remove God from active participation in the life of the world.[24]

Basilides' account of the world's origin seems to be grounded in a vision of divine transcendence in which creation from nothing provides a metaphysical basis for insulating God from direct contact with the created order. Since for Basilides the world that God creates "from nothing" is a "nonexistent" seed of pure potentiality, even the very moment of creation only approximates a genuine encounter between Creator and creature, and there is no possibility whatever for divine engagement with the world after this seed has been brought into being. By contrast, for Theophilus the doctrine of creation from nothing served precisely to highlight God's direct involvement with and responsibility for the world at every moment of its existence. Thus he posited his account of creation in opposition to Platonist cosmologies that he judged false because they failed to acknowledge the intimacy of God's engagement with the material realm. His specific target seems to have been a theologian named Hermogenes, who apparently was unique among early Christian writers in defending a Platonist understanding of creation from preexisting matter as an *alternative* to the idea of creation from nothing.

Although Hermogenes is not mentioned in Theophilus's extant writings, we know from the church historian Eusebius that Theophilus composed a treatise

23. See, e.g., Hippolytus, *Refutatio* 7.22.1 and 24.5, where the evolution of the sensible world from the primordial seed is described, respectively, as a matter of necessity (*anankaiōs*), and as a process in which particulars emerge "when and as and how they ought to be" (*hote dei kai hoia dei kai hōs dei*), without any supernatural activity subsequent to God's primordial creative act.
24. "Basilides's understanding of the world and of creation is essentially different from the Christian conception. True, the world comes into being through a single divine act of creation, but the unfolding of what is in time follows according to a plan laid down at the creation of the world-seed, and in this God takes no further part. . . . In the end his God is much more like the '*heimarmenē*' [fate] of the Stoics than the God of the Bible" (May, *Creatio ex Nihilo*, 80–81). In this way, Basilides reduces the creation-from-nothing notion to a theory about the world's origin that is only peripheral to the central significance of the doctrine for later Christians, for whom it grounds a theology of God's ongoing engagement with the world.

against him.[25] Because this lost work was almost certainly used by Tertullian, whose own book *Against Hermogenes* is the earliest known defense of creation from nothing in Latin, it is reasonable to suppose that Theophilus's lost treatise also focused on that topic.[26] According to Tertullian, Hermogenes made his case for a Platonist cosmology by setting out three possible approaches to the doctrine of creation: either God created the world out of God's own being, or God created the world out of nothing, or God created the world out of something else. Hermogenes rejects the first of these options on the grounds that it implies that God can be divided. The second is ruled out because anything entirely dependent on God's will for its existence would necessarily be as good as God is, but the material universe is evidently imperfect. It follows, therefore, that God made the world out of something that is neither God nor created by God, and Hermogenes identifies this something (the source of the world's imperfection) with unformed matter.[27]

In making this argument, Hermogenes seems to have been offering a theoretical analysis rather than responding to any position actually maintained by some other theologian.[28] Given that his broadly Platonist cosmology appears to have had a considerable following among catholic thinkers up to that time, there is little reason to suppose that he would have understood his position as especially controversial.[29] Nevertheless, Hermongenes's strategy of defending the Platonist account by contrasting it with creation from nothing seems to have clarified, for Theophilus, theological problems with the Platonist approach that had not occurred to earlier theologians. In arguing against the Platonist model, Theophilus insists that it is not possible to maintain God's lordship and matter's eternity at the same time:

> Now Plato and those of his school confess that God is uncreated, Father, and maker of all things, but then they argue that God and matter are both uncreated, and they say that matter is coeternal with God. But if God is uncreated, and matter is uncreated, God is (according to the Platonists) not

25. Eusebius of Caesarea, *Ecclesiastical History* 4.24, in *Nicene and Post-Nicene Fathers*, 2nd ser. (hereafter *NPNF²*), ed. Philip Schaff and Henry Wace, 14 vols. (1890–1900; repr., Peabody, MA: Hendrickson Publishers, 1994–99), 1:202.

26. The fact that the doctrine of creation from nothing is treated in *To Autolycus* as a well-established position suggests that Theophilus wrote it after his lost book against Hermogenes, though this is disputed. See the discussion in May, *Creatio ex Nihilo*, 156–59.

27. Tertullian, *Against Hermogenes* 2, in vol. 3 of *ANF*. In *Against Hermogenes* 3, Tertullian also reports a second argument against ex nihilo: if God is unchangeable, then God has always been Lord, and it is therefore necessary to conclude that there has always existed something (viz., matter) over which God has been Lord. Although this argument plays no part in Theophilus's defense of creation from nothing in *To Autolycus*, Tertullian rejects it as a category confusion, arguing that because "Lord" is a relational term, it cannot properly refer to God's unchanging essence.

28. May argues that Hermogenes' disjunctive syllogism is best viewed as a purely theoretical analysis, in line with the parallel in Plutarch, *Platonic Questions* 4 (1003AB). See May, *Creatio ex Nihilo*, 141.

29. In addition to Justin, the cosmology of the apologist Athenagoras, who seems to have been roughly contemporary with both Hermgenes and Theophilus, also follows the lead of Plato's *Timaeus*. See Athenagoras, *A Plea for the Christians* 10, 15, in *Early Christian Fathers*, 309, 313.

the maker of all things, nor (so far as they teach) is God's monarchy maintained. Furthermore, in the same way that God, because uncreated, is also
unchangeable, so also if matter were uncreated, it too would be unchangeable and equal to God. For that which is created is variable and changeable;
but that which is uncreated is unvarying and unchangeable.[30]

For Theophilus it is the postulate of uncreated matter that turns out to be
theologically unacceptable because it effectively makes matter equal to God and
thus fatally compromises God's status as the sole ground of being (the technical
meaning of "monarchy" in this context). The doctrine of creation from nothing
thus emerges as the only account of the world's origin that does justice to the
Christian conviction that there is only one God.

IMPLICATIONS AND PROBLEMS

In deciding for creation from nothing, Theophilus pays a conceptual price. If
Tertullian is to be believed, Hermogenes rejected ex nihilo because it implied
that God was responsible for the evident imperfections in the created order,
thereby undermining Christian convictions regarding God's goodness and wisdom. For him (like the gnostics) the doctrine of creation provided a solution to
the problem of evil: if God is not responsible for the existence of matter, then the
evils that attend material existence cannot be blamed on God; to put it colloquially, God cannot be expected to make a silk purse out of a sow's ear. In short,
while the gnostics used the doctrine of creation as a theodicy, for Theophilus it
no longer plays this role. Evil cannot be explained as a natural consequence of
creation. It is rather a deeply irrational perversion of creation that emerges as the
result of the inexplicable fact that creatures reject God's will for them.[31]

Instead of using the doctrine of creation to generate a theodicy, Theophilus
turns it to the service of soteriology. This is not to say that for Theophilus creation *is* salvation, as though making the world were itself God's means of defeating evil. Such a perspective would only reaffirm the basic structure of Platonist
cosmology, because treating God's creative work as a form of resistance to evil
implies some (evil) reality existing alongside of God "in the beginning."[32] The
soteriological cast of Theophilus's account of creation from nothing is more
indirect. It is not that creation is itself salvific (since only what already exists can
be saved, and creation from nothing means precisely that things exist only after

30. Theophilus, *To Autolycus* 2.4, in PG 1052A–B.
31. Theophilus holds that Satan had rebelled against God and then induced human beings to do
the same through the serpent described in Gen. 3. See *To Autolycus* 2.28.
32. In the last century the Danish theologian Regin Prenter offered a defense of this perspective
as a means of affirming the inseparability of creation and redemption as equally a "struggle against
the enemies of God," but he was able to defend the consistency of this view with the doctrine of
creation from nothing only by arguing that the *nihil* of *creatio ex nihilo* is not "an empty nothingness
. . . but . . . that unfathomable abyss which surrounded God prior to creation." See his *Creation and
Redemption* (Philadelphia: Fortress Press, 1967), 199.

they have been created), but that creation from nothing is a necessary implication of Christian confidence in God's ability to save. In Theophilus's work this
is revealed in the following attempt to explain the origins of the word "God":
"'God' [*theos*] is so named because he has placed [*tetheikenai*] all things in dependence on the security he provides; and because he runs [*theein*], and this running
means giving all things power, motion, activity, nourishment, ends, direction,
and life."[33]

The novelty of this perspective cannot be underestimated. The difference
from Platonist views is evident from comparison with Justin, who is led by his
belief in the ontological independence of matter to argue that God is unable
to act directly on or be immediately present to creation: God is and remains
outside of the phenomenal world.[34] No less striking, however, is the difference
from the vision of creation from nothing developed by Basilides, who also argues
(albeit on different metaphysical grounds) against the possibility of direct divine
involvement with the created order. Over against both these positions, Theophilus refuses to equate God's transcendence of creation with remoteness or discon-
nection from the material order. Although God's immensity means that God
cannot be confined to a particular place, this does not signal divine absence but
rather points to the fact that "the heights of heaven, the depths of hell, and the
ends of the earth are in [God's] hand."[35]

This feature of the catholic doctrine of *creatio ex nihilo* is even more prominent in the slightly later writing of Irenaeus of Lyons. He, too, describes the
whole of the created order as in God's hand, arguing that God's power as Creator means that God contains the whole of creation: "There is nothing either
above [God] nor after [God]; nor . . . [was God] influenced by anyone, but of
his own free will he created all things, since he is the only God, the only Lord,
the only Creator, the only Father, alone containing all things, and himself com-
manding them into existence."[36]

For Irenaeus, a crucial corollary of this all-containing immensity is God's
incomprehensibility: because nothing is outside of God, the divine cannot be
encompassed by human thought.[37] And yet far from placing God at a distance

33. Theophilus, *To Autolycus* 1.4, in PG 6:1029A–B.
34. "He who has but the smallest intelligence will not venture to assert that the Creator and
Father of all things would leave behind everything above heaven and appear on a little portion of the
earth." See Justin Martyr, *Dialogue with Trypho* 60, in ANF 1:227, trans. alt.; cf. 1:263 (chap. 127):
"For the ineffable Father and Lord of all neither has come to any place, nor walks, nor sleeps, nor
rises up, but remains in His own place [*chōrai*], wherever that is." Here and elsewhere all alterations
to the translations found in the ANF series are based on the Greek (or, for much of Irenaeus, Latin)
text, as found in the relevant volumes of PG.
35. Theophilus, *To Autolycus* 1.4, in PG 6:1029B. Here and there in *To Autolycus*, 2.22, in PG
6:1088A, Theophilus characterizes God's transcendence with the phrase "There is no place where he
rests" (*ouk esti topos katapauseōs autou*), which suggests both that God cannot be contained in any
part of creation and that God is never absent from any part of creation.
36. Irenaeus, *Against Heresies* 2.1.1, in ANF 1:359, trans. slightly alt.); for further references to
God's containing all things, see 2.1.2; 4.3.1; 4.20.1–2, 6.
37. "For the one who fashioned you cannot be contained within limits [*indeterminabilis*]; nor, if
you were to measure the whole world and come through all of his creation, and consider everything

from the world, this divine fullness establishes the most profound intimacy between Creator and creature: the same God "who fills the heavens and views the depths . . . is also present with everyone of us. . . . For his hand lays hold of all things, . . . is present in our hidden and secret parts, and publicly nourishes and preserves us."[38] God's transcendence does not imply distance from creatures, but is rather the ground for God's engagement with them.[39]

This intimacy is central to the way in which, for both Theophilus and Irenaeus, the idea of creation from nothing turns the focus of the doctrine of creation from theodicy to soteriology. At one level this leads to a profoundly anthropocentric theology of creation. For once creation is understood as the free act of God's will, the question naturally arises as to the purpose for which God willed it, and Theophilus has no doubts here: God made the world so that through it God might come to be known by human beings,[40] a view in which Irenaeus concurs.[41] Crucially, however, the fulfillment of this purpose is dependent on God's presence and power within the created order: "Give yourself over to the physician, and he will clear the eyes of your heart and soul. Who is the physician? It is God, who gives healing and life through Word and Wisdom. For God through his Word and Wisdom made all things."[42] God can and should be trusted because God holds all things in God's hands.[43]

All this is not to claim that appreciation for God's power to save emerged only after Christians formulated the doctrine of creation from nothing. Justin, for example, was no less able than Theophilus or Irenaeus to cite Jesus' claim that "for God all things are possible" (Matt. 19:26) and thus to affirm the principle that God's power exceeds all human expectation.[44] Yet as much as a theologian like Justin could stress God's power as a matter of piety, his emphasis on matter's ontological independence of God rendered him conceptually incapable of viewing God as directly active in creation. Like Hermogenes (even if not as explicitly), he sees the character of matter as fundamentally incompatible with God's unmediated presence to it, even though he affirms God's lordship over it.

---

in it in its depth and height and length, will you conceive another above the Father himself." Irenaeus, *Against Heresies* 2.25.4, in *ANF* 1:397, trans. alt.

38. Irenaeus, *Against Heresies* 4.19.2, in *ANF* 1:487, trans. alt.

39. "What makes God different from every creature—his eternal and ingenerate simplicity—is thus, for Irenaeus, precisely what assures his direct and intimate involvement with every creature." R. A. Norris Jr., *God and World in Early Christian Theology* (New York: Seabury Press, 1965), 86.

40. Theophilus, *To Autolycus* 1.4, in PG 6:1029B; see note 1 above.

41. See, e.g., Irenaeus, *Against Heresies* 4.5.1; 5.29.1.

42. Theophilus, *To Autolycus* 1.7, in PG 6:1036A. At the same time, the fact that in the following chapter Theophilus uses the example of the formation of the human being from a single drop of semen as an illustration of creation from nothing indicates that he is still capable of reverting to the colloquial sense of creation from nothing found in Rom. 4:17 and Heb. 11:3.

43. "If the farmer trusts the earth, the sailor the boat, and the fevered the doctor, do you not wish to trust God when you have so many pledges from him?" Theophilus, *To Autolycus* 1.8, in PG 6:1037A; cf. Irenaeus, *Against Heresies* 5.1.3: "For never at any time did Adam escape the hands of God."

44. Justin Martyr, *First Apology* 19; cf. Theophilus, *To Autolycus*; and Irenaeus, *Against Heresies* 4.20.5; 5.5.2.

By contrast, Irenaeus's defense of creation from nothing makes it easier for him to affirm, as a matter of logic (and not simply of piety), that nothing constrains God's ability to effect what God wills.[45] For him, as for Theophilus, it is not simply that God's power is greater than human imagination, but that there simply is no factor independent of God that might limit that power.

Irenaeus goes on to explore some of the implications of this position, and in the process effectively answers Hermogenes' primary objection to creation from nothing: How is it, if God is both good and omnipotent, that creation is so obviously imperfect? For Irenaeus the world's imperfection in no way impugns God's benevolence or power, but is simply a corollary of its having been *created*: "Created things must fall short of the one who created them, from the very fact of their later origin; for it was not possible for things only just created to have been uncreated. And because they are not uncreated, for this very reason they fall short of the perfect."[46]

Irenaeus acknowledges the imperfection of the created order, but he does not attribute this to matter's ontological independence, as Hermogenes thought had to be done in order to avoid tracing the world's imperfections back to some deficiency in God. For Irenaeus, the world's imperfection is simply a matter of logic: that which is created cannot by definition possess the property of being uncreated.[47] Nevertheless, creatures can acquire something of God's perfection as the result of subsequent modification of their created status over time. According to Irenaeus, creatures come to participate in God's uncreated being through God's commitment to perfect their created existence—something that can only happen after God has first brought them into being, when God, through God's utterly gracious love for creatures, gives them the glory of uncreated existence through God's own loving presence to them.[48]

---

45. See, e.g., Irenaeus, *Against Heresies* 5.5.2, in *ANF* 1:531: "Neither the nature of any created thing, . . . nor the weakness of the flesh, can prevail against the will of God. For God is not subject to created things, but created things to God; and all things yield obedience to his will."

46. Irenaeus, *Against Heresies* 4.38.1, in *ANF* 1:521; cf. 4.38.2: "Humanity was not uncreated [*agennōtos*] because of anything impossible for or lacking in God, but because humanity's having been only just created [*neōsti gegonota*]" (my trans.; see PG 7a:1107B).

47. "This . . . is not a limitation imposed on God by some external condition, such as the existence of a refractory 'matter.' It is a limitation of a *logical* order. That created things should be uncreated is a logical, not a physical, impossibility." Norris, *God and World*, 93. Cf. Maximus the Confessor: "Nothing that came into being is in itself perfect and complete. If complete it would have the power of action, but because it has being from what is not, it does not have power of action. That which is perfect in itself is uncaused." From *Ambiguum 7*, in *On the Cosmic Mystery of Jesus Christ: Selected Writings from St. Maximus the Confessor*, trans. Paul Blowers and Robert Louis Wilken (Crestwood, NY: St. Vladimir's Seminary Press, 2003), 49.

48. "For inasmuch as these things having been created, they are not uncreated; but by their existing [*paramenein*] throughout a long course of ages, they shall receive the faculty of the uncreated, through God's granting them the gracious gift of eternal existence [*tēn eisaei paramonēn*]. And thus in all things God has the preeminence, who alone is uncreated . . . and the primary cause of the existence of all, while all other things remain under God's subjection. But being in subjection to God is continuance in immortality, and immortality is the glory of the uncreated One." Irenaeus, *Against Heresies* 4.38.3, in *ANF* 1:521, trans. alt.; cf. 3.20.2.

In this way, Irenaeus understands the world's present imperfection as a function of its subjection to God's will rather than evidence that matter lies outside the scope of that will.[49] Given God's own perfection, moreover, for Irenaeus it is integral to God's ongoing work in and with the world that creation's imperfection will ultimately be overcome: God will act so that human beings will be "accustomed gradually to partake of the divine nature,"[50] and since human beings subsist as creatures within and dependent on the wider panorama of created being, this work of perfecting will include the whole of the created order.[51] At one level, the result is a remarkably confident and optimistic cosmology, in which God's power ensures not only the existence, but also the ultimate well-being of all things. At the same time, this stress on God's power can also be viewed as problematic in at least two respects: first, it raises the specter of divine despotism, in which God's sovereignty is so uncompromising that it threatens to undermine belief in creaturely freedom; and second, it fails to fully confront the problem of evil, since creation's present imperfection is not simply a matter of immaturity, but of extraordinary pain and suffering, which is capable of inflicting apparently irrevocable damage to creatures' well-being. Admittedly, neither of these problems seems to worry either Theophilus or Irenaeus, both of whom go out of their way to insist on creaturely freedom before God as a defining feature of rational creatures in particular and as the source of evil in the world.[52] But it is certainly possible to question whether this position is finally coherent, whether the emphasis on divine sovereignty that attends these two theologians' support of creation from nothing is consistent with their emphasis on human freedom.[53] Similarly, if one follows them in tracing the origin of evil to the necessary imperfection (and thus mutability) of created beings, this naturally raises the question of whether or not evil is to be viewed as somehow "natural" and therefore ultimately good.[54] Although the doctrine of creation

49. Irenaeus can go so far as to describe God's will as the "substance" (*substantia*) of all things in *Against Heresies* 2.30.9, in *ANF* 1:406.
50. Irenaeus, *Against Heresies* 5.32.1, in *ANF* 1:561.
51. "For since there are real men, so must there also be a real establishment, that they vanish not away among nonexistent things, but progress among those which have an actual existence." Irenaeus, *Against Heresies* 5.36.1, in *ANF* 1:566.
52. See Theophilus, *To Autolycus* 2.17; and Irenaeus, *Against Heresies* 4.37, 39–40; 5.23–25.
53. For example, is it possible, e.g., to square Irenaeus's claim that "all things yield obedience to [God's] will" (*Against Heresies* 5.5.2; see note 47 above) with the principle that "God made the human being free, possessing his own power, even as he does his own soul" (*Against Heresies* 4.37.1, in *ANF* 1:518, trans. alt.)? Irenaeus himself clearly thinks so, since he accuses those who deny human freedom with "present[ing] the Lord as destitute of power, as if . . . he were unable to accomplish what he willed" (*Against Heresies* 4.37.6, in *ANF* 1:520, trans. alt.), but it remains unclear exactly how for Irenaeus a strong emphasis on human freedom can be anything but an impediment to God's ability to accomplish whatever God wills.
54. "Irenaeus's attempt to solve the problem of evil by an appeal to creaturely finitude raised a whole host of questions and difficulties. . . . Was his solution to be taken as asserting that sin is simply a matter of 'nature'? Surely not. But if this is not what it means, then does it really offer a solution at all?" Norris, *God and World*, 97. For an attempt to interpret Irenaeus as asserting precisely the "naturalness" of the fall, see John Hick, *Evil and the God of Love*, 2nd ed. (New York: Palgrave Macmillan, 2007), 211–15.

from nothing triumphed in the wider church, these questions have continued to generate problems for its defenders.

A CONTEMPORARY CHALLENGE

In response to these problems, proponents of process theology have argued that Christians would do better to abandon the doctrine of creation from nothing.[55] Working with the metaphysics introduced by the philosopher Alfred North Whitehead, process theologians effectively reclaim the doctrine of creation proposed by Hermogenes, arguing that creation ex nihilo creates insuperable problems for Christian theodicy and defending instead a model of creation from chaos, in which God's role is that of bringing order to reality.[56] Going beyond what we know of Hermogenes' theological commitments, they also object to the model of divine omnipotence associated with creation from nothing as morally problematic (since it renders God's decisions to intervene in some situations rather than others arbitrary), scientifically incredible (since it makes no sense to suppose that a God who could bring into existence any state of affairs immediately would instead take billions of years to do so by means of the slow processes of cosmic and biological evolution), and incompatible with creaturely freedom (since a God who effects all states of affairs is necessarily the only free agent).

Especially given some process theologians' enthusiasm for Hermogenes' cosmology,[57] it is tempting to view them as latter-day Platonists. But although Whitehead was a great admirer of Plato (he famously characterized the whole of the Western philosophical tradition as a series of footnotes to the latter's work),[58] process thought also makes a break with Platonist metaphysics. For as

55. Not all Christian writers who reject creation from nothing identify themselves as process theologians, and some explicitly distance themselves from process thought (e.g., Ruth Page, *God and the Web of Creation* [London: SCM Press, 1966], 46–49); but process theology remains the most widespread and well-developed alternative to creation from nothing within contemporary Christian theology.

56. It is only fair to note that process theologians do not necessarily reject the language of creation from nothing, so long as it is interpreted according to the "loose" sense adopted by Jewish and Christian sources prior to Theophilus. See, e.g., David Ray Griffin, "Creation out of Nothing, Creation out of Chaos, and the Problem of Evil," in *Encountering Evil: Live Options in Theodicy*, ed. Stephen T. Davis (Louisville, KY: Westminster John Knox Press, 2001), 121: "Prior to the emergence of . . . enduring objects, there would have been no 'things' in the ordinary sense of *enduring* things. For those who like the phrase, . . . it can be said that our world was created out of 'no-thing.' It was not, however, created *ex nihilo* in the sense that this phrase took on in post-biblical times." Cf. John B. Cobb Jr. and David Ray Griffin, *Process Theology: An Introductory Exposition* (Louisville, KY: Westminster John Knox Press, 1976), 65: "Process theology rejects the notion of *creatio ex nihilo*, if that means creation out of *absolute* nothingness."

57. See, e.g., Griffin, "Creation out of Nothing," 112–14; and Catherine Keller, *Face of the Deep: A Theology of Becoming* (New York: Routledge, 2003), 47–49.

58. Alfred North Whitehead, *Process and Reality: An Essay in Cosmology* (New York: Macmillan, 1929), 63.

much as process theologians endorse the model of creation from chaos,[59] their underlying metaphysical framework is different from Plato's. In all its various forms, Platonism is marked by a sharp distinction between the eternal, change-less world of Being and the temporal, mutable realm of Becoming. Especially for the later forms of Platonism that influenced early Christians like Justin, God belongs squarely in the realm of Being and is for that reason precluded from direct engagement with the material sphere of Becoming. As we have seen, one of the theologically appealing features of creation from nothing for thinkers like Theophilus and Irenaeus was that it raised no such metaphysical barriers to God's interacting with the world: because matter is God's own creation, its difference from God does not imply a distance from God, the crossing of which would compromise the immutable perfection of divine Being.

Process theologians, too, highlight God's ability to interact with matter. Whereas proponents of creation from nothing make this point by stressing God's absolute sovereignty over the material realm, however, process thinkers stress rather the interdependence of God and creation. Behind this process understand-ing of God lies a rejection of the classical Platonist dichotomy between Being and Becoming in favor of a metaphysic in which reality is defined as Becoming ("pro-cess"), in relation to which the idea of a changeless realm of Being is an unreal abstraction.[60] Becoming is not conceived as a defective form of existence that at best can only approximate the timeless and immutable perfection of Being, but rather as the most metaphysically fundamental principle, such that in process thought an entity is constituted by its becoming, not by a changeless substrate that underlies and is unaffected by the process of becoming. And because becom-ing means change, every entity can be characterized in terms of two dimensions (or "poles") that condition the change it undergoes at any given moment: the accumulated effects of its past history (the "physical pole") and its openness to new possibilities (the "conceptual pole"). Both are necessary since absent a physi-cal pole, there is no identifiable entity of which "becoming" can be predicated, and without a conceptual pole an entity is incapable of becoming (i.e., of moving beyond its past) and so ceases to exist. This framework, in turn, highlights the fundamentally relational character of process metaphysics. Where becoming is central, an entity's being is defined by its relationships with other entities. The physical pole is the precipitate of past relationships, while the conceptual pole encapsulates an entity's sphere of freedom for new relationships. Becoming is the result of the interaction of these two poles from moment to moment, as present possibility builds on past history to produce a new configuration that, in turn, generates a new set of possibilities for further development.

This dipolar metaphysics constitutes a significant shift from classical Platonist understandings of God and matter alike. On the one hand, matter is no longer

---

59. Griffin, echoing Justin, identifies the model of creation from chaos as common to both Plato and the Bible, in "Creation out of Nothing," 119, 125.

60. "To be actual is to be a process. Anything which is not a process is an abstraction from pro-cess, not a full-fledged actuality." Cobb and Griffin, *Process Theology*, 14.

the purely passive object of external forces, but possesses its own irreducible integrity as a locus of spontaneous activity—although the scope of freedom exhibited by any particular material entity will vary enormously depending on its organizational complexity (so that, for example, a dog has a much wider range of possibilities associated with its conceptual pole than does an electron).[61] On the other hand, God is not defined by contrast with the realm of becoming as an utterly impassive being who exists independently of all external relationships, but rather as that entity whose range and richness of relationships is unsurpassable.[62] In this way, God is not an exception to, but the supreme exemplification of, the metaphysics of becoming, immediately related to all other entities in the universe, knowing their past histories and present possibilities with a depth that goes beyond the bare facts of their existence to include their experience of joy and pain. This radical intimacy with all other entities makes God supremely responsive to them, seeking at every point to influence their becoming in a way that maximizes the flourishing of all.

Because all entities have a range of freedom that is irreducible to past determination and thus escapes external control, God cannot guarantee that they will follow the divine lead. The God of process thought is therefore not omnipotent. All things do not yield to God's will; indeed, in important respects God's will is determined by creaturely willing. For although God's goodness means that God always wills all creatures' maximum enjoyment, the fact that creatures' decisions are not under God's control means that the particular content of God's will (i.e., the concrete possibilities that God presents to creatures for their actualization at any given moment) constantly shifts to reflect changing circumstances, in which the decisions creatures make (decisions God can neither predict nor prevent) open up new possibilities and preclude others. Because the conceptual pole of every individual entity is fundamental, God's power is not absolute and controlling, but relative and persuasive. It is both present to and directly affects all other entities, but does not determine their future, which thus remains radically open—for good or for ill.

With its stress on God's intimacy with every creature, process thought thus shares, with the doctrine of creation from nothing, a refusal to distance God from world. Yet process theologians do not simply view their perspective as a neutral alternative to creation from nothing, but as superior to it. One important reason for this judgment is exegetical: process theologians claim that their

61. In process thought the presence of a conceptual pole is associated with individuals only. Genuine individuals may be composed of smaller entities, provided the resulting compound has an organizing center (so that an amoeba is a compound of molecules and a human being a compound of cells). Where such a center is lacking and the combination of lower-level individuals simply produces an aggregate without any organizing center that coordinates the responses of the constituent parts (e.g., rocks), then there is no conceptual pole, and the aggregate cannot be said to possess any capacity for self-determination.

62. For this reason (and in deliberate opposition to characterizations of God as "Absolute"), the process philosopher Charles Hartshorne described God as the "Surrelative." See Charles Hartshorne, *The Divine Relativity: A Social Conception of God* (1948; repr., New Haven, CT: Yale University Press, 1964), 21 and passim.

model of creation from chaos more accurately reflects biblical depictions of God's creative activity. As already noted, however, they also cite a range of other reasons for the superiority of their position, all of which are correlates of process theology's rejection of divine omnipotence. While these objections include concerns about theodicy, human freedom, and scientific credibility, they share a common core: the claim that creation from nothing renders God *arbitrary*. An omnipotent God could prevent evil but doesn't, could have made creation perfect but didn't, could bring everyone to glory but won't. Even the worry that the model of divine omnipotence underlying *creatio ex nihilo* is inconsistent with creaturely freedom arguably turns on the same problem: God's relationship with human beings reduces to that of a puppet-master and thus lacks the basic conditions of personal relationship. In short, history under ex nihilo lacks the possibility of genuine drama and reduces to a capricious, and thus ultimately lifeless, game of divine charades.

A PRELIMINARY RESPONSE

While the whole of this book is my answer to this challenge, two preliminary observations, one logical and the other exegetical, will help to frame that answer. The logical point is fairly straightforward. Within process metaphysics, God's ability to interact with the world is conditional on a fundamental metaphysical continuity between God and all that is not God. Only if God and the world operate on the same metaphysical plane is it possible for God to engage the world both directly and without compulsion. According to process thinkers, if God is transcendent in the way implied by creation ex nihilo, other entities lose the autonomy required if their actions are to avoid being subsumed without remainder into God's activity. This line of reasoning reflects the fact that as much as process thought breaks with Plato's privileging of Being over Becoming, it fully shares the Platonist conviction that the two represent exhaustive and mutually exclusive alternatives. Therefore, in order to secure the possibility of God's direct and noncoercive engagement with the realm of becoming, process thinkers must render God subject to its laws. The metaphysical framework that defines becoming as the measure of all reality is primary, and God too is bound by its structures—even if God relates to them from a position of vastly greater knowledge and power than other entities and is, correspondingly, able to engage them with unsurpassable range and intensity.[63]

---

63. Griffin recognizes some ambiguity in process thought on this subject. On the one hand, Whitehead himself taught that the fundamental metaphysical categories were the product of a primordial decision by God and so denied that God was intrinsically bound by them; on the other, Hartshorne argued that the basic metaphysical categories belong to God's essence—a position that Griffin judges to be both more coherent and more consistent with the tenor of Whitehead's own thought. See David Ray Griffin, *God, Power, and Evil: A Process Theodicy* (1976; repr., Louisville, KY: Westminster John Knox Press, 2004), 297–300. Hartshorne wanted to argue that locating these categories in God's essence sidesteps the question of whether God or the categories are metaphysically

A crucial implication of this postulate of metaphysical continuity is that God is not finally sovereign over creation.[64] It was in opposition to this conclusion (promoted in the second century on different grounds by Platonists and gnostics alike) that Theophilus and Irenaeus insisted on creation from nothing. For these theologians the claim that the ontological autonomy of matter marked a fundamental limit on God's sovereignty was inconsistent with Christian confidence in God's power to save, and they posited *creatio ex nihilo* as a means of affirming that no reality was ultimately capable of thwarting God's will. In so doing, they implicitly rejected the either/or of Platonist metaphysics by refusing to make God's ability to engage directly with the world of change conditional on God's inclusion within it.[65] The upshot was a God conceived neither in opposition to nor as an example of becoming, but as its sole, direct, and immediate source. Because (in the words of a later theologian) "all things are distant from God not by place, but by nature," God's engagement with the world is neither impeded by nor subject to the metaphysics of becoming.[66]

Early promoters of creation from nothing like Theophilus and Irenaeus were far from being either comprehensive or even altogether consistent in addressing the issues raised by the doctrine.[67] Nevertheless, insofar as their theologies point to God's transcendence of the Platonic contrast between Being and Becoming, it is precisely the metaphysical *discontinuity* between Creator and creature (a discontinuity marked for both Theophilus and Irenaeus by the fact that God does not depend on existing materials in order to create) that becomes for them

---

prior, on the grounds that God cannot be said to be subject to categories that are coeternal with God's own individuality (Hartshorne, *Divine Relativity*, 41); but it is hard to see how one can avoid the conclusion that God *is* subject at least to the principle that God's power is intrinsically limited, since the finite realities that are the object of God's creative activity are themselves neither part of God's essence nor in their primordial "thereness" a product of God's will. Elsewhere Griffin himself claims that one corollary of the rejection of *creatio ex nihilo* is precisely the supposition "that there are some necessary principles, inherent in the very nature of things, about the nature of finite actualities, their relations to each other, and their relations to God" ("Creation out of Nothing," 122).

64. "Process theism . . . cannot provide the assurance that God's will is always done." Cobb and Griffin, *Process Theology*, 118.

65. Catherine Keller's claim that creation ex nihilo "depended upon platonic metaphysics" and so "locked into dogma a clean and simple form of Hellenistic dualism" (*Face of the Deep*, 46) is therefore baffling, given that dualism (viz., the affirmation of two ontologically ultimate principles) is precisely what creation from nothing was formulated to oppose. Cf. the way in which Kathryn Tanner *contrasts* the Christian idea of creation ex nihilo with the dualism that marks even the sophisticated metaphysics of the Neoplatonic philosopher Plotinus. See her *God and Creation in Christian Theology: Tyranny or Empowerment?* (Oxford: Basil Blackwell, 1988), 42–45.

66. John of Damascus, *On the Orthodox Faith* 1.13, in PG 94:853C. For an English translation, see vol. 9 of *NPNF²*. Process theologians would, of course, agree that God is not distant from any entity by place, but their insistence on metaphysical continuity between God and all that is not God limits their ability to affirm God's distance according to nature.

67. Most obviously, both evidently have difficulty in conceiving God as engaging directly with the realm of becoming, as is visible in their tendency (following earlier writers like Justin) to characterize the Word as a kind of ontological buffer between the unchanging God and the changeable world (see, e.g., Theophilus, *To Autolycus* 2.22; and Irenaeus, *Against Heresies* 5.18.2–3). At the same time, Irenaeus's references to Word and Wisdom (or Spirit) as God's two "hands" turns away from such Platonizing imagery by equating the Word with God's own presence in the world (see, e.g., *Against Heresies* 4.20.1; 5.6.1).

the basis for God's ability to interact directly with creatures.[68] It follows that the realm of becoming is not an inescapable feature of reality in the face of which God and the rest of us do the best we can, but a gift that is the proper mode rather than a more-or-less recalcitrant medium for creaturely flourishing.

To be sure, the identification of creation as a gift does not by itself answer the charge of divine arbitrariness: since it is part of the definition of a gift (in contrast to a wage or reward) that the giver is under no obligation to make it, it is certainly possible for the gift of creation to be arbitrary. God's creating the world would, on this reading, be analogous to my giving fifty dollars to a person chosen at random from a crowd. Indeed, some recent theorists have suggested that a genuine gift *must* be arbitrary. According to this line of argument, genuine gift giving can be distinguished from economies of exchange (in which "gifts" either function as payment for benefits received or impose an obligation of return) only when every motive has been eliminated—when the gift is not only anonymous but also made in complete ignorance of and disregard for the condition of the recipient. Otherwise the giver will always be suspected of a self-interest that vitiates the purity of the gift.[69] Interpreting creation as a gift in this sense would imply a divine indifference to creatures that is both unworthy of worship and incapable of inspiring it.

Whatever one makes of this account as a general theory of gift giving, it has serious implications for the doctrine of creation since Christian convictions about the freedom of God's creative work that underlie the interpretation of creation as a gift seem to render the act of creation inherently arbitrary. After all, if it is true that God creates from *nothing*, then God's desire to share the benefits of existence cannot be conditional either on any prior merits of the gift's recipients (since apart from God's gift of existence there is no recipient to which such merit might be ascribed) or on future benefits they might return (since in a world where everything is created by God, any possible return made by creatures will itself be rooted entirely and immediately in God's own action).[70] Therefore, insofar as the gift of created existence is, by virtue of its complete dependence on the will of giver, utterly unconditioned, it might well seem to be the epitome of arbitrariness.

One might counter that this case for divine arbitrariness is logically misplaced since it is based on an anthropomorphic model of choosing from a range of options external to the Creator (e.g., deciding to paint with oils rather than acrylics, or to construct a table instead of a chair). Such a picture arguably fails to reckon with the full implications of the claim that God creates from *nothing*,

---

68. For a particularly sharp statement of the ontological discontinuity between God and creation, see Irenaeus, *Against Heresies* 3.8.3: "But whatever things had a beginning, and are liable to dissolution, and are subject to and stand in need of Him who made them, must necessarily in all respects be described by a different term . . . so that He indeed who made all things can alone . . . properly be termed God" (in *ANF* 1:422, trans. alt.).

69. See Jacques Derrida, *Given Time: I. Counterfeit Money* (Chicago: University of Chicago Press, 1992).

70. See Kathryn Tanner, *Economy of Grace* (Minneapolis, MN: Fortress Press, 2005), 62–85.

which implies that in creating the world, God is not confronted by *any* reality, real or notional, in relation to which God may be said to "choose."[71] Even if this point is conceded, however, it is still possible to view the charge of divine arbitrariness as meaningful insofar as the essential goodness of creaturely existence is in doubt. How do we know that in creation, God is seeking the benefit of creatures? This question can only be answered by attending to the character of Divinity, showing what *kind* of creator this God is. An adequate defense against the charge that creation from nothing implies an arbitrary or tyrannical God will therefore need to combine analysis of the doctrine's logic with an exposition of the identity of the God who is its subject. Thus, in much the same way that it is possible in the human sphere to deflect the charge that a person is arbitrary by appeal to the character that underlies and shapes her actions, so, too, with God.[72]

Since Christians view Scripture as the definitive witness to God's identity, the claim that one can affirm creation from nothing while denying divine arbitrariness needs to be made on exegetical grounds. At first glance the prospects for success might seem limited, given both the lack of explicit biblical witness to the idea of creation from nothing and the undeniable presence of biblical passages seeming to suggest that God *is* arbitrary (see, perhaps most famously, Rom. 9:15–21; cf. Exod. 33:19). Of course, theology is not reducible to proof-texting, and a doctrine's orthodoxy does not hang on its being taught explicitly in the Bible. The fact that the doctrine of the Trinity is not spelled out in the Bible has not prevented the overwhelming majority of Christians for the last 1,500 years from viewing it as a thoroughly "biblical" concept. Likewise, the propriety with which the church teaches both creation from nothing and the fundamental graciousness of God's works will not be decided by citing texts apart from systematic consideration of the ways in which the confession of Jesus of Nazareth as Lord and Savior bears on the question of God's relationship to the world. Nevertheless, the importance of such systematic considerations does not obviate the need for careful attention to the meaning of particular biblical passages, especially a text as decisive for framing any putatively biblical understanding of creation as the first chapter of Genesis.

In undertaking such interpretation, however, it is important to insist that the proper content of the Christian doctrine of creation cannot be decided on the basis of a narrow focus on the Hebrew of Genesis 1:1. Even if this unusual

---

71. For further discussion of this point, see pp. 187–88 below.

72. Thomas Aquinas frequently appealed to the biblical accounts of God's nature, ways, and purposes to argue that although even the most theologically important features of God's work in the world could not be judged necessary (since God remains always utterly free to do as God wants), it is nevertheless possible to argue that they are fitting or appropriate. See, e.g., St. Thomas Aquinas, *Summa theologiae* 3.3.8, in Blackfriars ed., 61 vols. (London: Eyre & Spottiswood, 1964–81), on the fact that it was the second person of the Trinity who took flesh; and 3.46.1–4, on suffering as the means by which Christ freed humanity from sin.

Here and below, singular personal pronouns referring to persons (she, her, he, him, et al.) are generally intended to refer to any individual person, female or male.

construction were less ambiguous than millennia of competing interpretations suggest, for Christians who work with a two-Testament canon, its doctrinal significance cannot be assessed apart from texts like the first chapter of John, which gives its own account of "the beginning" with a grammar that (at least with respect to the opening prepositional phrase) is utterly unambiguous: "In the beginning was the Word, and the Word was with God, and the Word was God. He was in the beginning with God. All things came into being through him, and without him not one thing came into being. What has come into being in him was life, and the life was the light of all people. The light shines in the darkness, and the darkness did not overcome it" (John 1:1–5). [73]

For John, the authority of the Jewish Scriptures is clear, yet relative: on the one hand, they bear witness to Jesus (5:39); on the other, it is Jesus who unlocks their true meaning (see, e.g., 2:17). Consequently, John's "In the beginning . . ." does not merely echo Genesis 1 (in the way that elements of Genesis 1 may echo earlier Near Eastern creation myths like the *Enuma Elish*), but interprets it—a pattern repeated in various places throughout the Gospel.[74] Such interpretive elaboration of Old Testament is found throughout the New Testament and seems to be rooted in the conviction that Jesus is not only witnessed to by the law and the prophets (Acts 28:23; Rom. 3:21), but also provides an indispensable reference point for fully grasping their meaning. Given this conviction, it follows that if John 1 is accepted as canonical Scripture, its testimony about how the world came to be must be taken into account when developing a Christian doctrine of creation.[75]

What exactly does John 1 say about God's creating? The first thing to note is that the "beginning" in John 1:1 does not refer to the time "when God began to create" (which does not come into view until v. 3), but to the logically prior conditions that form the context of God's creative work. In describing these conditions, the evangelist makes no mention of any formless waste, water, or swirling deep alongside God; even darkness comes into play only after "all things" have already come into existence.[76] Yet there is one entity mentioned in addition to God: the "Word" (*Logos* in Greek). This Word is identified as that which

73. It is striking that Griffin does not mention John 1 in his exploration of the biblical evidence for ex nihilo in "Creation out of Nothing." Likewise, Keller's extensive exegesis of Gen. 1 in *Face of the Deep* (chaps. 6, 9–14) makes extensive use of the Babylonian *Enuma Elish* and the later Jewish kabbalah, but includes no discussion of John.

74. See, e.g., the reworking of the "Jacob's ladder" story in the context of Jesus' encounter with Nathanael (John 1:47–51; cf. Gen. 27:35; 28:10–12), the comparison between Jesus' being lifted up and Moses' lifting up of the bronze serpent in the wilderness (John 3:14–15; cf. Num. 21:9), and most striking of all, the various passages in which Jesus refers to himself as "I am" (John 6:20; 8:24, 28, 58; 13:19; 18:5–6; cf. Exod. 3:14).

75. For an argument that the opening of John's Gospel constitutes just this sort of interpretive midrash on Genesis 1, see Daniel Boyarin, "The Gosple of the Memra: Jewish Binitarianism and the Prologue of John," *Harvard Theological Review* 94 (2001): 243-84; cited in Blowers, *Drama of the Divine Economy*, 70.

76. If, as Raymond E. Brown suggests, the darkness in John 1:5 is a reference to the sin of Adam in Gen. 3, then its ontologically subsequent or derivative character is even more firmly established. See his *The Gospel according to John (i–xii)*, Anchor Bible 29 (Garden City, NY: Doubleday, 1966), 8.

was "with God" in the beginning (v. 1b)—a point evidently significant enough for the evangelist that it is repeated in verse 2. And sandwiched between this repeated claim is a further specification that upsets a straightforward interpretation of the Word and God as two distinct realities: "the Word *was* God" (v. 1c). No more than any other New Testament text does John contain the later doctrinal language of creation from nothing, but thanks to this final clause, the upshot of the Gospel's opening verse is that the sole precondition and only context for creation is God.[77]

And yet it remains a crucial feature of John's first verses that although God is the sole presupposition of creation, the God who creates is not solitary, since the Word who *is* God is also *with* God. In this way, at the same time that John 1 stands as the most explicit biblical statement of the unconditional character of God's creating work, it also signals that creation from nothing is not merely a claim about God's relation to the world, but also a statement about God's own identity. This latter point is crucial to addressing the charge that creation from nothing implies a domineering, tyrannical God: in light of John's Gospel, the claim that God creates from nothing means that God creates through the same Word (1:3) who, because of God's love for the world, "became flesh and lived among us" (1:14) "so that everyone who believes in him may not perish but have eternal life" (3:16). Following the lead of John, creation from nothing should not be understood in isolation, as an abstract claim about divine power, but as part of a broader story of God's ongoing commitment to the life of all that is not God.

So it is that where the doctrine of creation is concerned, evaluating what God does is inseparable from knowing who God is—knowledge that for Christians is inseparable from the person of Jesus Christ. For this reason, Christians cannot talk about creation apart from Christology, and this christological matrix, in turn, shapes whatever formal theological claims are made about God's nature and attributes. So, for example, in speaking of divine omnipotence, it will be important not to leap to abstract considerations of possible limits (logical, metaphysical, or moral, for example) on God's power. These sorts of questions obviously cannot be ignored, but Christians find a more plausible starting point for

---

77. Does this claim that John 1 is crucial for the doctrine of creation from nothing need to be tempered in light of the seemingly contrary witness of 2 Pet. 3:5 ("By the word of God heavens existed long ago and an earth was formed out of water and by means of water")? I do not think so. Aside from the fact that 2 Peter is, by comparison with the Fourth Gospel, a canonically marginal text (for it is possible to accept the judgment of 2 Tim. 3:16 that all Scripture is "inspired by God" and correspondingly "useful," without concluding that every biblical text is equally significant), the nature of this Petrine reference to creation gives it little dogmatic weight. In contrast to John (whose christological reworking of Genesis 1 sets the tone for the whole Gospel), Peter's reference to creation is incidental: his aim is simply to counter the skeptic's charge that "all things continue as they were from the beginning of creation!" (2 Pet. 3:4). Thus the emphasis on the watery context of creation in v. 5 is less a freestanding ontological claim than a rhetorical setup for the reference to the deluge in v. 6: the world made through water was also destroyed through water. That the water in question has no enduring ontological significance for the author is clear from v. 7 (cf. v. 12), where he claims that the present order will eventually be destroyed by fire.

reflection on what it might mean to say that God is omnipotent in a passage like John 10:29, where Jesus says, "My Father is greater than all by virtue of what he has given me, and no one can snatch out of the Father's hand."[78] While the Greek text of this passage is not without problems,[79] two things are clear: first (and in line with both Theophilus's and Irenaeus's defense of creation from nothing), there is no power capable of defeating God's will to save; and second, the indefeasibility of God's power is somehow bound up with the relationship between the Father and the Son. Clearly if omnipotence is understood in this way, the chief concerns of process thought regarding divine totalitarianism seem at the very least rhetorically misplaced. It remains, of course, to show both how these two aspects of the verse are related (*How* does God's power depend on God's identity?), and how their relation helps to address the charge that an omnipotent God is necessarily arbitrary (*What difference does it make* that God's power depends on God's identity?). That will be the task of the rest of this book.

78. My translation, based on Brown, *Gospel of John*, 401.

79. See John 10:29 NRSV: "What my Father has given me is greater than all else, and no one can snatch it out of the Father's hand." The chief textual problem with the verse has to do with variant readings of the relative pronoun (either *ho*, referring indefinitely to "what" the Father has given, or *hos*, referring to the Father, as in the RSV's "My Father, who has given them to me") and "greater" (which can apply either to "what the Father has given" [*meizon*], or to the Father himself [*meizōn*]). Strong witnesses can be cited for virtually every combination of these variants. The one I have chosen (*ho* plus *meizōn*) is supported by many of the more important uncial manuscripts (including the Codices Sinaiticus and Bezae) and can be defended as the most difficult reading, since the available alternatives are arguably driven by the desire to bring the pronoun and adjective into grammatical agreement with each other.

PART 1
EXITUS

2

God

A description of God's character as Creator naturally begins with an account of what Christians mean by the word "God." Broadly speaking, the whole of Christian theology is occupied with this question, since theology means "talk about God." And yet as soon as the would-be theologian seeks to go about this task, she is faced with a problem, for it is a long-standing Christian belief that God is not a kind of thing we can talk about. This is not to say that God is unknown. On the contrary, it is an equally long-standing feature of Christian belief that God is known both concretely and unsurpassably in Jesus the Christ, so that to be "Christian" entails making this same Jesus the measure of all talk about God. But this statement of principle only gets the theologian so far. What it means to make Jesus the measure of God-talk is not a matter of consensus among Christians, not least because the same Scriptures that Christians regard as the normative witness to Jesus warn against easy confidence in our ability to speak rightly of God:

> For my thoughts are not your thoughts,
>   nor are your ways my ways, says the LORD.

For as the heavens are higher than the earth,
so are my ways higher than your ways
and my thoughts than your thoughts.
(Isa. 55:8–9)

The God who is known in Jesus "dwells in unapproachable light, whom no one has ever seen or can see" (1 Tim. 6:16; cf. John 1:18; 6:46; 1 John 4:12). To be sure, even as they declare that God cannot be grasped by human thought or vision, such passages evidently talk about God and are found in the midst of a good deal more of the same. It remains the case, however, that the biblical account of God includes two prohibitions that pose stark limits to Christian God-talk: God is not to be depicted visually (Exod. 20:4–5; Deut. 5:8–9), and God's name is not to be spoken wrongfully (Exod. 20:7; Deut. 5:11).

The rationale behind the first of these commandments is clearly set forth in Scripture: a God who has no form cannot be given a form without being misrepresented (Deut. 4:15–18). To make an image of God is therefore to commit idolatry: to treat as God something that is not God. The same rationale cannot be applied in the second case, since God does have a name, which has been openly declared to God's people (Exod. 3:15). At the same time, the gift of God's name cannot be understood as a verbal replacement for visual or tactile representations of the divine. Although God has a name, that fact provides no basis for human efforts to limit, control, or define God. On the contrary, the fact that the revelation of the divine name is prefaced by God's declaration, "I AM WHO I AM" (or perhaps even better, "I WILL BE WHO I WILL BE," Exod. 3:14), indicates that God alone determines Who God is. For this reason, God—precisely as God—cannot be incorporated into human conceptual frameworks and ideological schemes. When this point is ignored, the "God" who results is no longer Israel's Lord, but an idol, even if an invisible one.[1] It follows that to invoke God's name, and thus to talk about God, rightly is not to claim any privilege over against God, but to recognize that who God is must be entirely God's affair.

Christians also confess that in Jesus, God has taken human form and has spoken human words. And yet Jesus himself makes it quite clear that the mere fact of talking about him, or even performing deeds of power in his name, is in itself no guarantee of fellowship with God (Matt. 7:21–23). The incarnation does many things, but it does not eliminate the risk of idolatry. On the contrary, God's assuming flesh arguably augments the risk of idolatry, even as it also opens up new possibilities for faithful God-talk. The fact of the incarnation therefore does not absolve Christians from needing to confront the challenge of speaking

---

1. "As I have often said, the trust and faith of the heart make both God and an idol. . . . Idolatry does not consist merely of erecting an image and praying to it. It is primarily in the heart, which pursues other things and seeks help and consolation from creatures, saints, or devils." Thus, even where the name of God is used, where God's freedom is not honored, "What is this but making God into an idol . . . and setting up ourselves as God?" Martin Luther, *Large Catechism*, in *The Book of Concord: The Confessions of the Evangelical Lutheran Church*, ed. and trans. Theodore G. Tappert (Philadelphia: Muhlenberg Press, 1959), 365, 367.

about God with a modesty that may at times seem rather austere. The point of such modesty is not to suggest that God is austere; on the contrary, God is not only inexhaustibly rich in God's self, but also endlessly profligate in sharing this divine plenitude with creatures. But precisely because God is so rich, we go astray whenever in our speech we limit God to a particular set of categories or concepts.

In order to avoid this danger, it is part of the strategy of this book to unfold God's richness gradually, through examination in successive chapters of the myriad ways in which that richness is disclosed (and yet, precisely because of its inexhaustible character, always only *incompletely* disclosed) in creation. Insofar as this chapter considers God as creation's sole and sufficient ground, and thus in abstraction from the ways in which the work of creation bears witness to the fullness of God's being, I will focus rather narrowly on the question of identifying God who is, in the hope that the exploration in the chapters that follow of what God does will bear ever more complete witness to God's glory as the Creator.

GOD AS TRANSCENDENT

Since the only words available to talk about God are the same words we use to talk about what is not God, all God-talk seems to be unavoidably idolatrous. To talk about something is to incorporate it into some conceptual scheme by subsuming it under some set of categories (big, square, red) in preference to others (small, round, transparent). This process of categorization makes possible the comparison and contrast of one thing with another that allows us to relate the various items of our thought and experience to each other into an ordered conceptual picture of the world. Talk about God is no exception: if we say anything about God at all, we incorporate God into our world-picture—and thereby implicitly define God in terms of created categories in a way that seemingly violates the basic principles of faithful worship as defined in the Decalogue.

In the late eleventh century the theologian Anselm (who later became Archbishop of Canterbury) gave expression to God's incommensurability with all created reality in his *Proslogion* by naming God as "that than which nothing greater can be conceived."[2] In order to appreciate Anselm's point, we need to distinguish this designation from the claim that God is "the greatest conceivable thing" or "the most perfect being." The latter options place God on the same metaphysical continuum as all other beings: even if they locate God on the

---

2. "Aliquid quo nihil maius cogitari potest." Anselm, *Proslogion* 2, in *S. Anselmi Cantuariensis Archiepiscopi Opera omnia*, 1:101, ed. Francis Salesius Schmitt (Edinburgh: Thomas Nelson & Son, 1946). In the course of the work, Anselm offers minor variations on this Latin phrase (e.g., "id quo maius cogitari non potest" later in the very same chapter), none of which affect the logic of his position. For an English translation, see Anselm, *Monologion and Proslogion, with the Replies of Gaunilo and Anselm*, trans. Thomas Williams (Indianapolis: Hackett Publishing Co., 1995).

extreme end of the scale, God remains subject to classification within a conceptual system, as part of the larger set of "things" or "beings." By contrast, "that than which nothing greater can be conceived" points to the limits of all human conceptual systems, because that to which it refers does not fit within any scale of rank or value, and so is not a "kind" of thing or being.

To grasp the distinctiveness of Anselm's language here, consider that the concept of "the greatest conceivable thing" stands in no tension with the rest of our thinking. Our experience of the world may or may not persuade us that that there actually exists in reality something corresponding to whatever concept lies at the upper limit of our conceptual framework. Either way, however, our concept of such an entity remains part of, and thus fits together with, the rest of our concepts. However great it may be, such an entity presents no challenges to our way of thinking about the world, because as an extrapolation of our concept of greatness, it is part of the way we think about the world. By contrast, "that than which nothing greater can be conceived" does not correspond to any item within a conceptual system. Instead, "that than which nothing greater can be conceived" is significant precisely because it destabilizes whatever conceptual system we may have by positing a distinction between the "that" it names and *anything* that we can conceive, so that the attempt to conceive of "that than which nothing greater can be conceived" is a sign that the phrase has been misunderstood. In short, to identify God as "that than which nothing greater can be conceived" is to insist that the *reality* of God invariably disrupts our *concept* of God in a way that anything defined in terms of our operative conceptual frameworks (such as the "most perfect being" or "greatest conceivable being") does not. In this way, Anselm's language can function as a kind of grammatical therapy for the theologian, reminding her that to whatever extent her talk about God treats "God" as a token within a conceptual system (and no talk about God can avoid this), her talk will, to that extent, fail to bear appropriate witness to God.[3]

The claim that God is *transcendent* is a traditional way of acknowledging that God cannot be incorporated into any conceptual system. So understood, "transcendence" is more a formal than a material property of Divinity: it is invoked to suggest certain protocols for talk about God and not as a direct description of the divine nature. Medieval theologians summarized the linguistic implications of divine transcendence in the Latin phrase "*Deus non est in genere,*" which

---

3. In this context—and whatever one makes of the validity of Anselm's attempt to derive an argument for God's existence directly from logical analysis of "that than which nothing greater can be conceived"—note should be taken of the fact that the whole of the *Proslogion* (in contrast to Anselm's earlier *Monologion*, not to mention virtually every other subsequent attempt to "prove" God's existence) is written as a prayer, as direct address *to* God rather than an abstract piece of ratiocination *about* God. Cf. Dietrich Bonhoeffer, *Act and Being: Transcendental Philosophy and Ontology in Systematic Theology*, vol. 2 of *Dietrich Bonhoeffer Works*, trans. H. Martin Rumscheidt (1931; repr., Minneapolis: Fortress Press, 1996), 131: "Because theology turns revelation into some*thing* that exists, it may be practiced only where the living person of Christ is itself present and can destroy the existing thing or acknowledge it."

may be loosely translated, "God cannot be categorized."[4] But this merely brings us back to the question with which we began: given that talk about any entity entails predicating certain attributes of, and thereby categorizing, that entity (e.g., as immaterial rather than material, or wise rather than foolish), how is it possible to say anything about God without immediately undermining the claim that God is transcendent?

A classic answer to this question is to maintain that attributes are predicated of God *analogously*. Normally we expect a speaker to use terms *univocally*. When a term is used univocally, its meaning is stable across different contexts, so that its various uses can easily be related to one another and correspond to a single overarching definition. Thus, when I describe a fifth grader, a particular elm tree, the Empire State Building, and the Himalayas as "tall," the meaning is consistent and readily transferable across all these instances (viz., "above average height for a given class of entities"), even though the actual measurements involved may vary enormously from one item to the next. If I am using the word "tall" univocally, you will have some idea of what I mean by a tall widget, even if you don't know what a widget is. Univocal predication stands in direct contrast with an *equivocal* use of terms, where nothing can be determined about the meaning of a term in one context from its use in another (as when I describe both the number 3 and my uncle Joe as "odd").

Now, to use a term univocally of God and a creature would be to locate both within the same conceptual framework, so that (e.g.) God's wisdom would be conceived on the same scale as human wisdom, albeit on the extreme upward end of that scale. That perspective, however, evidently violates the principle of divine transcendence. On the other hand, to say that when applied to God, words like "good" or "wise" are used equivocally would make them meaningless since I would have to conclude that the wisdom whereby "God is wise" bears no relationship whatever to creaturely examples of wisdom. Analogy is an attempt to split the difference by positing a mode of predication that honors the principle that terms cannot be predicated of God and creatures univocally while avoiding pure equivocation. In his *Summa theologiae*, Thomas Aquinas offers the word "healthy" as an example of analogical predication in everyday speech.[5] It is possible, he states, to describe a person as healthy, her diet as healthy, and her urine as healthy. The word "healthy" is clearly not being used univocally here since it is not possible to derive what it means to say that either a diet or urine are healthy from knowledge of what it means for a person to be healthy. At the same time, these various uses of healthy are not simply equivocal either: a physician

4. See, e.g., Thomas Aquinas, *Summa theologiae* (hereafter *ST*) 1.3.5, in Blackfriars ed., 61 vols. (London: Eyre & Spottiswood, 1964–81): "Genus est prius, secundum intellectum, eo quod in genere continetur. Sed nihil est prius Deo, nec secundum rem, nec secundum intellectum. Ergo Deus non est in aliquo genere." Cf. Kathryn Tanner, *Christ the Key* (Cambridge: Cambridge University Press, 2010), 156: "Monotheism means . . . that divinity is not a class term; divinity is not a kind of thing whose defining characteristics might be displayed by many things to a greater or lesser degree."
5. See Thomas Aquinas, *ST* 1.13.10.

who understands how all three instances of "healthy" are used can see and articulate the relationship between them (viz., that a healthy diet promotes health in a person, and that healthy urine reflects it). To claim that certain attributes may be predicated of God by analogy is to argue that a similar relationship holds between attributes predicated of God and creatures. On the one hand, Christians confess that God exists, and that the existence of creatures derives from God's existence; on the other hand, in confessing that God is transcendent, they acknowledge that God's existence is so radically different than that of creatures that they do not know exactly what it means to say that God exists. Nevertheless, insofar as they hold that they are justified in applying the term "existence" to God, they remain confident that it applies most properly to God and only derivatively to creatures—similar to the way that "healthy" applies preeminently to living organisms and only secondarily to things like diet and urine.[6]

While analogy provides a means of honoring divine transcendence without relinquishing God-talk, its limitations are obvious. Although Thomas characterized analogy as a middle way between univocal and equivocal predication, as a matter of logic it veers closer to being equivocal, since it is "impossible to predicate anything univocally of God and creatures."[7] Moreover, since we are not yet in glory and so cannot see how particular attributes apply both to God and to us, the question immediately arises of how we know exactly *which* attributes are to be predicated of God. To take God's transcendence seriously is, seemingly, not only to deny that the attributes I predicate of God carry the same sense they have when I apply them to objects in the world, but also to confess profound ignorance of the sense in which they may be affirmed of God. If this is the case, on what basis is the theologian to prefer any one term for God over another?

Initial reflection on the logic of divine transcendence itself suggests that there are at least two classes of terms that are appropriate for theological use, even allowing for our inherent inability to categorize God. The first is comprised of

6. For this reason, the extent of the dissimilarity between our understanding of a term and its meaning when applied to God cannot be stated too sharply: "The term 'existence' applies affirmatively, substantially, and properly to God with regard to that which it names or signifies in *his language*, but it does not apply to him *at all* with regard to what it means or signifies in our language. . . . While to say that God 'exists' is to say that there is a conceptual framework in terms of which the proposition 'God exists' would be intelligible, it is nevertheless true that the proposition is *not* intelligible in terms of *our* conceptual framework, and thus, insofar as 'exists' plays an intrasystemic role in our language, it must be *denied* of God." Victor Preller, *Divine Science and the Science of God: A Reformulation of Thomas Aquinas* (Princeton, NJ: Princeton University Press, 1967), 173–74. Cf. the famous judgment of the Fourth Lateran Council, in 1215: "For between Creator and creature no similitude can be expressed without implying a greater dissimilitude." DS 806 (DS = H. J. D. Denzinger [first editor], Enchiridion symbolorum, definitionum et declarationum de rebus fidei et morum, a progressively updated compendium of basic texts of Catholic dogma [1854–]), cited in *The Christian Faith in the Doctrinal Documents of the Catholic Church*, ed. Josef Neuner and Jacques Dupuis, rev. ed. (New York: Alba House, 1982), 109.

7. "Impossibile est aliquid praedicari de Deo et creaturis univoce." Thomas Aquinas, *ST* 1.13.5 (the language of analogy as a "middle way" [*modus . . . medius*] comes from the same article). In *Divine Science* (243), Preller characterizes the analogies that Thomas promotes as "appropriate equivocations." In *ST* 1.13.10.4, Thomas himself notes that Aristotle's use of the term "equivocal" includes the analogical.

negations. This is hardly surprising, even if we are unable to say how any conceivable quality might meaningfully be affirmed of God, it obviously remains possible to deny various things of God. Many of the traditional "divine attributes" are negations of this sort. Thus, in contrast to creatures, which we identify by reference to their composite features and corresponding location in time and space (e.g., "the small red car with the dented fender that was parked on the south side of Elm Street yesterday afternoon"), a transcendent God is eternal (not bound by time), immense (not confined in space), and simple (not subject to analysis in terms of component parts or aspects). As logical corollaries of transcendence, negative attributes like eternity, immensity, and simplicity are rightly predicated—and indeed are literally true—of God; but they add nothing positive to our knowledge of God. On the contrary, they merely restate God's essential unknowability.[8]

A seemingly more useful set of predicates includes the so-called transcendentals: unity, goodness, and truth. Transcendentals are so named because they "transcend" the categories by reference to which we conceive of particular entities. Categories are the means by which we recognize the ways in which the various things we encounter in the world differ from each other: with respect to substance, quality, place, time, and so forth. The transcendentals, by contrast, name features that all entities have in common: insofar as something exists at all, it is one (i.e., *this* thing rather than some other), good (i.e., desirable as the thing that it is), and true (i.e., knowable as the thing that it is). In short, the transcendentals may be predicated of any entity that exists because they are intrinsic aspects of (and so, in the language of medieval Scholasticism, "convertible" with) existence itself. Thus, insofar as God may be said to exist, God may also be said to be one, good, and true. Indeed, insofar as God exists supremely, God may and must be said to be supremely one, good, and true. Yet these transcendental attributes, like the claim of existence on which they depend, may be predicated of a transcendent God only by analogy; this fact means that they do little to contribute to our knowledge of God beyond affirming the "thatness" of "that than which nothing greater can be conceived."[9]

8. The list of negative attributes of God can be expanded well beyond the three listed here and include, e.g., the claims that God is infinite (not finite, and so neither limited nor constrained by any nondivine reality) and that God is pure act (i.e., not containing any potential needing to be actualized by some other reality).

9. "The transcendentals . . . are used to name or signify something which is actually true of God in his own being. Since, however, the terms as they really apply to God have intelligible meaning only as analogues in a postulated and unknown conceptual system, and not in our conceptual system, we must simultaneously deny that we use them to intend the specific and intelligible intensional [connotative] content that they possess for us." Preller, *Divine Science*, 167.

GOD AS LIVING

Taken by itself, then, the claim that God is transcendent does not give any positive account of God, but only signals the obstacles to any such account that follow from the impossibility of locating God within any creaturely conceptual frame. As already noted, it is at bottom a formal rather than a material claim. A transcendent God, who cannot be subsumed under any concept or category, is ineffable, but ineffability is not a positive quality. Along with attributes like eternity and simplicity, it is "apophatic" in character: a negative claim grounded in the conviction that we "are closest to the truth when we deny of God that which we have consciously 'in mind.'"[10] The transcendental attributes of unity, goodness, and truth seem at first blush to be more helpful, but their character as transcendentals—and thus true of all beings—means that they are of little help in distinguishing God in any positive respect from other entities. Indeed, insofar as the transcendentals are predicated of God only analogously, they offer just another example of God's fundamental incommensurability with human conceptual frameworks. The upshot of the claim that God is transcendent therefore turns out to be little more than a matter of conceptual ground clearing: far from giving us tools to help us talk about God, it only highlights our incapacity to say what God is like.[11]

How then do Christians presume to make claims about God that are both positive (i.e., not pure negation) and substantive (i.e., not just transcendental), claims that describe God in terms of particular qualities to the exclusion of possible alternatives? If, following the lead of Exodus 3:14, we take the position that God's identity is entirely God's affair, then good theology is finally a surrendering of one's words and thoughts to God, in line with the advice Jesus gives his disciples: "When they hand you over, do not worry about how you are to speak or what you are to say; for what you are to say will be given to you at that time" (Matt. 10:19; cf. Luke 12:12). Given the impossibility of mapping God onto any conceptual framework, in the last analysis the theologian can only pray that her thoughts and words will be acceptable to God (Ps. 19:14). But this does not mean that she is utterly without guidance in determining which claims about God are to be judged "orthodox" (literally, that which gives "proper praise"). That God alone determines God's identity means that appropriate language for God must derive from God, and Christians hold that God has provided the

10. Ibid., 271.
11. In this context, Karl Rahner's charge (see his *The Trinity*, trans. J. Donceel [New York: Herder & Herder, 1970], 16–17) that Thomas Aquinas subverts the logic of the Christian faith by beginning his reflections in the first part of the *Summa theologiae* with God's oneness (in qq. 2–26) and only later moving on to the Trinity (qq. 28–43) is not altogether fair, since the earlier questions function far more in this ground-clearing mode than as positive statements about God's nature. As William Placher has put it, Thomas's analysis of the divine attributes in the *Summa* constitute "not a *metaphysical system* that would place God within our understanding of the world and specify the meaning of our language about God, but *metalinguistic rules* that remind us of the limitations of our language about God." William C. Placher, *The Domestication of Transcendence: How Modern Thinking about God Went Wrong* (Louisville, KY: Westminster John Knox Press, 1996), 31.

ground for such language by taking flesh in Jesus of Nazareth (John 1:14) and leading a fully human, historical, and perceptible life. It is the further conviction of Christians that God has provided a trustworthy witness to this act of divine self-disclosure in Holy Scripture, which, because it is "inspired by God," is "useful for teaching, for reproof, for correction, and for training in righteousness, so that everyone who belongs to God may be proficient, equipped for every good work" (2 Tim. 3:16–17; cf. 2 Pet. 1:20–21).[12] In short, if God's transcendence leaves us without any means of fitting our language to God, it does not prevent God from making use of our language to teach us about God where and as God pleases, appropriating human words to speak truly of divine reality.[13]

Because the words of Scripture are human words, the same words we use to speak of everyday realities like shoes and ships and sealing wax, they have no inherent capacity to speak of God. Christians receive Scripture's words as authoritative out of the conviction that, in bearing witness to Jesus, they communicate God's Word. But since God's Word is none other than God (John 1:1) and so shares fully in God's transcendence, even when made flesh its fullness cannot be exhausted by any number of human words (John 21:25). Consequently, Scripture cannot be taken as a static repository of truths about God, as though faithful witness to God could be reduced to the recitation of Scripture.[14] Instead, God's self-presentation in Jesus renders the words of Scripture both supremely authoritative for Christian God-talk (since in speaking of Jesus, Scripture speaks of nothing less than God) and yet strictly subordinate to the Word who is the object of their witness, to the extent that faithful witness to God may involve words that go beyond the specific vocabulary found in Scripture.[15] The Christian conviction that Scripture speaks of God is therefore inseparable from

12. If Scripture's authority in the church depends on its witness to Jesus, then Jesus' identity as the Christ (Matt. 16: 16–20 and pars.; John 1:18; 20:31) dictates that the Christian canon include the Old Testament no less than the New; for "Christ" (Greek for "Messiah") is a Jewish title that refers to the hope of Israel, and the content of this hope can only be discerned through engagement with Israel's Scriptures. So (to give just one of many examples from within the New Testament itself) Paul takes pains to argue that to know who Jesus is means to know him as the fulfillment of God's promises to Abraham (Gal. 3:6–29; Rom. 4:1–25; cf. Gen. 12:1–3, 7; 15:5–6; 17:4–6; 22:17–18). Thus, even though the Old Testament does not speak explicitly of Jesus, it is no less crucial a witness to Jesus' identity, and thus to God's identity, than the New Testament.

13. "To the question of how we come to know God by means of our thinking and language, we must give the answer that of ourselves we do not come to know Him, that, on the contrary, this happens only as the grace of the revelation of God comes to us and therefore to the means of our thinking and language, adopting us and them, pardoning, saving, protecting, and making good." Karl Barth, *Church Dogmatics* (hereafter *CD*), ed. G. W. Bromiley and T. F. Torrance, 13 vols. (Edinburgh: T&T Clark, 1956–75), II/1:223.

14. Even biblical words do not all bear witness to God in the same way. As Thomas noted (*ST* 1.13.3.1), terms that carry an explicit reference to a created mode of existence ("rock," "warrior") can only apply to God metaphorically, while those that do not ("living," "good") may be understood as literally true of God (albeit by analogy).

15. A classic, and in its time quite controversial, example is the use of the nonbiblical Greek term *homoousios* ("of the same substance") to describe the relation between the Father and the Son in the Nicene Creed. For a sophisticated account of the way in which fidelity to God's own self-disclosure may assume new and surprising forms over time, see Kevin W. Hector, *Theology without Metaphysics: God, Language, and the Spirit of Recognition* (Cambridge: Cambridge University Press, 2011).

the equally firm conviction that Scripture is not God. The God who declared to Moses, "I AM WHO I AM"—and who in that same gracious freedom willed to live a human life among us (John 8:58)—is no more constrained or ruled by Scripture than by any other creaturely reality. Precisely in and as the incarnate Word, God is the Lord of Scripture, too.

It follows that Scripture does not furnish the church with a conceptual framework within which God becomes comprehensible. Even when Christian use of Scripture succeeds in giving true witness to God, God remains transcendent. And since the transcendent God remains unknowable to creatures, there can be no viable claim that their commitment to the truth of Scripture gives Christians any more success in grasping God's essence than non-Christians. When Christians bind themselves to the words of Scripture, they do so out of trust in and obedience to God, and not because they are able to establish the adequacy or appropriateness of those words by their own effort or skill.[16] Conscious of the gap between their vision of Divinity and God's reality, they trust that their talk about God is true insofar as God creates an analogy between what they intend to say of God and what God intends to communicate through them. On the basis of this analogy between their words and God's Word (following the Greek of Rom. 12:6, it may be called the "analogy of faith"), Christians may speak truly of God, but with two provisos: First, apart from grace (which they can never secure for themselves) nothing they say about God can be true, however much it may refer either to Scripture (Matt. 4:6) or to Jesus himself (Matt. 7:21). Second, even where they succeed, by grace, in speaking truly of God, they cannot claim to know *how* it is true that their words correspond to God.[17]

And yet however incomprehensible God remains even when described in the light of Scripture, and however constant the threat that human perversity or carelessness will misapply the words of Scripture, Christians claim that through Scripture they have genuine knowledge of God. This knowledge remains analogical, because Christians cannot claim to grasp the full significance of what they know about God. But insofar as God enables what they say to bear genuine witness to God, there is no "gap" between the theological truths that Christians

16. While by definition the fact that believers take the truth of what they say on authority means that they do not know how it is true, this does not imply any qualification in their conviction of its truth, for just as "a person with scant learning is far surer [*certior*] of something he hears from an expert than he is of his own opinion," so "anyone is far surer of what he hears from the infallible God than of what he sees with his own fallible reason." Thomas Aquinas, *ST* 2/2.4.8.2. Cf. John Calvin, *Institutes of the Christian Religion*, trans. Ford Lewis Battles, 3.2.14 (Philadelphia: Westminster Press, 1960).

17. In this respect they are "like infants mouthing scraps out of Shakespeare or the *Principia mathematica*, parrot-like, by rote. Only occasionally do they have inklings of the meanings of the words they utter." George A. Lindbeck, *The Nature of Doctrine: Religion and Theology in a Postliberal Age* (Philadelphia: Westminster Press, 1984), 61. Donald D. Evans makes a similar point regarding our inability to specify the similarity between God and any attribute we may predicate of God and our corresponding dependence on the authoritative testimony of someone else for knowing which attributes to predicate of God—in *The Logic of Self-Involvement: A Philosophical Study of Everyday Language with Special Reference to the Christian Use of Language about God as Creator* (London: SCM Press, 1963), 133.

manage to say and what God is, as though the claim (e.g.) that "God is Lord" were true only as an approximation.[18] At the same time, because it is God alone who enables words to communicate such knowledge, God remains free with respect to theological language, which therefore cannot be used to acquire conceptual leverage over against God (as though the meaning of "God is Lord" were bound by our finite and sinful conceptions of lordship). Through the activity of the Holy Spirit in the writing, reading, and preaching of Scripture, God's Word and human words can and do coincide, so that in and through human words, we may hear God speaking.

So understood, the Bible serves as the natural basis for Christian God-talk. In this context it is significant that Jesus himself counters the faithless use of Scripture precisely by citing Scripture against it (Matt. 4:7 and pars.).[19] This temptation story illustrates the church's conviction that by virtue of the gift of Scripture, the church's talk about God is not haphazard. Although the need to wait on the Spirit means that theological speech will always have a certain ad hoc quality about it, the task of surrendering one's thoughts and words to God remains inseparable from engagement with these texts. Faithful reading of Scripture is correspondingly *systematic*, not in the colloquial sense that it treats the Bible as a "system" in which everything to be said about God can be determined by following some set of procedural protocols, but in the etymological sense that it pushes the reader to test how any particular claim she finds herself inclined to make about God "stands together" (Greek *syn-histēmi*) with the broadest possible range of other features of the biblical witness to God's nature and character. Following this view of Scripture as a means provided and used by God to enable faithful witness to God, perhaps the most fundamental thing that may be said about God is that God is *living*: the One who is never at our disposal, but who is known rather in graciously anticipating and enabling our disposing.

The claim that God is living is biblically very well supported (see, e.g., Deut. 5:26; Josh. 3:10; Pss. 42:2; 84:2; Dan. 6:26; Matt. 16:16; Acts 14:15; 1 Thess. 1:9; 1 Tim. 4:10; Heb. 3:12; 12:22; Rev. 7:2), but its theological significance

18. God remains incomprehensible even in being known, "But," as Hans Urs von Balthasar puts it, "here 'incomprehensibility' does not mean a negative determination of what one does not know, but rather a positive and almost 'seen' and understood property of him whom one knows. The more a great work of art is known and grasped, the more concretely are we dazzled by its 'ungraspable' genius. We never outgrow something which we acknowledge to stand above us by its very nature." In his *Seeing the Form*, vol. 1 of *The Glory of the Lord: A Theological Aesthetics*, ed. Joseph Fessio, SJ, and John Riches, trans. Erasmo Leiva-Merikakis (San Francisco: Ignatius Press, 1982), 186.

19. Elsewhere, especially in the so-called antitheses of the Sermon on the Mount (Matt. 5:22, 28, 32, 34, 39, 44), Jesus seems to place his word over that of Scripture. While it is tempting to take this language as evidence of God's lordship over Scripture, any such conclusion must be tempered by consideration of the context within which the antitheses are spoken. Before the first antithesis is uttered, Jesus explicitly states that, far from abolishing the law or the prophets, he has come to fulfill them (5:17). Given that the antitheses are immediately preceded by Jesus' warning that the righteousness of his hearers must exceed that of the scribes and Pharisees, it seems most consistent with the text to conclude that they are intended precisely to specify what the law's fulfillment looks like—and thus that they serve to uphold rather than to qualify Scripture's authority (cf. in this context Rom. 3:28–31).

cannot be derived simply by counting up the references in a concordance. Indeed, the propriety of singling out "living" as the transcendent God's chief positive attribute might seem rather questionable, given the evident disparity between the meaning of the word when predicated of creatures on the one hand and of God on the other. In a terrestrial context, living creatures are defined by certain locally contained chemical processes and are distinguished chiefly by the capacity to reproduce themselves through the internally regulated replication of long molecular chains. By contrast, when Scripture speaks of God as living, the focus is on God's irreproducible uniqueness: in contrast to idols that can be multiplied at will but are inert and utterly powerless, the living God is active in a way that is incapable of being augmented (Jer. 10:2–16; cf. Ps. 115:3–8). Moreover, while for any creature life is sustained by drawing energy and shelter from other creatures (Gen. 1:29–30; Pss. 104:14–18, 21–28), God stands in no such dependence on anything outside of God (see, e.g., Ps. 50:7–13; Isa. 40:28; cf. 2 Macc. 14:35). Even allowing that by the rules of analogy we can never know how any of the terms we predicate of God apply to God, in this case the difference seems so vast as to amount to sheer equivocation.

And yet this radical incommensurability between the life of God and the life of creatures makes it an appropriate test case for the principle that divine attributes are not simply quantitative variations on their creaturely analogues. As the terms of analogical predication dictate, the claim that God is living can neither be derived from nor justified by reference to human experience of life. For this reason, even though the most faithful exegesis of the biblical claim that God is living will not give us direct knowledge of God's life as such (since in this life our knowledge never encompasses God, but only propositions about God), it remains possible to defend the claim that God is living by offering an appropriately "thick" (i.e., thoroughly contextualized) description of its content, which clarifies the features of Christian belief that it includes and summarizes.[20] Following this strategy, to say that God is living is not for Christians in the first instance to speak of God as Absolute Being or First Cause or Intelligent Designer, all of which (however justifiable they may be in particular contexts) simply contrast God with that which is relative or subsequent to God. Instead, when Christians want to identify God as living, it is more illuminating for them to say that God is Trinity: Father, Son, and Holy Spirit.[21]

20. The phrase "thick description" originated with Gilbert Ryle (see his "Thinking and Reflecting" and "The Thinking of Thoughts: What Is 'Le Penseur' Doing?," in *Collected Essays, 1929–1968*, vol. 2 of *Collected Papers* [1971; repr., London: Routledge, 2009], 465–86), was appropriated by the anthropologist Clifford Geertz (see esp. his "Thick Description: Toward an Interpretive Theory of Culture," in *The Interpretation of Culture: Selected Essays* [New York: Basic Books, 1973]), and was initially proposed as an appropriate way of conceiving and doing Christian theology by George Lindbeck in *The Nature of Doctrine*, 115.

21. I use the traditional language for the three persons not because I believe it to be either unproblematic or unsubstitutable, but because it provides a ready point of semantic contact with past generations of Christians in relation to and dependence on whom I develop my own theological position in this book.

✴ The confession of God as Trinity is not a statement about God's relationship to the world, but about who God is eternally. Although the classical form of the doctrine, that God is one substance (Greek *ousia*) in three "persons" (Greek *hypostaseis*), is not found in Scripture, the traditional language of Trinitarian confession is taken from Matthew 28:19 (cf. 2 Cor. 13:13). The upshot of the doctrine is that although God is *one* (and thus neither divisible into parts nor capable of increase), God is not *alone*. Here again, the opening verse of John (1:1) is important: "In the beginning was the Word, and the Word was with God, and the Word was God." God's own life includes another, a Word who is "with" or "facing" (*pros*) God and yet is not other than God. Nor is God's life exhausted by this binitarian relation between God and God's Word. There is a third: "another Counselor," namely, "the Spirit of truth" (John 14:16–17), who "proceeds from the Father" (John 15:26 RSV) and who "searches everything, even the depths of God" (1 Cor. 2:10) in a way that is impossible for any creature (1 Cor. 2:11).

Interpreted through the lens of the Trinity, the claim that God is living reflects the belief that the divine being is not a static co-presence of the one whom Jesus calls "Father," the Word, and the Holy Spirit, but a pattern of dynamic and fully mutual intimacy traditionally described as "perichoresis" (a Greek word often rendered as "coinherence" or "mutual interpenetration").[22] The Spirit's searching the depths of God has already been noted. The Word's place in the Godhead is reflected in the fact that, having taken flesh and dwelled on earth as the human being Jesus of Nazareth, the Word is consistently named the "Son" of the Father (John 1:14; 3:35; 5:19–23, 26; 10:36; 17:1; cf. Matt. 11:27 and pars.; Luke 1:32). The character of this relationship is such that the Son is uniquely capable of revealing the Father (John 1:18; cf. 14:6; Col. 1:19), even as it is only through the action of the Father that anyone confesses the Son (John 6:44; cf. 1 John 5:1). So likewise, even as the Son glorifies (John 13:31–32; 14:13; 17:1) the Father, so the Father glorifies the Son (John 8:54; Acts 3:13), a pattern that is not restricted to the period of Jesus' earthly ministry but also characterizes the divine life eternally (John 17:5). The Spirit too, as the one sent to bear witness, glorifies the Son (John 16:14) by bearing witness both to Christ's lordship (1 Cor. 12:3; 1 John 5:6–8) and to the faithfulness of the Father (Heb. 10:15–17).

In this way, the confession of God as Trinity suggests that part of what it means for God to be (inherently) living is for God to be (inherently) in relation. Importantly, this is not to make relationality a criterion of life, as though God were said to be living *because* God is in relation. When Christians say that the living God is in relation, they are not specifying a condition, but simply giving a description: God lives as the One who exists in *this* way—as Father, Son, and

---

22. Given the frequency with which the contrary is affirmed, it is probably worth noting here that "perichoresis" is etymologically unrelated to the Greek word for dancing (*choreuō*), deriving instead from *chōreō*, "to make room for, contain."

Holy Spirit. The relational character of the Trinity thus interprets what it means to say that God is living but does not establish the truth of the proposition. For one thing, the various biblical accounts of the relationships between the Father, Son, and Spirit do not lay out anything like a comprehensive picture of what it means for the Trinitarian persons to live in relation. The handful of verses (almost all in John) that speak explicitly of mutuality among the persons are at best partial and suggestive (e.g., no mention of the Father or the Son glorifying the Spirit). They certainly fall far short of what would be needed to generate anything like an ontology of Divinity.

In this context, it is vital to remember that Trinitarian confession is not based on general ontological considerations, but derives rather from the desire to give an adequate account of the God depicted in the New Testament. Consequently, the significance of the Trinity is less descriptive than ostensive: although it certainly entails various claims about God that Christians hold to be true, its primary aim is to say *who* God is rather than *what* God is like. From this perspective, the ground of Trinitarian confession is simply the conviction that God is not just the one who sends Jesus and the Spirit; rather, Jesus and the Spirit are also God. In these instances (and in contrast to what holds for the prophets of the Old Testament and the apostles of the New) God is both the sender *and* the sent; and because the sending and the being sent are both real (so that the one who sends remains distinct from those who are sent, who are, in turn, distinct from each other), God is properly identified in terms of the relations between Father, Son, and Holy Spirit, the fullness of which we cannot (and need not) fathom, but which is illustrated by the way in which reference to any one of them immediately implicates the other two. For who is the Spirit but the one sent by the Father to bear witness to the Son (1 Cor. 12:3; 1 John 4:2)? And who is the Son but the one anointed (the meaning of the title "Christ") by the Spirit to proclaim the Father's kingdom (Luke 4:18; Acts 10:38)? And who is the Father but the one who has sent the Son in the power of the Spirit (John 3:34–35; Rom. 1:1–4; cf. Matt. 3:16–17 and pars.)? To do theology without reference to these relations is simply to have failed to identify the Christian God.[23]

If the relations among the three Trinitarian hypostases are the primary framework for the Christian interpretation of the claim—common to both Testaments—that God is living, they also provide the basis for understanding the specifically New Testament affirmation that God is love (1 John 4:8, 16; cf.

---

23. Importantly, it does not follow that it is necessary to use Trinitarian language in order to refer to God successfully. Even though the Old Testament does not refer to God in terms of the Trinitarian relations, Christians hold that it speaks of the same God as the New, on the grounds that it is logically possible to *refer* to the Christian God without *identifying* that God as Father, Son, and Holy Spirit (in the same way that I can successfully refer to "the woman who runs research and development" without knowing her name). From a Christian perspective a consistently non-Trinitarian reference to the God of Israel will be theologically deficient, but not necessarily idolatrous. For a nice discussion of this issue, see Bruce D. Marshall, "Christ and the Cultures: The Jewish People and Christian Theology," in *The Cambridge Companion to Christian Doctrine*, ed. Colin E. Gunton (Cambridge: Cambridge University Press, 1997), 95–98.

John 15:9–10).[24] Here, as with all divine predicates, we must recognize the analogical character of this claim and be careful to guard against projecting our notions of love (whether in its "tough" or sentimental forms) onto God. Exegesis of the claim that God is love must be controlled by the life of the Trinity, which is the concrete form of divine love. And once again, what the Bible tells us of the eternal, intra-Trinitarian dimensions of this love is no more than suggestive. The Father's love for the Son is described in terms of giving (John 3:35) and showing (5:20), and the Son's love for the Father as a matter of keeping and abiding (15:10). But in each case it is unclear to what extent these descriptions are bound to the particular circumstances of the Word's enfleshment; and there is no account at all of how the Holy Spirit participates in the divine love.[25]

Nevertheless, the affirmation that God is love is not vacuous. If a Trinitarian exegesis of the claim that God is living points in the first instance to the perichoretic mutuality of the relations among the divine hypostases, the lack of symmetry with respect to the biblical accounts of the love of the Father, Son, and Spirit honors their distinctiveness. As the this-worldly (or in the language of classic Trinitarian doctrine, "economic") distinction between Father who sends and the Son and Spirit who are sent rules out interpreting the equal divinity of the hypostases as a matter of interchangeable equivalences, so the eternal (or "immanent") predicate of love may be taken as an index of the way in which the dynamism of God's triune life is characterized by attention to the particularity of the one loved that blocks the temptation to view the hypostases as interchangeable. If the living God, though one, is not alone, the further claim that this God is love clarifies that the plurality of the divine life is no formulaic repetition of abstract perfections (as in a summing of infinities that only reproduces infinity), but a diversity that can only be named and never explained.[26] This presence of

24. In light of the persistent temptation posed to Christian orthodoxy by Marcionite theologies that contrast the loving God of Jesus with the judging God of Israel, it must be stressed that the fact that the sentence "God is love" is found only in the New Testament does not reflect any inconsistency or tension with God's character as depicted in the Old Testament. God is unreservedly and unswervingly loving throughout the whole of the Bible, but it is the revelation of God's Trinitarian character that displays the rootedness of God's love in God's own life.

25. This lacuna has led one whole line of Christian thought to conceive of the Spirit as the substance rather than an agent of divine love. The key figure here is Augustine, whose characterization of the Spirit as love (see esp. *The Trinity* 15.31, ed. John E. Rotelle, trans. Edmund Hill [Hyde Park, NY: New City Press, 1991], 420–21) has profoundly shaped both Catholic and Protestant thought. For an alternative to this functionalist approach that, taking its cues from Orthodox and Syriac theological traditions, treats the Spirit in more "personal" terms as a distinct biblical character with its own agency, see Eugene F. Rogers Jr., *After the Spirit: A Constructive Pneumatology from Resources outside the Modern West* (Grand Rapids: Wm. B. Eerdmans Publishing Co., 2005).

26. So, in the words of the Athanasian Creed, while it is true that "the Father is infinite; the Son is infinite; the Holy Spirit is infinite," still "there is one Father, not three fathers; one Son, not three sons; one Holy Spirit, not three spirits." Cf. Vladimir Lossky: "In speaking of three hypostases, we are already making an improper abstraction: if we wanted to generalize and make a *concept* of the 'divine hypostasis,' we would have to say that the only common definition possible would be the impossibility of any common definition of the three hypostases. They are alike in the fact that they are dissimilar." Vladimir Lossky, *In the Image and Likeness of God*, ed. John H. Erickson and Thomas E. Bird (Crestwood, NY: St. Vladimir's Seminary Press, 1985), 113.

irreducible diversity within the indivisible unity of God's own life reflects love's character as that which is neither envious of nor threatened by the otherness of the beloved, but rather remains faithfully committed to it (see 1 Cor. 13:4–5, 7). Insofar as creation from nothing implies that God's love extends beyond God's own life to include what is not divine, appreciating the Trinitarian form of the claim that God is living is a first step in defending the doctrine against the charge that it implies an arbitrary and tyrannical God: if diversity among the divine person is no threat to (and is, in fact, constitutive of) God's life, there is no reason to suppose that God would be any less faithfully committed to the diversity of creatures.

GOD AS PRODUCTIVE

At this point, however, the question naturally arises as to how a difference that is other than God should come to be. According to the doctrine of creation from nothing, whatever exists that is not God must arise from God: but on what basis should God do such a thing? If the Trinitarian confession that God is living affirms God's own exemplification of difference, it does not yet give any reason to suppose that this difference should move beyond the confines of Divinity. Granted that it is a central principle of Christian belief that the work of creation is free, so that there is no internal or external necessity compelling God to create, it is still important to show that God's work in and for the world (*ad extra* in Latin) corresponds to the eternal character of God's Trinitarian life *ad intra* (considered apart from relation to anything that is not God) if the charge of divine arbitrariness is to be countered. In this context, alongside the claim that God is living, it is no less important to affirm that God is *productive*.[27]

Although God's productivity is manifest in creation, in which God brings into being a reality that is other than God, the theological characterization of God as productive is justified principally as a claim about the character of God's own being, in which God gives rise to God. As with the claim that God is living, God's identity as Trinity serves as the ground and guide for explicating what it means to say that God is productive: in the same way that to confess God as living is at bottom simply to point to the unity-in-relation of the Father, Son, and Spirit, so to say that God is productive is just to describe these same relations from another angle. God is productive in that the structure of mutual commitment defining the life of the divine persons does not consist in the mere acknowledgment of God's triune diversity, but in its active generation, as the love that is God takes the concrete form of producing and sustaining the other. In this way, God's intrinsic productivity allows the claim that God's *being* Trinity takes form in God's *becoming* Trinity—so long as "becoming" is understood

27. Cf. David S. Cunningham, "What Do We Mean by 'God'?," in *Essentials of Christian Theology*, ed. William C. Placher (Louisville, KY: Westminster John Knox Press, 2003), 80–83, 86–91.

as a means of highlighting the dynamic character of the divine life rather than (as in the created sphere) its evolution from one state to another.[28]

The character of this triune productivity is given classical form in the language of the Nicene Creed, where it is confessed that the Son is "begotten" of the Father (cf. Acts 13:33; Heb. 1:5; 5:5; cf. Ps. 2:7), and that the Spirit "proceeds" from the Father (cf. John 15:26 RSV).[29] Like all terms predicated of God, the meaning of these two verbs is strongly analogical. The imagery of begetting obviously resonates with the biological relationship connoted by the terms "Father" and "Son," to the extent that the Eleventh Council of Toledo in 675 spoke of the Son as being "begotten or born . . . from the womb of the Father."[30] But Christian theologians have been both consistent and emphatic in arguing that such language, although indicative of the intimacy of the relationship between the Father and the Son, is not to be taken literally.[31] The language of the Spirit as "proceeding" from the Father is much less suggestive (so that the Spirit's generation is also described by using the more resonant imagery of "spiration"), and it is significant simply as a means of marking the distinctiveness of the Holy Spirit, who is not another Son, but a third hypostasis characterized by the Spirit's own unique set of relationships with the other two (Father and Son).[32]

While the difference between "begetting" and "proceeding" within the Trinity remains obscure,[33] their common theological import is that they are both

28. See Eberhard Jüngel, *The Doctrine of the Trinity: God's Being Is Becoming*, trans. Horton Harris (Edinburgh: Scottish Academic Press, 1976).

29. The original text of the Nicene Creed, in the form that was officially affirmed at the Council of Chalcedon in 451 and continues in use by the Orthodox churches, speaks of the Spirit as proceeding from the Father only. A complicated set of theological and political circumstances later prompted the Western church to modify this account of the Spirit's procession by adding the phrase "and [from] the Son" (*filioque*) to the Latin text of this creed, creating a source of conflict between the Catholic (and later, Protestant) and Orthodox communions that remains unresolved to this day. The theological issues at stake are serious, but beyond the scope of the present study, for which the crucial point is the fact rather than the character of the Spirit's procession.

30. DS 526, cited in Neuner and Dupuis, *The Christian Faith*, 103. The language of the Council seems less innovative when it is remembered that in wider Greek use the term *kolpos* in John 1:18, usually translated as "bosom," can also mean "womb."

31. As Athanasius, one of the principal architects of Trinitarian theology put it, "If the same terms are used of God and humanity in divine Scripture, yet the clear-sighted . . . will study it, and thereby discriminate, and dispose of what is written according to the nature of each subject, and avoid any confusion of sense, so as neither to conceive of the things of God in a human way, nor to ascribe the things of human beings to God." Thus, regarding divine begetting, "God, being without parts, is Father of the Son without partition or passion; for there is neither effluence of the Immaterial, nor influx from without, as among human beings." See his *Defence of the Nicene Definition*, in *Nicene and Post-Nicene Fathers*, 2nd ser. (hereafter *NPNF*[2]), ed. Philip Schaff and Henry Wace, 14 vols. (1890–1900; repr., Peabody, MA: Hendrickson Publishers, 1994–99), 4:156–57.

32. See, e.g., Gregory of Nazianzus, *Oration 39* 12, in Patrologia graeca (hereafter PG), 36:348B: "The Holy Spirit is truly Spirit, coming forth [*proion*] from the Father, but not as the Son does, for it is not a matter of 'begetting' [*gennētos*] but of 'proceeding' [*ekporeutōs*]."

33. See Augustine, *Trinity* 15.45. Earlier in this same work, Augustine had proposed that the difference between the production of the Son and the Holy Spirit within the Trinity consists in the fact that the latter "comes forth . . . not as being born but as being given," so that while the Son "is referred to the Father alone . . . and therefore . . . is the Father's Son and not ours too," the Holy Spirit "is referred both to him who gave and to those it was given to" and so "is both God's who gave it and ours who received it" (*Trinity* 5.15). But since explaining the distinctiveness of the Spirit's

understood to name relationships absolutely distinct from "creating." In creating, God produces that which is not God, and which God need not have brought into being; by contrast, the Father's begetting the Son and the Spirit's proceeding from the Father are precisely what it is for God to be God. What is produced in the begetting of the Son and the procession of the Spirit *is* God, such that apart from this dual production, it is not possible to speak of God at all. This does not mean that God has to be triune in order to be God (as though existence in three persons were an ontological condition of divinity), but simply to emphasize that the fact of God's being triune renders the production of the Son and Spirit constitutive of God's identity in a way that the production of the world is not. Whatever the content of their relationships named by "begetting" and "proceeding" (and, insofar as they are constitutive of the particularity of the Son and Spirit, one should not expect their content to be any more subject to generalized definition than that of the hypostases themselves), the terms are used to characterize the way in which God is God. As such, they are eternal: since God did not begin to be triune only at a certain point, the Son was not begotten once upon a time, but is eternally begotten by, even as the Spirit proceeds eternally from, the Father.[34]

Given the fact that the productive relationships within the Trinity all have their origin in the Father, it is natural to ask whether, strictly speaking, productivity should be ascribed to the hypostasis of the Father only. After all, classical Trinitarianism defines the Father as the "cause" (Greek *aitia*) or "principle" (Latin *principium*) of divinity within the Godhead, and this confession of the "monarchy" (from the Greek for "sole source") of the Father seems to imply that the productivity of the Trinity is a particular attribute of the Father.[35] Indeed, Gregory of Nazianzus, one of the principal architects of Trinitarian orthodoxy, argued that the Christian confession of divine unity was grounded in the Father

---

procession in terms of the Spirit's reception by human beings sidelines the Spirit's significance for the inner life of the Trinity, the agnosticism about the difference between the production of the Son and Spirit expressed in *Trinity* 15.45 seems the better course.

While Augustine also invokes the Spirit's character as gift to support his belief that the Spirit proceeds from both the Father and the Son (since "what is given also has him it is given by as its origin"; *Trinity* 5.15), he does not use this theory of double procession to explain the different ways in which the Son and Spirit come from the Father, presumably because "the Holy Spirit proceeds from the Father principally, and [only] by the Father's wholly timeless gift from them jointly" (*Trinity* 15.47; cf. 15.29).

34. While the Nicene Creed states explicitly that the Son is "eternally begotten of the Father," the eternal character of the Spirit's procession is left implicit, though clearly a corollary of the assertion that the Spirit is "worshiped and glorified" with the other two persons. This comparative reticence on the Spirit (also reflected in the fact that the Spirit is not described as "of one substance with the Father" as the Son is) seems to be due to the fact that the article's authors at the First Council of Constantinople (381) were seeking to avoid undue provocation and thereby secure consensus among various theological parties. See J. N. D. Kelly, *Early Christian Creeds* (1960), 3rd ed. (London: Continuum, 2006), 338–44.

35. Needless to say, in a Trinitarian context "monarchy" is to be understood exclusively as a transliteration of the Greek *monarchia* ("sole source") and does not imply any sort of sovereignty of the Father over the Son or the Spirit.

as cause of the Son and the Spirit.[36] Yet just as for Gregory the Father's unique role as cause in no sense compromises the divinity of the Son and Spirit, neither does it diminish their participation in the intrinsic productivity of the Godhead:

> Monarchy is what we hold in honor. It is, however, a monarchy that is not limited to one person. For although it is true that oneness becomes many when at variance with itself, this monarchy is established in an equality of nature, and an agreement of mind, and an identity of motion, and a convergence of its elements to oneness (which is impossible for created nature), so that though there is a distinction of number, there is no division of substance. In this way the unity, having arrived by motion from its source at duality, came to rest in Trinity. This is what we mean by the Father and the Son and the Holy Spirit. [37]

What Gregory calls the convergence (Greek *synneusis*) of the Son and the Spirit back on the Father is crucial for understanding the unique character of Trinitarian productivity. While among creatures, production causes a division of substance (e.g., in the numerical increase of living beings via biological reproduction), the life of the Trinity is one in which production establishes ontological unity.[38] Thus, although for Gregory the Father is the ground of unity in the Trinity, the conclusion does not follow that the generation of the Son and the Spirit compromises that unity in a way that can only be overcome by their ontological subordination to the Father. Rather, because for Gregory the production of the Son and the Spirit includes their convergence on the Father, it is constitutive of the Father's identity *as* Father (since the Father is Father precisely *in relation to* the Son, upon whom the Spirit rests). Consequently, the productivity of the Trinity is not limited to the Father but includes all three persons.

In this way, the concrete form of triune productivity indicates that the relationships defining the living God as Trinity, while characterized by the profoundest mutuality, are not undifferentiated but have a particular order, or *taxis*. This intra-Trinitarian *taxis* defines and preserves the irreducible particularity of the three hypostases within the unity of the divine life, so that identifying

---

36. "So it is my view that the one God [*heis . . . theos*] is preserved when the Son and the Spirit are neither combined nor blended, but are referred to one cause [*hen aition*], according to one and the same [*hen kai tauto*] motion and will of divinity (as I will call it), and preserving identity of substance [*tēn tēs ousias tautotēta*]." Gregory of Nazianzus, *Oration 20* 7, in PG 35:1073A; cf. *Oration 42* 15, in PG 36:476B: "The one nature [*physis . . . mia*] the three have is God. But their unity [*henōsis*] is the Father, from whom and to whom those who follow [*ta hexēs*; viz., the Son and Spirit] are referred."

37. Gregory of Nazianzus, *Oration 29: The Third Theological Oration—On the Son*, in NPNF² 7:301. On the basis of the Greek text in PG 36:76B, I have substantially modified this Victorian translation, which is rather free and not especially clear.

38. Thus, "what makes for the unity of this eternal dynamic is that the distinct issue (the Son and the Spirit) 'converge' on their source in unity, bringing about a union of divine nature, will, and action among all three," with the result that the "consubstantiality of the Son and the Spirit with the Father and the divine unity, as well as the distinct identities of the Father, Son, and Holy Spirit, are therefore the eternal result of the Father's divine generation." Christopher A. Beely, "Divine Causality and the Monarchy of God the Father in Gregory of Nazianzus," *Harvard Theological Review* (2007) 100: 209.

the relationships of Trinitarian productivity helps to highlight the conviction that the equal divinity of the divine persons does not render them interchangeable. So to claim that the Trinity is intrinsically productive is not to say that all three persons are productive in the same way. From the perspective of the inner dynamics of the triune life, only the Father is productive as cause; but this does not render the Son and the Spirit purely passive (and so unproductive) in the triune life. On the contrary, they are confessed as divine hypostases rather than as creatures precisely because in their going forth from the Father they are revealed as subjects rather than objects of the divine life—and thus as truly God.[39] In short, to affirm the Father as cause or principle of divinity within the Godhead does not imply the reduction of divine productivity to the first person of the Trinity, since (in line with John 5:26) to speak of the Father precisely as the cause of *divinity* is to affirm that divinity (whether considered in terms of life or productivity or any other divine attribute) is not reducible to the Father. God is productive in the acts of begetting and proceeding that, in their particular and unsubstitutable ways, involve the agency of all three persons.

As already recognized, this kind of productivity is not possible for created beings, for which generation implies ontological separation rather than convergence. For this reason, when considering the question of the conditions of the possibility of God's unique form of productivity, there is at one level nothing more to say than that the nature of God's productivity, like all other aspects of God's life, is finally ineffable, something we can only note with wonder and never explain. At the same time, in the same way that Scripture's "God is love" can serve as the basis for an explication (if not explanation) of what it means to say that God is living, so the productivity of God may be illumined by appeal to the biblical claim that "God is Spirit" (John 4:24; cf. 1:32–34). Jesus invokes this idea in response to a query over the relative merits of the worship practices of Jews and Samaritans, as a means of affirming divine transcendence of creaturely categories in terms of the typically Johannine opposition between the earthly and heavenly realms.[40] In line with the character of John's Gospel, this opposition is not a matter of physical location ("above" and "below" as directions) but of orientation: "spirit" is opposed to "flesh" as the realm of freedom disclosed by Christ (John 8:32; cf. 2 Cor. 3:17).

---

39. "On the basis of divine revelation Christian teaching affirms that the Father begets the Son eternally. This begetting is not the action of one subject upon another since this would in some sense make the latter into an object of the former. . . . Nor does the term 'proceed' indicate any passivity on the part of the Holy Spirit such as to make him the object of the Father in some respect. . . . The act of the Son's begetting and the act of the Spirit's procession are acts of a pure common subjectivity, the first proper to the Father and the Son, the second to the Father and the Holy Spirit. But within these common acts each Person has his own place." Dumitru Stăniloae, *Theology and the Church*, trans. Robert Barringer (Crestwood, NY: St. Vladimir's Seminary Press, 1980), 76–77.

40. Similarly, Gregory of Nazianzus cites God's incorporeality as the ontological basis for God's unique form of productivity (see *Oration 29* 4). Of course, insofar as angels, too, are incorporeal, God's transcendence is not reducible to immateriality as such. Although spirit is a mark of freedom, because there is also created spirit, what finally distinguishes divine freedom from that of every creature is God's being uncreated.

Human beings enter into the realm of spirit through the action of the Holy Spirit, who effects for them a rebirth that translates them from the realm of the flesh (John 3:5–6). In the case of God, there is no need for such rebirth: because God is Spirit, God is free. This freedom is disclosed in the Trinity's internal productivity. The Father, as cause or principle of divinity within the Godhead, is not defined or limited by his nature. Divinity is not a constraint on the Father's being, something that confines the Father to himself. On the contrary, divine freedom takes shape in the fact that the Father is Lord of the divine nature and is therefore free to communicate it fully to another (John 5:26).[41] So too, in receiving the Father's nature, the Son is not confined by it, but receives it with a freedom that is manifest in giving himself fully back to the Father (John 17:1, 5);[42] while the Holy Spirit expresses the Spirit's divinity precisely as eternal witness to the mutual love of the Father and the Son.[43] Thus, by confessing that God is Spirit, Christians affirm that divine freedom, like divine love, is not relative to some nondivine reality (which would, precisely as the reference point for divine freedom, define its limit), but is intrinsic to God's own triune life. God's freedom, correspondingly, does not consist in a theoretical capacity to dispose of what is not God (of the sort reflected in hypothetical questions about God's capacity to bring about a particular state of affairs); it is rather defined by the concrete reality of God's being Father, Son, and Holy Spirit. God is free in that the Father is not God by himself but is God with the Son and the Spirit, who in their turn are each God only with the other two divine persons. In short, God

41. "The Father is the cause of the other hypostases in that He is not His essence, *i.e.*, in that He does not have his essence for Himself alone." Lossky, *Image and Likeness*, 83. The confession that Father has bestowed the fullness of divine being on the Son is what Augustine uses to ground his theory of the double procession of the Spirit (see *Trinity* 15.47); but insofar as the Father's status as *principium divinitatis* is ascribed to his hypostatic distinctiveness rather than to the divine nature, the communication of the fullness of the divine nature to the Son implies nothing about the latter sharing the Father's status as cause of the Spirit.

42. In addition to these verses, which suggest that the Father's glorification of the Son has as its end the Son's glorification of the Father in time (John 17:1) as in eternity (v. 5), it is also worth mentioning Jesus' statement, "If you loved me, you would rejoice that I am going to the Father, because the Father is greater than I" (14:28). For while it is common to interpret this sentence in purely economic terms, as referring to the subordination of Jesus' humanity to the Father (see, e.g., Augustine, *Trinity* 1.15), Gregory of Nazianzus argues that it is more plausibly applied to the eternal relation between the Father and the Son: "For why should it be worthy of note that God is greater than a human being?" (*Oration 30* 7, in PG 36:113A).

43. Here again the economy of the incarnation reflects the eternal reality of the Trinity: just as the Spirit bears the Father's love by initiating (Matt. 1:20; Luke 1:35), revealing (Matt. 3:16–17), and vindicating (Rom. 1:4; 1 Tim. 3:16; 1 Pet. 3:18) Jesus' status as Son, so it is by the Spirit that the Son, in turn, gives glory to the Father (see, e.g., Luke 4:1, 14, 18; cf. Matt. 12:28). Even in the context of the Western theory of the Spirit's double procession, the Father's love for the Son remains logically prior to the Son's love for the Father because the Son comes from the Father (see note 29 above). At the same time, although the idea of the Spirit as a bond between the Father and the Son is associated with Augustine (see *Trinity* 6.7; 15.50), such language is not dependent on the theory of double procession, and an Orthodox theologian like Stăniloae can equally well speak of the Spirit as one who "unites" the Father and the Son by serving as a "bridge" between them (*Theology and the Church*, 94, 96).

is free precisely as one whose divinity is, and therefore may be, shared without loss or diminishment.

Insofar as it takes the form of sharing divinity, God's freedom as Spirit is a manifestation of God's love. Precisely as an expression of freedom, the sharing of divinity that takes place as the Father brings forth the Son and the Spirit is not a matter of necessity forced on God from without, as though God had to be triune in order to be divine.[44] But because this sharing is the concrete and eternal form of God's love, neither is it arbitrary, as though God could equally well be other than God is. That God's freedom is exercised in the mode of the Father's giving the Father's own life to the Son in the Spirit means that God's life is essentially a matter of generosity, or (to use a more specifically theological term) of grace, which, in light of the character of the Trinity, may be defined as freedom lived out in love.[45] The grace that structures the life of the Trinity is free in that it is not compelled (i.e., not a matter of the hypostases being constrained by their nature); but because it is shaped by love, it could not be other than it is (i.e., as though the hypostases had a logically prior existence as agents who create the divine nature) without being the freedom of a different God—which for Christians would by definition be no God at all.[46]

44. Among the many studies that have emerged in connection with the revival of Trinitarian theology in the latter half of the twentieth century, some seem to imply that the doctrine of the Trinity is necessary in order to secure the conceptual coherence of the Christian doctrine of God. I do not deny the philosophical sophistication of, as well as the many valuable theological insights contained in, the work of (1) Robert Jenson ("An actual infinite consciousness could only be one that encountered a genuine, resistant object, and so was centered, without thereby being impeded in his intension of other objects. . . . Just this is asserted of the Father and his Son"; in *The Triune Identity: God according to the Gospel* [Philadelphia: Fortress Press, 1982], 174), (2) Walter Kasper ("Is the radically conceived unity of God thinkable at all without at the same time thinking of a differentiation within God himself that does not cancel out the unity and simplicity of God, but on the contrary is required to make these meaningful?"; in *The God of Jesus Christ*, trans. Matthew J. O'Connell [New York: Crossroad, 1991], 241), and (3) Dumitru Stăniloae ("We can say that if the Two do not meet in the Third, their subjectivity is not truly a common subjectivity"; in *Theology and the Church*, 94); yet they all seem to me to be overly ambitious at this point. The fact that other monotheistic faiths have found no insurmountable conceptual problems raised by confessing one God without appeal to Trinitarian distinctions should remind us that God's transcendence of creaturely categories raises suspicions about the degree to which divine reality is constrained by our understanding of consciousness, unity, or subjectivity. Still more seriously, the attempt to argue that hypostatic plurality is a condition of God's essential unity invariably compromises the gracious character of divine life by making the Trinity a matter of metaphysical necessity. This does not disallow reflection on the inner logic of the Trinity as a necessary prophylactic against the charge of arbitrariness in the Christian doctrine of God, but it demands that such analyses be carried out as arguments from fittingness (*ex convenientia*) rather than from necessity.

45. Since the Father's being as Father is constituted by this self-giving (since the Father is only Father in relation to the Son), it has nothing to do with self-sacrifice, any more than the Son's return of glory to the Father entails any diminishment of the Son's being.

46. The insistence that God's life is free but not arbitrary is another way of affirming that within the Trinity, hypostasis and nature cannot be ranked in terms of relative priority. That God's life is free—manifest in the self-giving of the Father that is, in different ways, reciprocated by the Son and the Spirit—means that the divine nature is not an ontologically prior limit on the divine life but rather an expression of the mutuality of the three hypostases. At the same time, the insistence that this freedom is not arbitrary means that neither is the divine nature an ontologically subsequent creation of the hypostases; it is rather quite simply what they *are* as divine hypostases. "The one

GOD AS PRESENT

The perfect freedom of the Trinity, realized in the ordered self-giving of the Father, Son, and Holy Spirit, points to one further dimension of the Christian doctrine of God: that God is *present*. Like the category of freedom, presence at first glance appears to be a relative term, and thus properly descriptive of God only in relation to what is not God rather than an immanent characteristic of the Godhead. And it is true that God's presence to the creature is a defining feature of the doctrine of creation, reflected in the psalmist's wonder:

> Where can I go from your spirit?
>   Or where can I flee from your presence?
> If I ascend to heaven, you are there;
>   if I make my bed in Sheol, you are there.
> If I take the wings of the morning
>   and settle at the farthest limits of the sea,
> even there your hand shall lead me,
>   and your right hand shall hold me fast.
> If I say, "Surely the darkness shall cover me,
>   and the light around me become night,"
> even the darkness is not dark to you;
>   the night is as bright as the day,
>   for darkness is as light to you.
>   (Ps. 139:7–12)

Here, too, however, this affirmation of divine presence to what is not God has as its presupposition God's presence to God's self. Otherwise divine omnipresence could only be experienced by creatures as a terrifying, persistent, unwearied spying out that can never be escaped or avoided. That God's presence is good news—as the right hand that holds me fast rather than the panoptic gaze that undermines any possible sense of personal integrity—is a consequence of the fact that God's presence to us is rooted in God's presence to God's self as Trinity: the mutually productive presence of the Father, Son, and Holy Spirit in self-giving and sustaining love.

The mode of presence characteristic of God's internal life reflects still another dimension of the relations among the three divine hypostases. The Son's identity as the *Word* of God is particularly helpful in distinguishing this dimension of the divine life from God's status as living and productive because it reframes Trinitarian language in a noetic rather than biological register. God's Word is not just spoken without as the means of creation (in line with John 1:3) but also within the Trinity; indeed, it can only be heard from without as a genuine expression of God's will because it is already a feature of God's internal life.

---

nature and the three hypostases are presented simultaneously to our understanding, with neither prior to the other. The origin of the hypostases is not impersonal, since it is referred to the person of the Father; but it is unthinkable apart from their common possession of the same essence" (Lossky, *Image and Likeness*, 81).

Within God as outside of God, the Word is a perfect and complete expression of the Father's being, in the speaking of which the Father withholds nothing. And precisely as Word (Greek *Logos*) this expression is communicative: the Word does not merely contain the mystery of the Father, but the Word also makes that mystery known and, therefore, knowable (John 1:18; 14:9; cf. Col. 1:15). This is not to say that the Word is any less transcendent than the Father by whom it is spoken (if it were, it could not qualify as the Word of *God*); but it claims that in the Word, God's transcendence is revealed. Although Christ is no less a mystery than the God he proclaims, encounter with Christ somehow brings knowledge of this mystery (Col. 1:27; 2:2; 4:3; cf. Matt. 13:11 and par.; Eph. 1:9). So within the Trinity the coming forth of the Word enacts God's openness to God's self as the ground of God's openness to creation: if God is hidden (Isa. 45:15), this is due to human sin (Rom. 1:18–21) and not because of God's withholding of God's self:[47]

> For thus says the LORD,
> who created the heavens
>   (he is God!),
> who formed the earth and made it
>   (he established it;
> he did not create it a chaos,
>   he formed it to be inhabited!):
> I am the LORD, and there is no other.
> I did not speak in secret,
>   in a land of darkness;
> I did not say to the offspring of Jacob,
>   "Seek me in chaos."
> I the LORD speak the truth,
>   I declare what is right.
>   (Isa. 45:18–19)

Within the divine economy, this opening of the divine life to human understanding is the work of the Holy Spirit, especially as considered under the title of "Paraclete" (John 14:16, 26; 15:26; 16:7). Although the Greek *Paraklētos* is open to a range of possible English translations (e.g., "Comforter" in the AV, "Counselor" in the NIV and RSV, "Advocate" in the JB and NRSV), the Greek term points to the specifically hermeneutical dimension of the Spirit's role as one who is called (*klētos*) to stand alongside (*para*) in the role of helper, in the face of humanity's sin-induced blindness to God. Thus, with the Word having become flesh among us (John 1:14), the job of the Spirit is to "remind you of all that I have said to you" (14:26), to "testify on my behalf" (15:26), and thereby to "guide you into all truth" (16:13). Within the Trinity, of course, there is no sin to overcome; but the Spirit's work remains a matter of testimony: in

---

47. Of course God remains intrinsically incomprehensible by creatures by virtue of God's transcendence, but this is not a matter of God's being hidden, for God's incomprehensibility will be undiminished even in the light of glory.

resting on the Son, the Spirit witnesses to the Son's status as the Father's image and thereby through the Son glorifies the Father as the one whose divinity is expressed precisely in fully sharing the divine substance.

Understanding the living productivity of the Trinity in terms of the full and mutual presence of the three hypostases to one another points to the unconditioned character of the divine life (or in more traditional language, to God's aseity). God's life is unconditioned in a sense that goes beyond the implications of divine transcendence, where claims about God as unconditioned are purely formal (i.e., ruling out talk about God that reduces God to one in a series of beings). The doctrine of the Trinity clarifies that God's being unconditioned does not mean that God is amorphous. While the affirmation of divine transcendence means that God is not to be defined by contrast with nondivine beings, the doctrine of divine presence affirms that God's being is given its character by the ordered relations among the divine hypostases. To affirm this definition in terms of the hypostases' mutual *presence* to one another means that the intra-Trinitarian relationships are not properly characterized as relations of *opposition*: that the Father is the source of the Son and Spirit does not mean that the Son and the Spirit are defined by contrast with the Father (or with each other), since their production is precisely the repetition of the Father's own life, yet in a different manner. Mutual presence entails a radical intimacy in which each hypostasis experiences the life of the other two as its own. As a result, the characterization of God as unconditioned is not merely a negative statement about our creaturely inability to comprehend divinity, but also a positive feature of God's own intrinsically productive life.[48] As distinguished from all nondivine beings, God's action "originates with himself and is expressive of himself" and thus "has no other basis than himself."[49]

Understood in terms of the mutual presence of the three hypostases, divine self-determination, or aseity, does not mean isolation or indifference. This stands in stark contrast to the God of Aristotle, who exemplifies just these qualities as the logical condition of being the unmoved mover, since to turn to something else is to be moved by it and so to cease to be the source and ground of all movement. By contrast, the Trinity's life is characterized by an openness that, far from being threatened by relations with another, is constituted by them. For the Father to generate the Son is not to have his own being as Father diminished, but precisely to establish his identity as Father. So it is that the Father is God as he gives all that he is and has to the Son and (in a different manner) to the Spirit,

48. So Stăniloae argues that the intimacy of the intra-Trinitarian relations is properly expressed not in the opposition of I and Thou (even allowing that the "Thou" who is the object of the "I's" address is itself another "I"), but as a triad of "I's." He writes, "The divine 'I' as pure subject must be experienced as such by another divine 'I' and must also experience the other divine 'I' as pre subject. . . . The divine love and happiness of God consist in the fact that in God an 'I' which is the all contains other 'I's which are also the all, and that each of these 'I's' contains the other. These 'I's' do not encounter each other from the outside as is the case with human 'I's'" (in his *Theology and the Church*, 76, 87).

49. Robert H. King, *The Meaning of God* (Philadelphia: Fortress Press, 1973), 94.

even as it is in receiving all that God is and has from the Father that the Son and (in a different manner) the Spirit are God.

In this context, the intra-Trinitarian priority of the Father as source of divinity, far from risking the subordination of the other hypostases, highlights the specifically personal (and thus unsubstitutable) character of their equality. The equality of the hypostases is not metaphysical deduction from their being coeternal modifications of an underlying divine substance, but the free product of the Father's self-giving, reciprocated in distinct fashion by both the Son and the Spirit. In this way, God's divinity does not hinge on any sort of self-containment through which the divine nature must, in whole or in part, be held in reserve against the threat of contamination. Divinity is rather Trinity: the absolutely unreserved and distinctive presence of each hypostasis to the other two, with the Father present to the Son as the one who has given the fullness of his being in the Spirit, with the Son present to the Father as the one who returns this gift through the Spirit, and with the Spirit present to the Father and the Son as the one who affirms and instantiates this mutual self-giving as a relationship of love.

A potential problem with interpreting the life of the Trinity as one of full mutual presence is that it threatens to erase the distinctions between the hypostases. This line of critique is based on the idea that genuine relations between the hypostases presupposes some sort of distance between them. Considered from this perspective, the language of presence subverts the confession of relations by reducing the distance between the hypostases to zero and thereby brings theology back to the totalitarian nightmare of God as the "unblinking cosmic stare."[50] In response to this critique, it is vital to attend to the distinction between *ousia* and hypostasis in Trinitarian theology. Certainly the affirmation that the divine nature is one—possessed equally by the Father, Son, and Spirit, such that each is fully God—constitutes a fullness of presence that has no creaturely analogue; yet the term "hypostasis" affirms the irreducible distinctiveness of Father, Son, and Spirit as a matter of their subsisting in eternal and irreversible relations to one another that constitute their respective "modes of existence" (*tropoi hyparxeōs*). In this way, the confession that the Father alone begets, that the Son alone is begotten, and that only the Spirit proceeds makes for an eternal generation of difference within the Godhead that precludes equating the mutual presence of the hypostases to one another with their constituting an undifferentiated unity.[51]

Further reflection on the character of the relations among the hypostases highlights the role of the Spirit in particular in preventing their mutual presence from collapsing into totalitarian singularity. After all, the status of the Son as the "image" of the Father (2 Cor. 4:4; Col. 1:15), so perfect as to be "the exact

---

50. Dallas Willard, *The Divine Conspiracy: Rediscovering Our Hidden Life in God* (San Francisco: HarperSanFrancisco, 1998), 244–45.

51. "When . . . we acknowledge such a distinction in the holy Trinity that we believe that one is the cause and the other depends on it, we can no longer be charged with dissolving the distinction of the Persons in the common nature." Gregory of Nyssa, *An Answer to Ablabius: That We Should Not Think of Saying There Are Three Gods*, ed. and trans. Cyril C. Richardson, in *Christology of the Later Fathers*, ed. Edward R. Hardy (Philadelphia: Westminster Press, 1954), 267.

imprint of God's very being [*hypostaseōs*]" (Heb. 1:3), might seem to imply that the very fullness of the Father's self-giving to the Son finally negates the difference between them. Within this context, the procession of the Spirit from the Father realizes a "second difference" within the Godhead, which secures the integrity of the first since the Spirit's role is precisely that of confessing the Son as the Father's only-begotten (John 15:26).[52] Invoking the Johannine designation of the Son as God's Word, the Spirit can be understood as the hypostasis who both affirms the Word's status as the Father's and its difference from the Father by speaking it back to the Father.[53] In short, by proceeding from the Father and resting on the Son or Word, the Spirit both establishes the Son as the Father's very presence (John 14:9–10) and bears witness to the Son's distinctiveness (1 John 4:2–3).[54]

This immanent dynamic makes it clear that the mutual presence of the three hypostases is not a matter of juxtaposition, in which the three are conceived in some sort of equilateral equipoise. On that model, presence would be defined by mutual opposition and would, consequently, always carry the threat of the erasure of difference through the absorption of one hypostasis by another. By contrast, the particular shape of the relationships that mark the distinctiveness of the hypostases reveal the divine presence as a *making present*. The Father's begetting of the Son is distinguished from a self-giving that is either illusion (such that the giving simply reinscribes the identity of the giver) or dissolution (such that the giver is undone by the giving), distinguished by the simultaneous procession of the Spirit, who by bearing witness to the Son as the Father's image, makes the Son present to the Father and the Father to the Son. Nor is this work of presentation limited to the Spirit: so too, as the Father's image, the Son makes the Father present to the Spirit and the Spirit present to the Father;

52. See John Milbank, "The Second Difference: For a Trinitarianism without Reserve," *Modern Theology* 2 (April 1986): 230. Milbank's depiction of the Spirit as interpreting the Son or Word to the Father provides a compelling *ex convenientia* argument for God as being in three persons; but in line with my own emphasis on presence as an identifying characteristic of the Trinity, I part company with his claim that intra-Trinitarian difference implies absence. Insofar as Milbank correlates absence with an "infinite deferment of self-identity" within the Godhead, his point is clearly to maintain the permanence of the intra-Trinitarian distinctions and not to characterize the Trinity as "a 'bad infinite' of never completed understanding." Yet talk of "deferment" invariably suggests that (monohypostatic) self-identity is somehow the implied (albeit never realized) end of the divine life in a way that seems inconsistent with his own insistence (citing 2 Cor. 3:18) that "the vision 'face to face' is *also* the 'passing from glory to glory'" ("Second Difference," 231).

53. The idea that the Spirit, too, speaks God's Word does not encroach on the distinctiveness of the Father as *principium divinitatis* so long as it is affirmed that the Spirit does not speak the Word in the same way that the Father does. There is nothing inconsistent with traditional Trinitarian theology in affirming that while the Father speaks *forth* the Word as its source, the Son speaks *as* the Word who reveals the Father, and the Spirit speaks in *response*, affirming the Word spoken as the Father's own. See my discussion in Ian A. McFarland, "Christ, Spirit and Atonement," in *International Journal of Systematic Theology* 3 (March 2001): 83–93.

54. Importantly, this perspective neither needs nor should be contrasted with more traditional interpretations of the Spirit as the bond of union between the other two hypostases. Given that the unity of the Father and the Son is a crucial feature of the biblical witness (John 10:30; cf. 17:21–22), to specify the Spirit as the "second difference" is not to reject the Spirit's unifying role, but rather to say something about how the Spirit fulfills this role.

and the Father, as the source of the other two hypostases, makes the Spirit present to the Son and the Son present to the Spirit.

As the biblical designations of God as love and as Spirit help to interpret the claims that God is living and productive, so the third Johannine "definition" of God as light (1 John 1:5; cf. John 1:4–5; 8:12; 9:5; 12:46) brings into relief some of the salient features of divine presence. Created light must be separated from the darkness (Gen. 1:4), but such light is no more to be identified with God than creaturely productivity with that of the Godhead. While created light is a correlate of the darkness, the uncreated light of God is neither a response to darkness nor equiprimordial with darkness, but is ontologically fundamental. Darkness may be included among the things created by God (Isa. 45:7; cf. Amos 4:13), or, construed as a metaphor for sin, among those creaturely powers that resist God's will (Acts 26:18; cf. Matt. 6:23 and par.; John 1:5; Eph. 5:11). In either case, however, it is subsequent to God, in whose eternal light there is no darkness.

That the divine light is corollary to divine presence is reflected in its somewhat ambiguous effects on human beings. On the one hand, it is so brilliant as to be unapproachable (1 Tim. 6:16; cf. Matt. 17:2 and pars.; Rev. 1:14, 16). On the other, even as created light is the basis for vision of worldly realities, so God's light is the ground of all true seeing (Ps. 36:9; cf. 2 Cor. 4:6; Rev. 22:5).[55] This ambiguity presumably reflects that of human beings themselves, whose own complicity in the darkness of sin renders the experience of God's light painful, in much the same way that the eyes of someone who has spent a long time in physical darkness cannot bear the brightness of the day (John 3:19; Eph. 5:11–14).[56] Indeed, the effect of the darkness on human beings is so pervasive as to render them incapable of recognizing God at all, just as some cave-dwelling animal species have lost the ability to see (2 Cor. 4:4; 1 John 2:11). Considered from the perspective of God's own life, however, where the darkness of sin has no place,

55. In Orthodox theology, the divine light is equated with the uncreated divine energies, which, in distinction from the utterly transcendent and unknowable divine essence, may be participated in by creatures. According to Orthodox doctrine, this light is intrinsic to the divine life, representing "the visible character of the divinity, of the energies in which God communicates Himself and reveals Himself" (Lossky, *Image and Likeness*, 58). Cf. Nicholas of Cusa, *De li non aliud*, 3: "Perceptual light is in some way conceived to be related to perceptual seeing as the Light which is Not-other [is related] to all things which can be mentally seen."

56. Francis Watson observes that a further ambiguity has been introduced into the symbolism of light by the advent of atomic weaponry (which, he observes with some irony, was first used in wartime on the Feast of the Transfiguration). "By re-enacting and indeed surpassing the transfiguration after its own fashion, modern science has burdened the image of the light shining brighter than the sun with sinister, inhuman and demonic connotations. We cannot and must not dispense with Christian light-imagery; but it has undoubtedly been contaminated for us by the pseudo-miracles of light which John of Patmos . . . would correctly have identified as an epiphany of the beast that ascends from the bottomless abyss." From his *Text and Truth: Redefining Biblical Theology* (Edinburgh: T&T Clark, 1997), 283–84. Cf. Joseph Sittler, *Evocations of Grace: Writings on Ecology, Theology, and Ethics*, ed. Steven Bouma-Prediger and Peter Bakken (Grand Rapids: Wm. B. Eerdmans Publishing Co., 2000), 50: "Ever since Hiroshima the very term *light* has had ghastly meanings. But ever since creation it has had meanings glorious; and ever since Bethlehem meanings concrete and beckoning."

the language of light is consistent with the idea of Trinitarian presence as making the hypostases present to one another. Here it is not a question of dispelling darkness but of glorifying (or to use more colloquial language, highlighting) what is already inherently visible. As the words of the Nicene Creed have it, the Son comes from the Father as "light from light"; and even as this process of generation entails no decrease in the Father's light, so the Spirit's glorifying the Son to the Father implies no deficiency in the Son's light. The mutual illumination of the three hypostases constitutes just one light, but it shines within God's own life as the realization of the active and mutual presence of the three hypostases to one another; the particularity of each hypostasis is displayed within the divine life in its distinctive way (as Father, Son, and Holy Spirit) of being present to the others such that nothing of what any one hypostasis is can be hidden or held back from the rest.[57]

As the Trinitarian hypostases reflect their eternal presence to one another, the language of light also provides a salient link between God and the world that God creates. As already noted, this link is not a matter of ontological continuity that would blur the distinction between divine and created light. The two are distinct, and any relation between them must be viewed as analogical. Nevertheless, the analogy is significant. The conviction that before the light of God nothing is hidden or lost points to the hope that the divine light that is the presupposition of creation is also its destiny (see Rev. 21:25; 22:5). The identification of physical light as the first of God's creatures (Gen. 1:3) may be taken as sensible pledge of this hope: as the claim that God is light reflects God's intrinsic presence as Trinity, the phenomenon of created light is a sign that God is also present extrinsically to what God creates. For while God's acting outside of God's self to bring into being that which is other than God does not involve any blurring of the distinction between God and the creature, neither does it presuppose any sort of ontological barrier that might limit God's intimacy with creation. On the contrary, the light that stands at the beginning of God's creative work may be taken as indicative of God's commitment to be present to the whole of creation, which is thereby revealed as a theater of God's glory. What it means to characterize creation in this way, as utterly different from God and yet ever before God, is the subject of the next chapter.

---

57. "For [the three hypostases] are made one not so as to commingle, but so as to cleave to each other, and they have their being in each other without any coalescence or commingling, . . . just like three suns cleaving to each other without separating and giving out light mingled and conjoined into one." John of Damascus, *On the Orthodox Faith* 1.8, in *NPNF²* 9:11. Cf. the same imagery of three suns in Gregory of Nazianzus, *Oration 31: The Fifth Theological Oration—On the Holy Spirit,* in *NPNF²* 7:322. In order to emphasize the equality of the three hypostases, Gregory rejects the imagery of sun, ray, and light (which had been favored by Athanasius), "lest people should get an idea of composition in the uncompounded nature, such as there is in the sun and the things that are in the sun. And in the second place lest we should equate the *ousia* with the Father and deny hypostasis to the others, making them only powers of God, existing in him but not hypostatic. For neither the ray nor the light is another sun, but they are only effulgences from the sun, and qualities of its essence." *Oration 31,* 328, trans. slightly alt.

3

Creates

In the preceding chapter, God was characterized as intrinsically living, productive, and present. That God is so in God's self, it was argued, makes it fitting that God should create, since creation is simply the act by which God, who is already intrinsically living, productive, and present, determines also to be living, productive, and present to that which is not divine. Creation is not necessary for God (i.e., it is not a logical entailment of God's intrinsic divinity that God should also be God extrinsically), but it is fully consistent with God's identity that God should be so. For, as living, productive, and present, God is love (1 John 4:8, 16), and the inherent productivity of this love makes it natural that it should expand beyond the bounds of God's own being.[1] The creation of the world is just such an expansion, through which God proves to be love not simply in and for God's self, but also to and for that which is not God.

---

1. "It is proper for the ocean of Divine love to overflow its limits, and it is proper for the fullness of the life of Divinity to spread beyond its bounds. If it is in general *possible* for God's omnipotence to create a world, it would be improper for God's love not to actualize this possibility inasmuch as, for love, it is natural to love, exhausting to the end *all* the possibilities of love." Sergius Bulgakov, *The Lamb of God*, Russian ed. (1933), trans. Boris Jakim (Grand Rapids: Wm. B. Eerdmans Publishing Co., 2008), 120.

Because it is intrinsic to God's identity as living, productive, and present that God is the only condition of God's own being, it follows that God can only be God extrinsically insofar as God is also the only condition of the world's being. To conceive of a world that existed in any respect independently of God would be to imagine a world in relation to which God was not God (since some other factor—namely, the world's own intrinsic existence—would then contribute to God's being God), and thus to have failed to speak properly of *God*. So if creation is nothing other than God's being God to that which is not God, then it necessarily takes the form of God's giving existence to whatever is not God. Quite simply, that there should *be* anything other than God is possible only because God *gives* being, along the lines of the "Let there be" language found in Genesis 1. And that God should be able to give being in this way is, in turn, possible because being is intrinsic to God as the One who is living, productive, and present. Following the lead of Thomas Aquinas, we can say that the reason God can make that which is other than God to be is because God's own nature is simply "to be."[2]

The claim that creation is that act by which God allows the world to *have* what God eternally *is* (viz., "to be") stands in some tension with how creation is often conceived. In colloquial speech talk about "creating" has a strongly temporal character: to create something is to bring it into being in time, so that the act of creation can be described in terms of a "before" (prior to the existence of the thing created), a "during" (the process of creating itself), and an "after" (when the thing created is finished). Although the opening verses of Genesis and John alike make it natural to link the Christian doctrine of creation with the topic of cosmic origins, interpreting creation in terms of God's bestowal of existence (i.e., of making the world to be) fits somewhat uneasily with a focus on the temporal beginning of the world. Since the world only exists at any point in time only because God gives it being at that point, "we cannot properly say that God *created* the world but that God *creates* the world."[3] In other words, precisely because creation is the bestowal of existence where there was nothing existing before, it is not a process that can be described in terms of a sequence of events; it is rather a relationship. Nor is it a onetime act, but rather an enduring bond of intimate and complete dependence on God.[4] To speak of God as

2. "Similarly, anything that exists either is itself existence [*est esse*] or partakes of it [*habet esse*]. Now, God . . . exists. If then he is not himself existence [*suum esse*], and thus not by nature existent, he will only be a partaker of existence. And so he will not be the primary existent. God therefore is not only his own essence, but also his own existence [*suum esse*]." Thomas Aquinas, *Summa theologiae* (hereafter *ST*) 1.3.4, in Blackfriars ed., 61 vols. (London: Eyre & Spottiswood, 1964), vol. 2.

3. David Burrell, *Faith and Freedom: An Interfaith Perspective* (Oxford: Blackwell, 2004), 11. Burrell has no interest in denying that the world had a beginning in time (in fact, he takes the reality of a t = 0 to be axiomatic), but he uses the present tense as a means of emphasizing the profound disanalogy between God's creating and colloquial use of the verb, noting (e.g.) that owing to the fact that theologically creation refers to the giving and not just the shaping of being, God "would better be imagined *inside* the becoming which time measures than *outside* it" (*Faith and Freedom*, 10).

4. "There is nothing to be moved or changed [in creation], nothing in which a process could occur, prior to creation, if creation is perfectly comprehensive. Nothing is happening to you in any

creating is fundamentally to describe the world in terms of this ongoing relation, a description that can be given without reference to the question of its temporal beginnings.

THE BASIC CHARACTERISTICS OF CREATURES

As has already been suggested, the most significant thing that can be said about the world, as the object of God's creative work, is that it is other than God. Among creatures, spatial distance is perhaps the most obvious marker of otherness: that which is other than I am has a different location than I do, so that we most easily identify something other than ourselves by pointing to it, thereby distinguishing it from ourselves by virtue of where it sits in space. Leaving aside for the moment the particular issues raised by the doctrine of the incarnation (i.e., the claim that God personally assumed creaturely existence in Jesus of Nazareth), it is clear that God is not "other" in this way, whether with respect to any individual creature or to creation as a whole. The God who creates space has no place within it; rather, "He is His own place, filling all things and being above all things and Himself maintaining all things."[5] Moreover, as the one in whom "we live and move and have our being," God "is not far from each one of us" (Acts 17:27–28). Indeed, in light of God's transcendence of creaturely categories of opposition, Nicholas of Cusa went so far as to designate God as the "Not other," not meaning to suggest that God and the world are indistinguishable (i.e., "Not other" is not equivalent to "The same"), but rather to highlight that the kind of difference obtaining between Creator and creature has no ready analogue in our everyday experience of otherness. God is "not other," if by that one means *an*other item in a series of "others" that could be lined up on a shelf.[6]

And yet if spatial metaphors will not do, the ontological distinction between creature and Creator can nevertheless be spoken of as a sort of distance, in line with John of Damascus's dictum, "All things are distant from God not by place, but by nature."[7] That is, the fact that every creature is created makes it

---

ordinary sense of the term when you are being created. Furthermore, since God's creating is neither instigated by intervening motions . . . , nor found within the world of time and change, the temporal progression, the lapse of time, that goes with movement or change is absent from God's creating of the world." Kathryn Tanner, "Is God in Charge?," in *Essentials of Christian Theology*, ed. William C. Placher (Louisville, KY: Westminster John Knox Press, 2003), 123.

5. John of Damascus, *On the Orthodox Faith* 1.13, in *Nicene and Post-Nicene Fathers*, ser. 2 (hereafter *NPNF²*), ed. Philip Schaff and Henry Wace, 14 vols. (1890–1900; repr., Peabody, MA: Hendrickson Publishers, 1994–99), 9:15.

6. "It . . . would be improper to try to conceive of the creator as 'over against' the created universe, as though it were a separate being. . . . That is, no creature can *be* without its inherent link to the creator, so these 'two' can never be separable from one another, as individual creatures are." David B. Burrell, *Towards a Jewish-Christian-Muslim Theology* (Oxford: Wiley-Blackwell, 2011), 21–22. Cf. Nicholas of Cusa, *Nicholas of Cusa on God as Not-Other: A Translation and Appraisal of "De li non aliud,"* trans. Jasper Hopkins, 2nd ed. (Minneapolis: Arthur J. Banning Press, 1983).

7. John of Damascus, *On the Orthodox Faith* 1.13, in Patrologia graeca [hereafter PG], 94:853C; see p. 19 above.

different in nature—in the basic *kind* of entity it is—from God, who is uncreated. Most fundamentally (and as already noted), this "distance" between uncreated and created is constituted by the difference between God's being living, productive, and present in God's self, on the one hand, and God's being living, productive, and present to that which is not God, on the other.[8] Where God simply *is* "to be," other creatures can be said "to be" only as God grants them existence. Clearly, this difference in nature is of another order than those types that obtain within the created realm, by which we distinguish, say, a wasp as a different kind of thing from an angel or a mountain. It is another aspect of divine transcendence: the fundamental difference between Creator and creature that provides the framework within which creation may be described most generally as the set of all "beings" (i.e., individual creatures) of which we can predicate qualities univocally, in distinction from God, to whom we can ascribe such characteristics only analogically (and who thus cannot be identified as *a* "being").

Perhaps no one has so effectively highlighted creation's distinction from God as the fourteenth-century anchorite Julian of Norwich, who recounted the following vision of the whole world considered as a creature:

> [The Lord] showed me something small, no bigger than a hazelnut, lying in the palm of my hand, as it seemed to me, and it was round as a ball. I looked at it with the eyes of my understanding and thought: What can this be? I was amazed that it could last, for I thought that because of its littleness it would suddenly have fallen into nothing. And I was answered in my understanding: It lasts and always will, because God loves it; and thus everything has being through the love of God.
>
> In this little thing I saw three properties. The first is that God made it, the second is that God loves it, the third is that God preserves it. But what did I see in it? It is that God is the Creator and the protector and the lover.[9]

As Julian notes, creation is and may be conceived as "one" (and indeed, as shockingly "little" in its unity) in that it depends entirely upon on God's love both for its coming to be and for its continuation in being. Yet in addition to being one in distinction from God, creation's unity can also be considered in terms of certain properties common to all creatures by virtue of their status as

8. In this context Barth described creation as "the temporal analogue, taking place outside God, of that event in God Himself by which God is the Father of the Son. The world is not God's Son, is not 'begotten' of God; but it is *created*. But what God does as the Creator can in the Christian sense only be seen and understood as a reflection, as a shadowing forth of this inner divine relationship between God the Father and the Son." Karl Barth, *Dogmatics in Outline*, trans. G. T. Thompson (New York: Harper & Row, 1959), 52. Similarly, Kathryn Tanner (citing Athanasius) argues that all creatures image God, albeit as "a mere 'copy' and 'shadow' of the image of God that is God's own Wisdom" (*Christ the Key* [Cambridge: Cambridge University Press, 2010], 11).

9. Julian of Norwich, *Showings*, trans. Edmund Colledge, OSA, and James Walsh, SJ (New York: Paulist Press, 1978), 183 (chap. 5 of the Long Text); cf. 190 (chap. 8 of the Long Text): "I know well that heaven and earth and all creation are great, generous and beautiful and good. But the reason why it seemed to my eyes so little was because I saw it in the presence of the Creator. To any soul who sees the Creator of all things, all that is created seems very little."

identifiable "beings."|The absolute and unvarying character of dependence on God across all scales and types of created existence is such that all creatures, from the most exalted seraph to the most insignificant grain of interstellar dust, are *contingent*, subject to *movement*, and occupy a particular *place.* These three properties can be understood as the created corollaries of God's character as living, productive, and present, and as such, can define the ways in which God forms creatures to share by grace the being that God has by nature.[10]

The first of these properties is the most obvious, for if the existence of every creature is dependent on God's giving it existence, then it follows that created nature is inherently contingent. To describe something as *contingent* is to contrast it with what is *necessary*. While the necessary cannot not be, that which is contingent might not have been: that twice two make four or that the angles of a (Euclidean) triangle add up to two right angles is necessary; that there should have been a person named George Washington or even a planet Earth is not.[11] At a certain level the claim of creaturely contingency does not seem especially controversial. In line with the colloquial saying "There but for the grace of God" (not to mention popular interpretations of chaos theory or reflections on the implications of time travel), people tend to have a healthy, almost reflexive appreciation for the contingent character of phenomena. Few claims, seemingly, could be less controversial than that the existence of any one of us (and by extension, of any other created being) depends on a vast sequence of preceding and concurrent circumstances, variations in any one of which would lead to a very different outcome.[12]

And yet for all the apparent self-evidence of the idea that my or your existence is not necessary, it seems doubtful that anyone can empirically justify the claim that created reality is contingent. The fact that I can specify conditions under which a particular created entity would not have come to be does not in itself establish that those conditions could in fact have been changed. A thoroughgoing materialism can coherently affirm that every phenomenon in the universe takes the form it does necessarily, by virtue of a preceding set of causes that are

10. For an engaging exploration of the analogy between divine productivity and creaturely movement, see Simon Oliver, "Trinity, Motion, and Creation *ex nihilo*," in *Creation and the God of Abraham*, ed. David B. Burrell et al. (Cambridge: Cambridge University Press, 2010), 133–52.

11. In this context, it is advisable to resist the temptation to contrast creaturely contingency with divine necessity. While the idea of God as a "necessary being" has a venerable history, it is philosophically problematic and, in any case, is logically distinct from the specifically Christian theological claim that God is inherently living. Following the kind of noncontrastive understanding of divine transcendence encapsulated in Cusa's language of God as "Not Other," it seems preferable to limit the contrast between necessary and contingent to the created sphere (viz., "necessary" truths of reason as opposed to "contingent" truths of history) than to apply it to the difference between Creator and creature.

12. Here as elsewhere in Thomist metaphysics, angels constitute a special category. On the one hand, they have been created by God and so in that sense are as contingent as any other creature. On the other hand, as pure form they are contingent *only* with respect to God and not with respect to the sequence of cause and effect that brings material creatures in and out of existence. Because this independence of all other creatures renders them inherently incorruptible, in this sense Thomas Aquinas can call them necessary beings (see *ST* 1.50.5.3).

themselves determined with equal necessity. Even accepting what appears to be the majority view among physicists that at the smallest scale, created reality is genuinely contingent (because individual quantum events lack any created cause and thus cannot be viewed as determined by any set of pre-existing factors), the broader ontological significance of this judgment remains unclear, given that subatomic indeterminacies even out at macroscopic scales to produce a world governed by mathematically precise scientific laws.[13] And stepping back from the question of the contingency of individual events, it is very difficult even to specify how one, on the basis of experience, could establish the contingency of the world as a whole.[14]

Even if the grounds for affirming the contingency of creation cannot be divorced from faith, however, the significance of the claim is clear enough. Creatures do not and cannot subsist apart from God. Moreover, insofar as the means of creation is God's word of command (Ps. 33:9), God not only brings creatures into existence but also, in so doing, establishes a relationship of subordination, "so that the creature's very existence is 'obedience.'"[15] Within God's own life the Word is simply the eternal (or "immanent") expression of the divine life rather than its cause and so does not establish any relationship of subordination among the three persons; but spoken externally (or, in the language of classical Trinitarianism, "economically"), the Word acts precisely as cause, bringing the creature into the existence as an entity under divine command, subsisting only as it fulfills God's purposes. So Scripture insists that "all things are [God's] servants" (Ps. 119:91), existing by God's specific appointment for the ends God has determined.[16]

13. While chaos theory (i.e., the mathematical description of nonlinear systems far from thermodynamic equilibrium) is also frequently cited in discussions of contingency in nature, the fact that the mathematics of chaos theory are deterministic suggests that the "chance" character of chaotic systems is not a matter of ontological indeterminacy, even if the extreme sensitivity of such systems to initial conditions means that accurate prediction of any of its future states is practically impossible (viz., because such systems present science with an insuperable *epistemological* gap in causal explanation). John Polkinghorne has famously urged that this epistemological gap be taken as an indicator of genuine ontological indeterminism (see, e.g., his *Quarks, Chaos, and Christianity* [London: Triangle, 1994], 2nd ed. [London: SPCK, 2005], 68), but his views have met with stiff criticism, the most compelling (of which I am aware) being that by Nicholas Saunders, *Divine Action and Modern Science* (Cambridge: Cambridge University Press, 2002), 173–206.

14. Given the difficulty in specifying how the world's contingency might be inferred from experience (as witnessed by the seemingly intractable debates over the status of the so-called cosmological argument), David Kelsey proposes that matters like the world's contingency be understood as "claims about absolutely general features of the world, so general that they are the conditions of any experience of any part of the world rather than claims somehow 'based' on experience." See his "The Doctrine of Creation from Nothing," in *Evolution and Creation*, ed. Ernan McMullin (Notre Dame, IN: University of Notre Dame Press, 1985), 179.

15. Donald D. Evans, *The Logic of Self-Involvement: A Philosophical Study of Everyday Language with Special Reference to the Christian Use of Language about God as Creator* (London: SCM Press, 1963), 152.

16. In Gen. 1, e.g., the sky is created in order to separate the upper from the lower waters, while the heavenly bodies are created in order to mark the passage of time, and the plants are created to be food for animals. At the same time, and as stated with particular force in Job 38–41, God's purposes

To be sure, the ascription of "obedience" to all creatures requires that the term be applied somewhat loosely. According to the doctrine of creation, God gives existence to all creatures, but not all creatures are alive, and without life (and in fact, life characterized by a relatively high degree of internal complexity) there is no capacity for obedience in anything other than a highly attenuated sense of the term.[17] Moreover, in light of the authoritarian connotations that the term "obedience" carries, the "commandment" that creatures are enjoined to obey cannot, within the framework of creation from nothing, be viewed as the imposition of an alien will on an otherwise autonomous being, since in every case the content of God's command is simply that the creature should be just the sort of creature it is. In this respect, to say that creatures exist only insofar as they fulfill God's purposes is not to qualify their inherent value, but only once more to emphasize their contingency. For even if one takes the traditional position that the end of creation is the glory of God, the glory of God in creation consists precisely in the graciousness of God's giving existence to that which is not God.[18] Consequently, the character of God's creative work could perhaps be described more accurately in terms of permission than of command, as reflected in the "Let there be . . ." language of creation in Genesis 1.

In summary, while not everything that God creates is living, the contingency of creation establishes the possibility and limit of created life: where creatures live, it is because God has granted them life; and because their life is created, it is at every point contingent on God's gracious permitting. Moreover (and this brings us to the second common feature of created existence), this contingency is marked by *movement*. In its divinely sustained contingency, the world is not static. Creaturely movement is not to be understood as a sign of declension from a prior state of perfect stasis (as Origen of Alexandria thought). Instead, it is the mode by which creatures both exhibit and achieve their own peculiar and distinctively created sorts of perfection.

The idea that the creature, precisely by virtue of its status as created, has perfection as its goal rather than its beginning—this idea finds early expression in the work of Irenaeus of Lyons, who argued that because perfection is a property of God's *uncreated* being, it cannot be intrinsic to any *created* nature: it is just

---

in creating any being are not reducible to their utility for humankind (cf. Ps. 104:26, which states that Leviathan was formed purely for God's own amusement).

17. While Psalm 148, e.g., enjoins all creatures to praise God (and in v. 8 goes so far as to claim that the very elements fulfill God's command), there is presumably a significant difference between the "obedience" of "Mountains and all hills, fruit trees and all cedars!" (v. 9) on the one hand, and "Young men and women alike, old and young together!" (v. 12) on the other. Both classes of creatures are presumably thought to "obey" God insofar as they fulfill their existence as the creatures they are (viz., their very being praises God), but in the case of human beings, their particular form of created existence involves agency in a way that is not the case for nonliving entities and plants.

18. So in a specifically anthropological vein, Irenaeus famously opined that "the glory of God is a living human being," adding that "the manifestation of God which is made by means of the creation . . . affords life to all living in the earth." *Against Heresies* 4.20.7, in vol. 1 of *The Ante-Nicene Fathers* (hereafter *ANF*), ed. Alexander Roberts and James Donaldson (1885; repr., Grand Rapids: Wm. B. Eerdmans Publishing Co., 1985).

logically impossible for God to create that which is by definition uncreated.[19] Nevertheless it was possible, Irenaeus averred, for creatures to attain a creaturely analogue to divine perfection over time as a gift from God: though a creature can never (again by definition) be uncreated, it can take on the glory of divinity as an effect of God's communing with it over time.[20] Centuries later, Maximus the Confessor likewise insisted on movement as an intrinsic and therefore good feature of creatures that functions to bring them to their eschatological goal of perfect rest in God.[21]

In other words, while God's productivity is an expression of the inexhaustible richness of the divine life, creaturely movement derives from a fundamental lack: we move because we, as created beings, lack the fullness of existence that belongs properly to God alone but which God wills to share with us. Moreover, in sharp contrast to God's self-sufficiency, the being of creatures is at every point not only dependent on the sustaining power of the Creator who holds it in being, but also is affected by relationships with other creatures. These relationships shape the contours of creaturely movement, so that the process by which any creature becomes present to God is inseparable from its interactions with other creatures. Such interactions are an aspect of creatures' contingency and take many forms.[22] All matter is affected by the fundamental physical forces of gravity (which governs the interactions between bodies at the largest scales), electromagnetism (the

---

19. See pp. 13–14 above.

20. "Created things must be inferior to Him who created them, from the very fact of their later origin; for it was not possible for things recently created to have been uncreated. . . . For from the very fact of these things having been created, [it follows] that they are not uncreated; but by their continuing in being throughout a long course of ages, they shall receive a faculty of the Uncreated [dynamin agennētou], through the gratuitous bestowal of eternal existence on them by God." Irenaeus of Lyons, Against Heresies (hereafter AH) 4.38.1, 3, in vol. 1 of ANF. In AH 5.6.1, Irenaeus associates human perfection with the gift of God's Spirit, so that humanity is perfected when it lives not by its own, created ("natural") powers, but by the free gift of God's own being, which supervenes on human nature as created. For a contemporary version of this anthropology, see Tanner, Christ the Key, chaps. 2–3.

21. "So God is the source and end of every coming into being [genesis] and every motion [kinēsis] of beings, since they are created by him and are moved through him and will come to rest [stasis] in him. Now coming into being anticipates every natural motion of beings, and the natural motion anticipates its rest. If therefore the creation anticipates a motion that is in accord with nature, and the rest that is in accord with nature follows on that motion, it is clear that the states of coming into being and of rest do not exist simultaneously, but are naturally separated from one another by an intervening state of motion" (Maximus the Confessor, Ambiguum 15, in PG 91:1217C–D). Admittedly, Maximus associates creaturely motion specifically with life (Epistle 7, in PG 91:436C), and seems to view bodies as inert in themselves (Epistle 6, in PG 91:425B), but it remains the case that for him it is the need for motion as a means to attain rest that distinguishes created from uncreated being.

22. See chap. 6 below for a full account of how every creature's total dependence on God for its existence is consistent with its dependence on other creatures. As already discussed (see note 12 above), angels may constitute a special case, since (at least according to a Thomist angelology) they are—precisely because immaterial—irreducibly individual in a way that renders them ontologically independent of any reality other than their Creator. At the same time, even angelic beings are understood to relate to one another and to human beings, whether in tempting others to sin in the case of Satan and the fallen angels, or in the traditional imagery of the good angels' corporate service to God as a "host" or "choir."

basis of the chemical bonding that determines the properties of the substances we encounter in the world), and color force (which holds together the atomic nuclei that are the building blocks of matter). In living beings, interactions among creatures also include more complex processes like respiration and nutrition. And the same interactions that give creatures their particular identities also render them vulnerable to dissolution: living creatures die, and their bodies rot; rocks can be pulverized or melted; even atomic nuclei decay.

In this context of interactions among creatures, it becomes possible to identify a third dimension of creaturely existence: *place*. As noted in the preceding chapter, the three divine hypostases are fully present to one another as Trinity; and God's sustaining the whole creation in being implies that each creature is fully present to God as well. By contrast, all creatures are not immediately present to each other in this way. Instead, the possibility of creatures' presence to one another is a function of place, their relative locations in space and time. It is a characteristic of creatures to have place, and place is the condition of the possibility for their being present to one another, in the sense that a condition of mutual creaturely presence is proximity in space and time.[23]

The character of place (i.e., an entity's location in space and time) means that presence is for creatures relative. While all creatures might be said to be present to one another in the sense of being part of the same space-time continuum,[24] because each creature occupies a distinct place, no creature is present to any two others in exactly the same way: in relation to any one creature, others are situated at varying degrees of spatial distance from it, some are on the right rather than its left, above rather than below, before rather than behind, and so on.[25] And while

23. Even though Thomas Aquinas denies that angels are material (and so take up space), he argues that they do have place (since to argue otherwise would be to ascribe to them the divine attribute of omnipresence), though their incorporeality means that they relate to their place differently than embodied creatures. See Thomas Aquinas, *ST* 1.52.1–3. Austin Farrer refers to place as creatures' "mutual externality" and is dubious that it can be consistently maintained of purely spiritual beings. See Austin Farrer, *Finite and Infinite: A Philosophical Essay* (1943; repr., New York: Seabury Press, 1979), 246; cf. 279n1.

24. If there are parallel universes, as posited in some physical theories (e.g., "many worlds" interpretations of quantum theory), this claim of even the most attenuated mutual presence of all creatures to each other would not hold. It is, however, a crucial difficulty with such theories that they seem to lack any possibility of experimental confirmation, precisely because any parallel universe would by definition exist in a different space-time continuum, making any transfer of evidentiary data to our universe impossible. Some theoreticians hypothesize that gravity may flow between different universes in such a way as to enable some sort of communication between them, but in that case different universes do not occupy utterly separate continua.

Similarly, whether angelic beings and human who have died can be said to be present to the living depends on how heaven (and hell) are understood to relate to the phenomenal world of space and time. It will be argued in chap. 7 below that the presence of heaven to earth is an important feature of Christian belief that is well grounded in Scripture.

25. Insofar as creatures are composites, one can speak of their occupying the same place (e.g., the molecules of which I am composed occupy the same place that I do; my soul occupies the same place as my body). But this is precisely to deny that in such cases of composition we have to do with separate creatures (i.e., neither the molecules of which I am composed nor my soul are other than I am). Where there is a disintegration of the creature—e.g., if my arm is cut off in an accident, or (depending on how one understands what happens to the soul between death and resurrection) I

presence is a necessary condition for any interaction among creatures, different interactions require different degrees of presence. Certain sorts of interactions (e.g., the color force, human sexual intimacy) require that the creatures involved stand in extremely close physical proximity to one another. By contrast, the gravitational interactions between very massive material bodies are such that they may meaningfully be said to be present to one another even at vast distances of space and even time. And among human beings various means ranging from shouting to sophisticated forms of electronic communication establish modes of presence that also allow interaction from places separated from one another by significant stretches of space and time.

For the most part, however, spatiotemporal proximity is a necessary, if not entirely sufficient (since I can be near someone without being present to them, whether out of ignorance of their vicinity or by deliberately ignoring them), condition of mutual presence among creatures, so that creatures as a rule are more present to each other (and so have a greater capacity for mutual interaction) the more closely they are placed to each other. Although it is true that I can be present to someone on another continent by way of a video hookup, it is not as immediate as being in the same room with them (there are elements of my interlocutor's environment—whether physical features like temperature or emotional factors caused, for example, by the knowledge that the building she is in is in the path of a hurricane—that I cannot experience at a distance, even if I am made intellectually aware of them). In any case, the video hookup mediates presence precisely by collapsing, in certain respects, the distance between us, in a way analogous to that in which I might attempt to become present to someone by actually moving toward them, changing my place in order to be able to be present to them. The place a creature occupies is in this way decisive for its ability to affect and to be affected by other creatures: my place opens me to certain sorts of interactions and precludes others. In this sense, although place is here listed third among the fundamental characteristics of created being, place can be seen as encapsulating the other two: a creature's place defines its contingency (that it is in one place, one spatiotemporal location rather than another, is a function of a range of variable circumstances) and dictates the possibilities of its movement (viz., the transition from one place to another). In this sense, place encapsulates creatures' status as essentially *finite* beings: defined (and thus limited) by specific features that render them distinctly different from each other.[26]

---

die—then it does become natural to speak of occupying different places ("My arm is over there, but I am here," "My body is moldering in the ground, but my soul is in heaven"). In cases where co-location is not a matter of composition (e.g., a bacterium in my bloodstream, or a tapeworm in my intestines), the distinction of place between two creatures is named through the contrast between inside and outside, which is another spatial distinction.

26. This intrinsic "otherness" of creatures with respect to one another contrasts with God's status as "Not other," as described on p. 59 above.

THE DIVERSITY OF CREATURES

Contingency, movement, and place are features of the created order that shape and mediate the nature of all created beings. They identify crucial features that distinguish creatures from the Creator, even as they establish certain analogies between them. On a traditional interpretation of the Trinity, God is not contingent, God experiences the fullness of divine existence from eternity, and God is not limited by place. In their contingency, creatures participate in the existence that is proper to God, may exhibit their own forms of productivity through movement, and can be present to one another by virtue of their having a place in the world; yet they are not inherently alive, productive, or present as God is. In this sense all creatures share the fact of otherness from God and unilateral dependence on God, who is the sole source of the various forms of existence, movement, and place that creatures enjoy. The creation is one in that God holds it in existence, enables its movement, and gives it space and time as an interdependent whole that, in its contingency, motion, and locality, is other than God.

But if creation may be said to be one in its distinction from and dependence on God, it is not one as God is one. For Christians, God's unity excludes all talk of a plurality of gods. Although it is precisely *as* Trinity—Father, Son, and Holy Spirit—that God is one, it remains the case (in the words of the Athanasian Creed) that "there are not three eternal beings, but one who is eternal; . . . not three uncreated and unlimited beings, but one who is uncreated and unlimited; . . . not three almighty beings, but one who is almighty; . . . not three gods, but one God."[27] By contrast, creation's unity does not preclude talk of many creatures. Although all creatures are contingent, move, and have place, they have different motions and occupy distinct places, reflecting their irreducibly different forms of contingent existence. While in God all three hypostases are equally the subject of every divine action, creaturely actions are not shared in this way. Even where creatures' movements combine to produce a given effect, they do so as separate causes whose contributions are partial and distinct. Furthermore, although the existence of any one creature is bound up with that of every other (albeit with vastly different degrees of immediacy) by means of the physical forces that provide the basis for their mutual interactions, the existence, motion, and place of every creature pertain to that creature alone and are nontransferable. My own existence, motion, and place impact those of other creatures to a greater or lesser extent, but they cannot be identified with the existence, motion, and place of any other creature.[28]

---

27. Athanasian Creed, in *Lutheran Book of Worship: Ministers Desk Edition*, by Inter-Lutheran Commission on Worship (Minneapolis: Augsburg, 1978), 118–19.

28. This is not to deny that creatures can interact to form a unified system, as in (to give the simplest possible example) two bodies in space or (at a much higher degree of complexity) an ant colony, but only to note that all such systems are capable of being analyzed as the product of their component, creaturely parts in a way that is not true of the triune God.

Far more striking even than their numerical plurality, however, is the extent to which creatures differ from one another in *kind*, existing as qualitatively distinct types of entities that define and reflect the widest range of physical scales. In the first instance, this diversity is a function of the richness of God's own life. In God, this richness is eternally realized in the undivided unity of the Trinity. Creation is the enactment of God's will to share it; but because whatever God creates is other than God, no one creature can reflect all of God's perfections in itself. As Aquinas puts it, God

> brought things into existence so that his goodness might be communicated to creatures and reenacted through them. And because it was not possible for his goodness to be represented through any single creature, he produced many different ones, so that what was wanting in one expression of the divine goodness might be supplied by another; for goodness, which in God is single and united, in creatures is multiple and divided. Hence the whole universe shares and represents his goodness less incompletely than any one creature by itself.[29]

In this way, the diversity of creation can be understood as a function of God's transcendence. All perfections are one in God because God is infinite (i.e., unlimited by any nondivine reality), and since creatures are inherently finite (limited both in their own properties and, still more fundamentally, in that they derive their existence from God), they can reflect the multitude of divine perfections only by way of multiplicity.[30] Thus, insofar as God wishes to share God's life at all, this commitment naturally results in a range of created beings, each of which, in a finite yet unique and unsubstitutable way, reflects some aspect of God's infinite goodness.[31]

If the ultimate cause of creaturely diversity is God's will to share God's life as fully as possible with what is not divine, however, this diversity is realized in time and space through creatures' varied movements: the diverse ways in which they realize their several and mutually irreducible sorts of creaturely perfection.

29. Thomas Aquinas, *ST* 1.47.1, trans. alt. The conviction that the diversity of creatures reflects the fullness of God's goodness does not imply for Thomas that it is the best of all possible worlds, since "God's goodness is not bound to this universe in such a way that he could not have made another universe that was more or less good" (*Quaestiones disputata de potentia Dei* 3.16, in *On Creation*, trans. S. C. Selner-Wright [Washington, DC: Catholic University of America Press, 2011], 149).

30. Cf. Wolfhart Pannenberg, *Systematic Theology*, trans. Geoffrey W. Bromiley (1991; repr., Grand Rapids: Wm. B. Eerdmans Publishing Co., 1994), 2:61: "The creation of a reality that is distinct from God, but one that God also affirms and thus allows to share in fellowship with himself, is conceivable only as the bringing forth of a *world* of creatures. A single creature would be too tiny to face with God's infinity. As a finite creature it would have no lasting entity. A finite being is limited by other beings . . . [and] has its distinctiveness only vis-à-vis other finite things. Only in this distinction does it exist. Hence the finite exists as a plurality of what is finite."

31. Thus, while Scripture clearly views creation as "a single totality . . . willed and created by God, . . . the Old Testament has no word for this uniform conception of the 'world.' It occasionally uses (Ps. 8:6; Isa. 44:24) the expression 'the whole' (*hak-kōl*), but as a rule it can only enumerate the various elements." Karl Barth, *Church Dogmatics* (hereafter *CD*), ed. G. W. Bromiley and T. F. Torrance, 13 vols. (Edinburgh: T&T Clark, 1956–75), III/1:19.

As argued in the preceding section, creaturely motion is an analogue to the divine productivity by which God's perfection as the one God takes the form of the eternal, threefold repetition of the divine life. But whereas divine perfection is realized from eternity through a productivity that entails "no variation or shadow due to change" (Jas. 1:17), creatures achieve perfection by means of change, as they move by grace toward life in God, which they can only receive as a gift and never claim as an intrinsic part of their finite natures. As also noted in the preceding section, this creaturely movement toward God is never self-contained. Because created existence is characterized by interdependence, such that a creature subsists as the creature it is only in and through relationships with other creatures, the movement whereby creatures realize their individual perfection entails interaction with other creatures. These interactions, whose forms include varying degrees of repulsion, attraction, combination, disintegration, and transformation, provide the physical basis for the diversification of creaturely kinds.[32]

The process of creaturely diversification, as an effect of creaturely movement, can be understood as a further created analogy to the divine productivity. The analogy is, if anything, even more remote than that of the movement whereby individual creatures achieve their perfection, since while the Trinitarian repetition of the divine life in the three hypostases eternally establishes God's indivisible unity, the processes by which creatures proliferate confirms their irreducible plurality. This difference is important in several respects. First, it means that the experienced abundance of creatures that are genuinely and fully different from one another is not an illusion masking an underlying oneness (as in the Hindu "veil of Maya"). As Paul puts it:

> Not all flesh is alike, but there is one flesh for human beings, another for animals, another for birds, and another for fish. There are both heavenly bodies and earthly bodies, but the glory of the heavenly is one thing, and that of the earthly is another. There is one glory of the sun, and another glory of the moon, and another glory of the stars; indeed, star differs from star in glory. (1 Cor. 15:39–41)

Such claims echo themes well established from the outset in the Old Testament, where God is described as having created the variety of plants and animals, "each according to its kind" (Gen. 1:11–12, 21, 24–25 RSV), and in the flood similarly seeks to preserve them all "according to their kinds" (6:20; 7:14 RSV).[33]

---

32. Diversity among spiritual beings may constitute an exception to this claim, depending on one's angelology. Thus for Thomas Aquinas, e.g., because angels lack any material dimension and are thus pure form, every angel is a distinct species, which means that angelic diversity is the product of God alone, without the involvement of any creaturely causes (see *De potentia Dei* 3.9.27, in *On Creation*, 94; cf. *ST* 1.50.4). By contrast, Gregory of Nyssa evidently viewed angelic diversity as a product of a specifically angelic form of reproduction. See Gregory of Nyssa, *On the Making of Man* 17.2–3, in vol. 5 of *NPNF²*.

33. These translations follow the RSV, which, in turn, reflects the even more literal rendering of the AV ("after his/their kind") for the Hebrew *lĕmîn*. Except in the catalogues of clean and unclean

Also, since creation's material diversity is characterized as "good," both in its component parts (1:4, 12, 18, 21, 25) and as a whole (Gen. 1:31; cf. 1 Tim. 4:4), neither diversity nor materiality can be interpreted as a sign of declension from a state of primordial, purely spiritual unity, as apparently was the case for at least some of the so-called "gnostic" cosmologies of the early Christian centuries. For while the Bible also seems to teach that the multiplicity of creaturely types derives from a primordial, undifferentiated uniformity (the *tōhû wābōhû* of Gen. 1:2; cf. Jer. 4:23), it depicts such diversifying as a deliberate and benevolent process of ordering and enrichment, rather than as an accident that would better have been avoided.

Of course, the accounts of creation found in Genesis view divine fiat rather than immanent processes of creaturely interaction as the source of creation's diversity. By contrast, while contemporary science also derives the complexity of the present universe from an earlier state of relative homogeneity (the relative uniformity that obtained in the first fractions of a second of the big bang), it ascribes the resulting diversification of creatures—from galaxies thousands of light-years across to atomic nuclei many orders of magnitude smaller than a grain of sand—to the accumulated effects of the mutual interaction of forces and particles over billions of years through cosmological and biological evolution. Processes at these scales are not envisioned in Genesis.[34] Yet at the same time, according to Genesis, God creates both plants and animals by means of the creaturely realities of earth and water: "Let the earth put forth vegetation. . . . Let the waters bring forth swarms of living creatures. . . . Let the earth bring forth living creatures of every kind" (Gen. 1:11–12, 20–21, 24–25).[35] This understanding does not in any way diminish God's sovereignty in the work of creation (on the fifth and sixth days alike, the invitational "Let . . ." is followed by "So *God* created the great sea

animals in Lev. 11:22, 29, the NRSV makes use of alternative English expressions (see also Deut. 14:13–18; Ezek. 47:10). These alternatives do not reflect so well the consistent use of this Hebrew phrase, which (in line with the emphasis on taxonomic precision characteristic of the priestly writers) highlights the distinctiveness of the types of creatures enumerated. (I am indebted to David Petersen for his help in clarifying the significance of the Hebrew idiom.)

34. Nor should Christians be surprised that they are not envisioned there, since the point of the Genesis stories is to introduce the story of God's election and redemption of Israel (and through Israel, all nations), not to provide a complete natural history. As Calvin put it long before churches were torn apart by debates over biblical inerrancy, Moses "everywhere spoke in a homely style, to suit the capacity of the people, and . . . [therefore] did not treat scientifically of the stars, as a philosopher would; but he called them in a popular manner, according to their appearance to the uneducated, rather than according to the truth." John Calvin, *Calvin's Bible Commentaries: Genesis, Part I*, trans. John King (1847; repr., Charleston, SC: Forgotten Books, 2007), 182, on Gen. 6:14.

35. In the case of the aquatic creatures and birds, God goes on to give them charge of their own proliferation with the blessing, "Be fruitful and multiply and fill the waters in the seas, and let the birds multiply on the earth" (Gen. 1:22). While the land animals also multiply through biological reproduction (Gen. 6:19–20; 7:2–3; cf. 8:19), they are not given a separate blessing in Gen. 1, most likely because the inclusion of human beings on the sixth day complicates the rhythm of the narrative: on the fifth day the blessing of the creatures follows immediately on God's judgment of their goodness; in vv. 26–27, on the sixth day, the sequence is interrupted by the creation of human beings (who do receive the divine injunction, "Be fruitful and multiply" in v. 28) immediately after the designation of the land animals as "good" in v. 25.

monsters and every living creature, . . . with which the waters swarm" [v. 21], and "*God* made the wild animals" [v. 25]), but it indicates that in creating God both can and does make use of creaturely causes rather than necessarily overriding them.[36] The productive capacity of creation in its nonliving as well as its living forms is an expression of creaturely movement that is described as a matter of wonder at various points in Scripture (see Job 38–40, Pss. 104; 148), and which Jesus himself invokes as a sign of God's blessing on the world (Matt. 6:26–30). Likewise, in a manner that clearly goes beyond but does not seem in principle opposed to the narrative of Genesis 1, the evolutionary diversification of living beings across generations can be seen as a further mode of creaturely production, according to which creatures' multiplication is not limited to the reproduction of existing forms, but actually gives rise to new kinds of being.[37]

And yet the specter of evolution only heightens what is perhaps the most profound and troubling disanalogy between divine and creaturely productivity. For whereas the Trinitarian diversification of the Godhead entails neither diminution of the Father as source nor competition among the hypostases that are constituted through the acts of begetting and proceeding, the dynamics of creaturely diversity entails both: the flourishing of some creatures invariably comes at the expense of others. To be sure, biblical narratives of the original creation and of eschatological hope seem to envision a universal vegetarianism (Gen. 1:29–30; Isa. 11:7; 65:25) without hostility between species (Isa. 11:6, 9),[38] but however attractive this picture may be, it does not reflect the structure of any ecosystem that has existed during the half a billion years of multicellular life on earth. On the contrary, the best contemporary understanding of evolutionary dynamics seems to mark the world of organisms in particular and creation more generally as a zero-sum affair that stands in the sharpest possible contrast to the divine life: the begetting of the Son may be an expression of rather than a threat to the inexhaustible richness of the Father's life, but creaturely begetting entails

---

36. See Basil of Caesarea, *Hexaemeron* 8.1, in vol. 8 of *NPNF*[2]. Of course, the theological claim that God enables and directs the evolutionary processes that lead to the diversification of creaturely kinds exceeds any possible findings within the natural sciences, in which causal explanations are restricted to the phenomenal realm (the principle of "methodological materialism"); but insofar as Christians refuse to assimilate God to created causes, the fact that God's action in creation cannot be inferred directly from the fossil record should not be an occasion for theological concern. See the discussion of *concursus* and *gubernatio*, including their implications for the relationship between theological and scientific truth claims, in chap. 6 below.

37. While not in any exact sense an anticipation of modern evolutionary theory, Augustine introduced the category of "seminal reasons" (*rationes seminales*) to explain the possibility of novelty in the course of natural history as the product of "seeds in a sense of future realities, destined to germinate in suitable places from hidden obscurity into the manifest light of day through the course of the ages." In *The Literal Meaning of Genesis* 6.17 (p. 10); cf. 9.31–32 (p. 17), in *On Genesis*, trans. Edmund Hill, OP, ed. John E. Rotelle, OSA (Hyde Park, NY: New City Press, 2002).

38. Of course, from a modern evolutionary standpoint, vegetarianism does not remove the problem of creaturely competition, since plants are also subject to natural selection and develop various "strategies" (e.g., thorns) to protect themselves from being eaten; but from the perspective of the priestly writer, plants are clearly in a different category from animals, whose blood makes their ingestion, though permitted, morally risky (see Gen. 9:4–5).

a reallocation of resources that diminishes the parent (to the extent that in the case of octopuses, for example, the mother literally gives her life so that her brood may hatch) and represents a threat to others of the same species (through competition for food and living space), quite apart from the ways in which the conditions of the flourishing of one type of organism may require that another be harmed (e.g., by way of predation or parasitism).

In this context the characteristic of place emerges as a particularly striking source of disharmony within creation, since no two creatures can occupy the same place.[39] God's own mode of presence as Trinity does not exclude the presence of others but is the condition of the presence of others: thus the Father, present as the One who begets and spirates, makes present the Son and the Spirit; the presence of the Spirit glorifies (and thus makes present) the Son as the Father's image; and the presence of the Son is a bearing witness to the Father's presence in the power of the Spirit. Nor in creating the world is God's presence in competition with that of creatures. On the contrary, the doctrine of divine omnipresence is a corollary of creation from nothing: it is by virtue of God's transcendence of space and time (such that every creature is immediately present to God) that God sustains each individual creature in its place. Yet within the created order, individual creatures' location in space and time appears to constitute an arrangement in which one creature's having a place in the world invariably leads to the displacement (whether actual or potential) of others.[40] From this perspective, the fact of creaturely diversity is not in itself self-evidently a manifestation of the richness of the divine life; observation of nature might equally well lead to the conclusion that the diversity of creation is simply a jumble, in which the plurality of creaturely forms both derives from and is productive of an endless cycle of division and destruction, where talk of mutual enrichment is simply evidence of wishful thinking.[41]

---

39. Again, this is true even of nonmaterial creatures like angels, as well as those cases where one material creature is inside (and thus, so to speak, partially displacing) another. See notes 23 and 25 above.

40. "Nature may be compared to a surface covered with ten thousand sharp wedges, many of the same shape and many of different shapes representing differing species, all packed closely together and all driven by incessant blows: the blows being far severer at one time than another; sometimes a wedge of one form and sometimes another being struck; and one driven deeply in forcing out others; with the jar and shock often transmitted very far to other wedges in many lines of direction: beneath the surface we may suppose that there lies a hard layer, fluctuating in its level, and which may represent the minimum amount of food required by each living being, and which layer will be impenetrable by the deepest wedge." Charles Darwin, *Natural Selection: Being the Second Part of His Big Species Book Written from 1856 to 1858*, ed. R. C. Stauffer (1856–58; repr., Cambridge: Cambridge University Press, 1975), 208; cf. the parallel, shorter passage in his *On the Origin of Species* (London: Murray, 1859), 67, in chap. 3.

41. While the basic features of competition among creatures for resources is not a matter of dispute among evolutionary biologists, there is debate over the vision of nature constructed from consideration of this process. While many hold fast to the brutality of Darwin's wedge imagery (see, e.g., Richard Dawkins, *The Selfish Gene* [New York: Oxford University Press, 1976]), others interpret the complex interconnections between organisms and environment that have developed over time as evidence that the biosphere is a self-regulating system that moves toward points of

THE UNITY OF CREATURES

In order to view creation's diversity as good rather than a stochastic product of natural forces or, worse, as a manifestation of evil on a cosmic scale, it is necessary to frame one's (always partial) experience of the world in terms of a larger and harmonious whole. Given the ephemeral character—and often violent end—of individuals, species, and even entire classes of creatures, any affirmation of such harmony in the world is necessarily a matter of faith. In his own context, Irenaeus faced a religious perspective that was inclined to view material reality in strongly negative terms, and he offered the following characterization of the world's wholeness:

> Now inasmuch as created beings are various and numerous, they are indeed well fitted and adapted to the whole creation; yet when viewed individually, they are opposed to one another and inharmonious, just as the sound of a lyre, although it consists of many and opposite notes, through these differences gives rise to one harmonious melody. The lover of truth therefore ought not to be deceived by the interval between each note, nor should he imagine that one was due to one artist and author, and another to another. . . . And those who listen to the melody ought to praise and extol the artist, to admire the tension of some notes, to attend to the softness of others, to catch the sound of others between both extremes, and to consider the special character of others, so as to inquire at what each one aims, and what is the cause of their variety, never changing the rule [of faith] by either wandering from the artist, or casting off faith in the one God who made all things, or blaspheming our Creator.[42]

This kind of reasoning is always dangerous, since appeal to the harmony and order of the "big picture" can easily lead to a Panglossian optimism that fails to take seriously the reality of evil (let alone human complicity in it).[43] But at some level it is unavoidable: to see the world as good is to construe it in a particular way, as a wonderful gift to be received with gratitude in spite of the fact that certain features of the world may induce feelings of fear or loathing.[44] The doctrine of creation counsels that the world be seen in just such terms: as a

---

homeostasis (see, e.g., James Lovelock, *Gaia: A New Look at Life on Earth* [New York: Oxford University Press, 2000]).

42. Irenaeus, *AH* 2.25.2, in PG 7a:798B–799A, trans. slightly alt. Athanasius uses the same simile to describe the Word's integration of creation's disparate parts into a coherent whole in his *Oratio contra gentes* (*Against the Pagans*) 42, in PG 25b:85A.

43. Augustine's use of the big-picture analogy swerves dangerously in this direction: "All have their offices and limits laid down so as to ensure the beauty of the universe. That which we abhor in any part of it gives us the greatest pleasure when we consider the universe as a whole. . . . The colour black in a picture may very well be beautiful if you take the picture as a whole." Augustine, *Of True Religion* 76, in *Augustine: Earlier Writings*, ed. and trans. J. H. S. Burleigh (Philadelphia: Westminster Press, 1953), 264. See also his *Enchiridion on Faith, Hope, and Love* 10. For an extensive discussion of evil, see chap. 5 below.

44. For an excellent discussion of this point, see Kelsey, "Creation from Nothing," 176–96.

coherent whole, ordered by God for the benefit of creatures (Isa. 45:18).[45] From this perspective the diversity of creation is properly interpreted as an integrated unity, in which the flourishing of the many different kinds of creatures is both desired by God and achieved through relationships of mutual interdependence.

Given both the limits on our perceptual capacities and the immeasurable extent of creaturely suffering, a properly theological vision of creation's wholeness needs to be presented in very measured terms. Most important, in light of Christian conviction regarding the goodness of everything God has made, appeals to the harmony of the whole cannot be framed in such a way as to demean the significance of any part. Instead, talk about the wholeness of creation must affirm the integrity of every creature in God's sight, such that (1) no creature exists merely for the sake of some other one (as though its value were reducible to another's flourishing), since (2) each has its own inherent value before God as something meant to flourish in its own right, though (3) each is so constituted that it cannot flourish in isolation from other creatures. In line with this principle, Augustine insisted that it is only in taking stock of the diversity of creatures in their interrelatedness that creation's goodness is fully manifest:

> Seven times I have counted Scripture saying you saw that what you made is good. But on the eighth occasion when you saw all that you had made, it says they were not merely good but "very good"—as if taking everything at once into account. For individual items were only "good," but everything taken together was both "good" and "very good." This truth is also declared by the beauty of bodies. A body composed of its constituent parts, all of which are beautiful, is far more beautiful as a whole than those parts taken separately; the whole is made of their well-ordered harmony; though individual, the constituent parts are also beautiful.[46]

The goodness of creation applies to every individual creature, but it is fully visible only when creation is seen as the totality of these individuals. One important dimension of a doctrine of creation is to provide an account of the world that allows its various creaturely components to be seen in this way, and the rest of this chapter is an effort toward that end.

The extent of creation's diversity means that the various types of creatures can be classified in many different ways, and Jesus' declaring all foods clean in spite of clear scriptural teaching to the contrary (Mark 7:19; cf. Acts 10:15; Lev. 11:1–47) shows that no one system of classification, even one rooted in the biblical texts themselves, can be considered final or definitive. Various schemes

45. Michael Welker characterizes creation as "*the construction and maintenance of associations of different, interdependent creaturely realms,*" such that "God creates by bringing different creaturely realms into fruitful associations of interdependent relations that promote life." See his *Creation and Reality,* trans. John F. Hoffmyer (Minneapolis: Fortress Press, 1999), 13.

46. Augustine, *Confessions* 13.43. Augustine's count of seven for "God saw that it was good" in the creation story reflects the Old Latin version of Genesis (based, in turn, on the Greek Septuagint), which includes the phrase in Gen. 1:4, 8, 10, 12, 18, 21, 25. The Masoretic Text (the Hebrew on which most English Bible translations are based) lacks the phrase in v. 8.

will prove serviceable in different contexts (so that, for example, biologists' classification of organisms answers to different needs, and is based on correspondingly different criteria, than a system based on their nutritional value for human beings), and from the start Christians will, correspondingly, do well to abandon the goal of finding a definitive classificatory framework, striving instead to "pursue what makes for peace and for mutual edification" (Rom. 14:19). If articulating the goodness of the world in terms of a "big picture" always carries risks, Christians can address some of them by holding to any such account with a suitably light touch.[47]

But if no one taxonomy can claim to be suitable for every situation, some are more useful than others in theological discussions that seek to highlight the ways in which the creation is related to God. Traditional Christian creedal formulations, for example, follow the lead of Genesis 1:1 in highlighting a fundamental division within creation between "heaven and earth." In the Nicene Creed this distinction is given further specification, so that its focus is not the spatial distinction between physical locations above and below the terrestrial atmosphere but two distinct dimensions of created existence: the "visible" and the "invisible," all that can be seen on the one hand, and the unseen on the other. This specification reminds the church of two complementary points. First, creation is not limited to the phenomenal world that is subject to scientific observation. Traditionally, the invisible creation is associated with angelic beings, who are understood to be "extraterrestrial," not in the sense of being native to another planet, but rather as having their natural "place" as creatures altogether outside of the space-time continuum within which planets are found.[48] But there is no theological reason to limit the invisible creation to those beings called angels in the Bible. Because the "invisible" refers to everything that is not naturally accessible to the senses, it seems appropriate to maintain a healthy dose of agnosticism about its contents. In this sense it is profoundly foreign to us. And yet for that reason it is not a sphere that does not concern us. As the very title "angel" (Greek for "messenger") indicates, the spheres of visible and invisible are connected, with the invisible serving at least in part to further God's purposes in and with the visible, and both in their respective spheres serving the end of God's glory.[49] In this context—and this is the second point connected with the distinction between visible and invisible—the unseen creation, however expansive it may be

47. Here in particular the warning issued in the preface (above) against the idea of a "Christian" worldview needs to be heeded.

48. In light of the biblical witness to angelic appearances (e.g., Gen. 19:1; Luke 1:26–38), Christians have taken it for granted that angels' natural invisibility does not preclude their assuming physical form and performing actions within time and space as part of their service to God (see, e.g., Thomas Aquinas, *ST* 1.51.2).

49. Westermann argues that in the Old Testament there is a clear distinction between God's messengers ("angels" in the etymological sense) and the heavenly creatures who comprise God's court (the cherubim and seraphim) and who, as such, "are not messengers of God, but are in the message of the messenger." Claus Westermann, *God's Angels Need No Wings*, trans. D. L. Scheidt (Philadelphia: Fortress Press, 1979), 23. For further discussion of angels' place in creation, see chap. 7 below.

and however much it may exceed human experience, is also *created*.[50] Notwithstanding the biblical insistence that God is invisible (e.g., Rom. 1:20; Col. 1:15; 1 Tim. 1:17; cf. John 1:18), invisibility is not in itself the measure of divinity.[51] The realm of the invisible may be incomparably greater and more mysterious than anything that can be seen, but it is not divine and must not be confused with God (see Heb. 1:3–14). When pious people in the Bible do confuse the two, they are immediately corrected (Rev. 19:10; 22:8).

The biblical and creedal distinction between heaven and earth provides an initial indication of the enormous range of creaturely types: everything we can see—and a further realm of unknown extent beyond that![52] In so doing, it also establishes a framework within which to address the problem of how the goodness of creaturely diversity can be reconciled with the restrictions on creatures' flourishing posed by place. While it remains true that no two creatures can occupy the same place, framing creation in terms of the spheres of heaven and earth points to the capacity of the created order to accommodate vast numbers of creatures, each with its own place, by presenting a vision of creation as fundamentally *spacious*. The sequence of creative acts that follow the opening declaration of the heaven-and-earthly scope of God's work in Genesis 1 marks out the scope of that spaciousness within the earthly sphere (the spaciousness of heaven being left undescribed, in a manner suitable to its essential invisibility).[53] In particular, the work of the first three days defines the created regions (sky, water, land) within which the diversity of creatures formed on days four (sun, moon, and stars), five (aquatic creatures and birds), and six (land animals) exist. Moreover, the divine command that the living creatures multiply (Gen. 1:22, 28) suggests that these spaces can and should contain multitudes.[54]

50. For a discussion of the ways in which the unseen creation may be understood to exhibit the creaturely characteristics of contingency, movement, and place, see notes 23–25 above.

51. "There could also be *heavenly* revelations, that is, revelations of that invisible and inconceivable reality of creation, with which we are girt about. This world . . . of the impalpable and invisible is conceived in continuous movement toward us. Truly there are occasions of wonder there too. . . . But neither do these heavenly revelations have the character of ultimate authority; they too are in fact creaturely revelations" (Barth, *Dogmatics in Outline*, 83).

52. Insofar as it reflects the conviction that the extent of God's goodness in creating is incalculable, the traditional view that the realm of the invisible is of much greater extent than that of the visible (see, e.g., Thomas Aquinas, *ST* 1.49.3.5) is not without theological merit, even if it lacks explicit biblical foundation.

53. Robert W. Jenson correlates the spaciousness of creation with the intrinsic "roominess" of the triune God, who "can, if he chooses, distinguish himself from others not by excluding them but by including them." See his *The Triune God*, vol. 1 of *Systematic Theology* (New York: Oxford University Press, 1997), 226.

54. Catherine Keller rightly notes the significance of animal diversity in Gen. 1: "Loving presentation of the wild beasts had been an earmark of Gen. 1, indeed distinguishes the priestly narrative from the *Enuma Elish*, which for all its parallelism [with Genesis] features a noticeable absence of animals. While the divine love of the wild does not homogeneously characterize Hebrew Scriptures, the Genesis human emerges as the image of God amidst a dense company of other animals." From her *Face of the Deep: A Theology of Becoming* (New York: Routledge, 2003), 132. Along similar lines, in Gen. 2 God sets apart a limited space on land as a garden for human flourishing (vv. 7–8), which includes a wide variety of trees (v. 9), along with all types of animals and birds (v. 19; note that in this account they are created together rather than on separate days). Thus, in the second creation story

And yet part of the ambiguity surrounding the human experience of creatures' diversity is bound up with the fact that the multiplication of creatures is coupled with (and from a purely biological perspective, needed to compensate for) their regular destruction: rather than persisting in the capacious environments that God provides, living creatures, whether considered as individuals or as classes, die, so that, for example, only a small fraction of the terrestrial species that have existed in the half-billion years since the emergence of multicellular life survive today. Yet this fact in itself need not be viewed as inconsistent with creation's goodness. Although death has most often been viewed in Christian tradition as a punishment for Adam's transgression, Genesis 3:19, 22 (cf. 6:3) may also be read as teaching that humans (and by extension, other earth creatures) naturally return to the dust from which they were taken unless some other factor intervenes (see Gen. 2:7, 17; Ps. 103:13–16; Eccl. 3:19–20). Certainly there is nothing inconsistent with the goodness of creation that the "place" occupied by every creature should have temporal as well as spatial boundaries, entailing a limited life span no less than limited bodily dimensions; indeed, such temporal limits actually enhance the capaciousness of creation, since two creatures *can* occupy the same space if they do so at different times. Death can certainly be experienced as a violation of life and so as a curse, but Scripture also can speak of a kind of death that is a life's natural conclusion, in which an individual dies "old and full of days" (Gen. 35:29; 1 Chr. 29:28; Job 42:17; cf. Gen. 25:8; Isa. 65:20).[55] Insofar as extinction of a species is the analogue to the death of an individual creature, one might equally conceive of classes of creatures—trilobites or dinosaurs, say, both of which thrived for tens of millions of years before becoming extinct—as having experienced this sort of death.[56] In this way we can understand death as temporal finitude, as a means by which the fullness of creation is arranged along a temporal axis as well as within contemporary physical spaces: as Ecclesiastes says, there is to every matter under heaven a time no less

---

even a small part of the earth seems to be conceived as ample for containing an enormous diversity of creaturely forms.

55. Thomas argues that it is part of the character of creation that various degrees of goodness are realized among different creatures, such that some (viz., angelic existences) possess a degree of goodness that makes it impossible for them to lose existence (i.e., they are incorruptible), whereas the goodness of others is of a degree that they can and do fall out of existence (i.e., they are corruptible). He interprets this loss of existence as a form of evil (*ST* 1.48.2; 1.49.3.5), but insofar as he defines the good as that by which "each real thing tends to its own existence and completion" (*ST* 1.48.1), it is not clear that the "completion" of a particular existence should exclude its having a finite term of existence. Thomas himself adverts to this possibility when he says in *ST* 1.48.3 that the absence of a good is only evil when a deprivation, and not when one creature merely ceases to possess the perfection of another. See *ST* 1.49.2: "God's principal purpose in created things is clearly that form or good which consists in the order of the universe. This requires . . . that there should be some things that can and sometimes do fall away. . . . But we read also, 'God has not made death' (Wis. 1:13), and the meaning is that he does not will death for its own sake."

56. Of course, the particular circumstances of any given species' death can raise theodical problems similar to those posed by the death of individual creatures. Both trilobites and dinosaurs, e.g., seem to have gone extinct as the result of global environmental catastrophes, though dinosaurs appear to have been already in decline when an asteroid impact delivered the coup de grâce.

than a place (3:1), and the goodness of created existence is experienced within that time (3:12–13, 22; 5:18–19; 8:15; 9:9).[57]

Still, to make a case for creation as an identifiable whole in which all have a place, it is necessary to take account of a further feature of the biblical creation stories: the fact that in Genesis 1 and 2 alike (albeit in rhetorically very different ways), one creature, the human being, is depicted as the center or climax of God's creative work. "Good" though other creatures may be, only human beings are said to have been created "in the image of God" (Gen. 1:27; cf. 5:1; 9:6). This undeniably anthropocentric emphasis is often (and not unnaturally) seen as diminishing the significance of other creatures, with the result that the spaciousness of creation is conceived as one-sidedly oriented to the benefit of human beings. Even where Scripture is explicit that God's covenant with creation includes nonhuman creatures (e.g., Gen. 9:11; Hos. 2:18), human beings appear to be the focus of divine concern.[58] In order to make sense of the anthropocentrism of the biblical accounts without undermining their emphasis on the goodness of creation as a whole, a further articulation of the Christian "picture" of creation is needed. The proposal of the seventh-century theologian Maximus the Confessor is particularly striking:

> The saints . . . say that the substance of everything that has come into being is divided into five divisions. From the uncreated nature, the first of these divides created nature (considered as a whole), which receives its being from becoming. . . . The second division is that by which the whole of nature that receives its being through creation is divided by God into that which is perceived by the mind and that which is perceived by the senses. The third is that by which the nature perceived by the senses is divided into heaven and earth. The fourth is that by which the earth is divided into paradise and the inhabited world, and the fifth, that by which the human person (who stands over all as a kind of workshop most fit for joining everything together, naturally mediates between the extremities of each division, and encompasses everything according to its origin in a good and fitting way) is divided into male and female.[59]

---

57. "If things have their due times and intrinsic value, [the "wastefulness" of the evolutionary process] is not necessarily a problem, any more than it is necessarily wasteful that a species of fungus produces millions of spores only a few of which, if any, germinate. Much depends on what is conceived as waste, what as the liberality and overflowing generosity of God." Colin E. Gunton, *The Triune Creator: A Historical and Systematic Survey* (Edinburgh: Edinburgh University Press, 1998), 189.

58. Barth's characterization of the creation as "the external basis" of God's covenant is a notorious (though not especially atypical) example of this tendency, though Barth certainly did not view this fact as justification for human exploitation of other creatures (see Karl Barth, *CD* III/1:94–228). His great rival, Emil Brunner, can be even more extreme (see his *Revelation and Reason: The Christian Doctrine of Faith and Knowledge*, trans. Olive Wyon [Philadelphia: Westminster Press, 1946], 33n).

59. Maximus the Confessor, *Book of Difficulties* 41, in PG 91:1304D–1305B; ET in Andrew Louth, *Maximus the Confessor* (New York: Routledge, 1996), 156–57, trans. alt. There is no clear antecedent to Maximus's fivefold scheme. His mention of "the saints" probably refers to Gregory of Nyssa, who lists the distinction between created and uncreated as "the highest division of all beings," in *Against Eunomius* 3.6.67, in PG 45:793C; yet earlier (*Against Eunomius* 1.270, in PG 45:333B) he had awarded this same status to the distinction between intelligible and sensible. See Gregory of Nyssa, *Opera*, ed. Werner Jaeger, 2 vols. (Leiden: E. J. Brill, 1960).

At first glance the sequence of divisions described by Maximus may appear to be nothing more than a christianized version of the Neoplatonic "chain of being," according to which creatures' goodness is a function of their nearness to God, growing more coarse and intractable as one descends from the intelligible world of immaterial being to matter; but this appearance is deceiving. After all, the sequence ends with human beings, who clearly do not stand at the bottom of the ontological scale for Maximus. On the contrary, humanity lies at the center of creation, as a "workshop" (*ergastērion*) that mediates between and thereby brings together all the various divisions.[60] Instead of marking a declension from divinity, Maximus's representation of the various dimensions of creaturely diversity are better seen as a peeling back of complementary layers, like a Russian nesting doll. On this model the variety of creation is a mark of God's never-diminishing intimacy with creatures of every type rather than indicative of any variation in divine presence.

Maximus's sequence of divisions also stands in a clear, if loose, relation with the opening chapters of Genesis, which also include the distinctions between heaven and earth (1:1; 2:1; cf. 1:6–7), paradise and the rest of the world (2:8; 3:23–24), and male and female (1:27; cf. 2:21–22). While Maximus alters the biblical taxonomy (both by ignoring the divisions of waters in Genesis 1:6–7 and adding the distinction between the sensible and intelligible), his version retains the anthropocentric thrust of the narrative, in which the sequence of creative acts has the effect of focusing attention on human beings as the culmination of God's work (quite straightforwardly in Gen. 1, but also, albeit by way of a more complicated narrative path, in Gen. 2). As already noted for Maximus, humanity's location at the end of the sequence indicates an intensification of theological weight—humans have a distinctive role to play in the divine economy—but the claim that human beings are created in God's image does not entail that they are to be understood as ontologically closer to God than other creatures (a point emphasized by such Old Testament texts as Job 40:15). It does, however, suggest that human beings play a pivotal role within the created order. In Genesis 1 this role is characterized as that of exercising "dominion" (vv. 26, 28; cf. Ps. 8:3–8), a rather broad and imprecise remit that in Genesis 2 is given some definite content in the description of humanity as being put into the garden of Eden "to till it and keep it" (v. 15), and then naming the animals (vv. 19–20).[61]

In light of contemporary worries that the language of dominion establishes a basis for human abuse of the nonhuman realm, it is noteworthy that Maximus's

60. See also Barth, *Dogmatics in Outline*, 63: "Man is the place within creation where the creature in its fullness is concentrated, and at the same time stretches beyond itself." In a more specifically christological vein, see Tanner, *Christ the Key*, 142: "The exceptional character of human beings would be as placeholders . . . for creation generally, focal points for the worldwide imaging of the second person's relations with the other two."
61. Importantly, neither task is depicted as though its purpose were to benefit humanity directly, even if the naming of the animals is a by-product of God's attempt to find the first human being a suitable partner. For evidence of God's concern for the land and its animals in their own right, see Joel 2:21–22; cf. Prov. 12:10–11.

interpretation of humanity's role in creation does not involve any appeals to lordship, sovereignty, or the manipulation of other creatures. Instead, he depicts humanity more as the keystone to creation's order than as its master (or even its steward). As in a round arch, where the keystone's role is a matter of relative position rather than any intrinsic properties of the stone itself, humans' special status seems to derive from their location in the overall structure and thus is primarily a function of their relation to other creatures rather than evidence of any inherent superiority.[62] To be sure, Maximus believes that human beings have this mediating role because they are composed of spirit and matter. It is by virtue of this ontological fact that they may be characterized as a microcosm, or world in miniature, bridging the realms of the intelligible and the sensible and thus serving as the "linchpin" of creation as a whole.[63] But the point remains that for humanity to fulfill this role does not entail performing a particular set of tasks on or toward other creatures, but simply being the creature that humanity was created to be.[64] It is, in short, simply by maintaining a proper relation to the rest of creation—a relation that necessarily includes acknowledging the integrity of other creatures before God—that humans secure creation's relationship to the Creator.[65]

Fine words, and fine words butter no parsnips. After all, the reason the affirmation of creation's wholeness is so difficult is that our experience as human

62. This is not to say that Maximus is free of anthropocentricism. He sees no problem, e.g., in claiming that it is for the sake of human deification that "there exists and abides the system of created things" (*Epistle 24*, in PG 91:609C; cited in Maximus Confessor, *The Ascetic Life; The Four Centuries on Charity*, trans. Polycarp Sherwood [New York: Newman Press, 1955], 71). The point remains, however, that Maximus consistently presupposes a high degree of integration between the human and the nonhuman creation in humanity's movement to glory, and he explicitly speaks of God's will to deify the whole creation in *Quaestiones ad Thalassium* 2, in PG 90:272B. Cf. Thomas Aquinas, *ST* 1.47.2.3: "Inequalities arise in order to achieve the perfection of the whole, not because of any preceding inequality either of merits or even of material dispositions. You see this in works of art; for instance, the difference between the roof and the foundations of a building does not lie in the materials they are made of, but arises from the purpose, namely, a house complete of all its parts; it is in order to achieve this that the builder procures different materials." It remains an open question whether the kinds of *differences* among creatures to which Thomas refers are best described by using the language of *inequality*.

63. Though the term "linchpin" (*syndesmos*) is taken from *Ambiguum 41*, in PG 91:1305B, the image of the microcosm remains largely implicit in that text. For explicit use of this language, see esp. Maximus, *The Church's Mystagogy* 7, in PG 91:684D–685A; ET in *Maximus Confessor: Selected Writings*, trans. George C. Berthold (New York: Paulist Press, 1985), 196. For an extended discussion of the theme of the microcosm in Maximus's writings, see Lars Thunberg, *Microcosm and Mediator: The Theological Anthropology of Maximus the Confessor*, 2nd ed. (LaSalle, IL: Open Court, 1995), 137–42.

64. Maximus does speak of human mediation as an "ascent" (*anabasis*) through the various divisions of creation to God, but this is achieved by humanity "through the perfect knowledge of its own *logos*, in accordance with which it is" (*Difficulties* 41.157, in PG 91:1305C–D).

65. "The result is that . . . the one God, Creator of all, is shown to reside proportionately in all beings through human nature. Things that are by nature separated from one another return to a unity as they converge together in the one human being. When this happens, God will be *all in all* (1 Cor. 15:28), permeating all things and at the same time giving independent existence to all things in himself." *Ambiguum 7*, in PG 91:1092C; ET in *On the Cosmic Mystery of Jesus Christ: Selected Writings from St. Maximus the Confessor*, trans. Paul M. Blowers and Robert Louis Wilken (Crestwood, NY: St. Vladimir's Seminary Press, 2003), 66.

beings is not that of creaturely harmony, but rather a combination of help-lessness and complicity in the face of creation's evident disorder and violence. Maximus himself recognizes full well that, in their sinfulness, human beings do not fulfill the role for which they were created, and thus God must take on the responsibility for securing the functional unity of creation through the incarna-tion.[66] At the same time, Maximus's vision of the work of the incarnate Word in healing the divisions that through sin have distorted the intended harmony of creaturely differences ties in directly with his vision of creation's Trinitar-ian ground and allows him to present his doctrine of creation in profoundly nonanthropocentric terms. Following John 1, Maximus understands creation as grounded in the eternal divine Word (Greek *Logos*) whose enfleshment will later bring it to fulfillment. In a manner analogous to Thomas's image of the diffrac-tion of the divine unity in a plurality of created beings, for Maximus the one divine *Logos* gives rise to a multitude of creatures, each with its own individual *logos* that constitutes a fragmentary, spatiotemporal reflection of the divine:

> The Word of God is like a grain of mustard seed: before its cultivation it appears to be very small, but when it has been properly cultivated, it shows itself to be so big that the noble *logoi* of sensible and intellectual creatures, like birds, find rest in it. For the *logoi* of all things, as finite beings, are set in [the Word], but it is limited by none of them.[67]

A creature's *logos* defines its essential character, by attending to which we are drawn to contemplation of God. Yet because of the ontological distance between creature and Creator, we are unable to move on our own from the con-templation of any one creature—or even any indefinitely large set of creatures—to God.[68] Considered by themselves, the *logoi* of creatures are like words of a

66. Maximus holds with the wider Christian tradition in attributing this disorder to human sin: if creation as a whole has been endowed by God with a structural unity that allows its most distant extremes to be unified in human being, then the bewildering diversity of particulars encompassed by these extremes is such that when the human center fails to hold, the various, divinely instituted *dif-ferences* among creatures come to be experienced as matters of *division*, in which patterns of mutual flourishing give way to opposition and conflict (see Maximus, *Difficulties* 41, in Louth, *Maximus*, 158–59; and in PG 91:1308C–D). Since we now know that creaturely disorder and violence ante-date the appearance of human beings, this explanation will not hold, and the problem of creation's subjection to futility (Rom. 8:20) is correspondingly more intractable.

67. Maximus the Confessor, *Chapters on Knowledge* 2.10, in PG 90:1129A; ET in Maximus, *Selected Writings*, 149–50, trans. alt. Also cf. 2.4, in PG 90:1125D–1128A: "Just as the arrangement of straight lines which radiate outward [from a circle] appears entirely undivided at the center, so the one who has been made worthy to be in God will perceive with a simple and undivided knowledge all the *logoi* of created things preexisting in him" (148, trans. alt.). See also *Difficulties* 10, in Louth, *Maximus*, 154.

68. Austin Farrer makes this same point in speaking of the ways in which the multiplicity of creaturely perfections relate to their unity in God: "We do not know how these predicates are con-tained in the mode of perfection which is somehow their archetype, and to enumerate them is to give an inventory of the world from which we have drawn them, not of the God to whom we know not how to assign them." Austin Farrer, *Finite and Infinite: A Philosophical Essay* (1943; repr., New York: Seabury Press, 1979), 40.

novel taken out of context, the significance of which cannot be understood apart from some prior grasp of the one divine *Logos* who is their source and end.[69]

It is crucial to Maximus's proposal that no creaturely *logos* enjoys any advantage or priority with respect to any other: all abide equally in the one divine *Logos*, and none provides access to the *Logos* apart from the grace of divine illumination.[70] To be sure, the divine *Logos* is revealed through its taking flesh as the human being Jesus of Nazareth; this fact is ontologically relevant since it is by renewing the human nature that was created to be the unifying center of creation that Christ renews the created order as a whole. The scope of Christ's work, however, remains creation as a whole, so that the point of the incarnation is not for Christ to displace other creatures as the object of our vision, but rather to enable the mind "to see with knowledge what is [already] in front of it" by placing the multitude of creaturely *logoi* in their relationship to Christ as the one divine *Logos*.[71] For Maximus, the proper framework for understanding this process is provided by the story of the transfiguration, where the disciples' experience of Jesus' glory as divine *Logos* allows them also to see God's glory in the *logoi* of created beings.[72] While the light from the face of the Lord is unbearably bright (since creatures cannot perceive the glory of the *Logos* directly), in shining forth it illuminates Jesus' garments, which for Maximus symbolize the creatures made by God, in a way that allows us to see them as they truly are.[73] In short, the light streaming from Christ enables us to understand the world as God's creation, thereby confirming Jesus as the necessary reference point for all human knowledge of God and the world alike.

69. "The whole world is defined by its *logoi*, and we attribute place and time to whatever dwells within it. It has modes of contemplation inhering in it by nature that can produce a partial understanding of God's wisdom over all things. So long as these serve for perception, there cannot be anything but a middle and partial understanding. But when what is partial ceases with the appearance of what is perfect, all mirrors and hidden meanings pass away." Maximus, *Chapters on Knowledge* 1.70, in PG 90:1109A; and in Louth, *Maximus*, 140, trans. alt. Maximus uses the analogy of the interpretation of a written text in his discussion of biblical interpretation in *Chapters on Knowledge* 2.73, in PG 90:1157C.

70. See Maximus, *Chapters on Knowledge* 1.31, in PG 90:1093D–1096A; see Louth, *Maximus*, 134: "Indeed, the human mind as such would not have the strength to raise itself to apprehend any divine illumination did not God himself draw it up, as far as possible for the human mind to be drawn, and illumine it with divine brightness." Cf. 2.83.

71. Maximus the Confessor, *Difficulties* 10, in Louth, *Maximus*, 107.

72. "The knowledge of all that has come to be through Him is naturally and properly made known together with Him. For just as with the rising of the sensible sun all bodies are made known, so it is with God, the intelligible sun of righteousness, rising in the mind: although He is known to be separate from the created order, He wishes the true meanings of everything, whether intelligible or sensible, to be made known together with Himself." Maximus, *Difficulties* 10, in Louth, *Maximus*, 125–26.

73. "Thus, ascending the mountain of the divine Transfiguration, we shall behold the garments of the *Logos*, by which I mean the words [*hrēmata*] of Scripture, and the creatures that appear to us, and which are…rendered splendid by the divine *Logos* for exalted contemplation…. All the intelligible thoughts that derive from his goodness we shall know as a body, and all creatures perceived through the senses as a garment." Maximus, *Difficulties* 10, in PG 91:1132C–D; from Louth, *Maximus*, 112, trans. alt.

The creation is a whole insofar as, to use Maximus's analogy, it serves as the temporal clothing of God's eternal Word. Here its unity is not conceived (as was the case in the first section of this chapter) in terms of the certain characteristics shared by all creatures, but rather by reference to the Word, in relation to whom the creation acquires its shape as a garment, and apart from whom its true form cannot be perceived. Seen in its proper relation, the diversity of creation is a source of inexhaustible delight. Maximus himself ventures the following analogy between the believer's experience of creatures and the story of the disciples gathering grain on the Sabbath (Matt. 12:1–8 and pars.):

> The one who imitates the Lord's disciples is not deterred on account of the Pharisees from walking through the fields on the Sabbath and plucking the ears of grain, but having come through discipline to a state of detachment, he gathers up the *logoi* of creatures and is in a sacred manner nourished with a divine knowledge of beings.[74]

And yet if it is only in the light of the *Logos* that the *logoi* of creatures can be gathered with profit (so that it is impossible to understand the glory of creation apart from Christ), then it is necessary to say something more about the relationship between the one *Logos* and the many *logoi*. This chapter has affirmed that creatures (considered both individually and all together) reflect the *Logos* but are nevertheless absolutely distinct from it. It is this distinction that makes it impossible for human beings simply to extrapolate from their experience of the many created *logoi* to the one *Logos* who is their source and end. The first part of this chapter noted several features of this distinction between Creator and creature, including especially the contingency of created being. But to characterize their distinction in such contrastive terms makes all the more pressing the question of their relationship. What language can characterize the enormous variety of finite creatures as utterly dependent on and yet not less radically discontinuous with God, such that the talk of created *logoi* subsisting in the uncreated *Logos* can be viewed as more than a theological conceit? The answer to this question leads to the center of the Christian doctrine of creation. Because the unity of creation can be established only in the *Logos* and not through reference to any feature of created being considered by itself, it is not enough to say that God created the world, but it is necessary to specify that God created it *from nothing*.

---

74. Maximus, *Chapters on Knowledge* 1.32, in PG 90:1096A; from Louth, *Maximus*, 134, trans. alt.

4

From Nothing

A reader who has made it this far might well be inclined to wonder whether my initial claims for the distinctiveness and significance of the doctrine of creation from nothing were overstated. After all, much of what was said about creation in the preceding chapter is fully consistent with Plato's *Timaeus*, which also speaks of one God giving rise to a diversity of temporal beings. Most of it could also be affirmed by process theologians, whose rejection of creation from nothing does not prevent them from affirming, in the strongest terms, both the astounding diversity and profound integration of the created order. With such comparisons in mind, it may seem theologically unnecessary to introduce ex nihilo as a further qualification of the Christian doctrine of creation, especially given that the account of creation presented so far is thoroughly christocentric, since Christ—the one divine *Logos*, who is the source and end of the multiplicity of created *logoi*—has already been presented as key to understanding both the unity and the diversity of creation.

To be sure, one major point of divergence between the picture presented thus far and theologies that reject creation from nothing lies in the fact that the Creator described in chapter 2 (above) was characterized in chapter 1 as radically transcendent. Yet it is not self-evident that even quite radial affirmations of divine transcendence require commitment to creation from nothing, given that some of the strands in the Christian tradition that are most insistent on God's ineffability (including, e.g., Dionysius the Areopagite and Nicholas of Cusa) are indebted to Platonic thought. In order to show the significance of creation from nothing in this context, it is necessary to say something more about the character of the relationship between God and the world.

The central role of the second person of the Trinity in both chapters 1 and 2 (above) is suggestive of the degree to which a specifically Trinitarian doctrine of God is crucial to my account of the ground and work of creation. It is the goal of this chapter to develop this point by arguing that it is Christ's status as the incarnate Word of God (and thus both Creator and creature) that underlies Christian understanding of creation's status as an utterly gracious gift of God. Briefly, I will argue that Christology is the ground of the Christian claim that the world is created from nothing, because it is in Christ that creation is revealed as a matter of grace alone, and thus as grounded solely in God's love.[1]

Before launching that argument, however, some terminological clarification is in order. A millennium ago Anselm of Canterbury recognized that the phrase "from nothing" was a grammatical oddity. When in everyday speech we say, "x is made from y," we mean that y is the material out of which x is formed (as when, e.g., we say that a table is made from wood, or that bronze is made from copper and tin). As such, y both preexists x and is ontologically continuous with it (i.e., the wood of which the table is made existed before the table was crafted and continues to exist in the table). In short, to say that x is made from y is to ascribe to y the status of being a cause or condition of x. But this normal way of understanding does not work when applied to the sentence "God created the world from nothing." Quite the contrary, inserting "nothing" into the phrase troubles the normal sense of "made from y."

Anselm considered three ways in which the phrase "God made the world from nothing" might be understood.[2] First, one might take the term "nothing" as a simple negation (Anselm uses the example that someone who is not talking at all can be described as "talking about nothing") and conclude that saying the world is made from nothing is equivalent to saying that the world doesn't exist. But that interpretation of the phrase is inconsistent with the basic premise of the inquiry: that the world is *something*, the existence of which is to be accounted for by reference to God's creative work.

Second, one might interpret "nothing" as itself a kind of substance, and thus a cause or condition of the world's existence analogous to the way copper is a condition of there being bronze. But this option is disallowed because "nothing"

---

1. Karl Barth, *Church Dogmatics* (hereafter *CD*), ed. G. W. Bromiley and T. F. Torrance, 13 vols. (Edinburgh: T&T Clark, 1956–75), III/1:40–41.

2. For the following, see Anselm, *Monologion* 8, in *Monologion and Proslogion with the Replies of Gaunilo and Anselm*, trans. Thomas Williams (Indianapolis: Hackett Publishing Co., 1995), 20–22. Thomas Aquinas refers to Anselm in his own discussion of *ex nihilo* in *Quaestiones disputatae de potentia Dei* 3.1.7, in *On Creation*, trans. S. C. Selner-Wright (Washington, DC: Catholic University of America Press, 2011), 10–11.

is by definition not a *thing* (i.e., any kind of existent) out of which something might be made.

Anselm therefore advocates a third possibility, according to which the phrase "from nothing" is understood adverbially. According to this approach, "nothing" does not refer either to the world as created (as under the first option), or to some prior condition or cause of the world's existence (as under the second); rather, it indicates the *manner* of the world's creation: affirming that it was made, *but not out of anything*. In other words, whereas the sentence "The carpenter made the table from wood" posits two conditions, the carpenter and the wood, as contributing to (and thus as antecedent conditions of) the table's existence, the confession "God made the world from nothing" is intended to affirm that God is the *only* antecedent condition of the world's existence. In this way the doctrine of creation from nothing posits a profound disanalogy between God's creation of the world and all creaturely acts of making: creaturely making always require some factor in addition to the agent who does the making, but God's creating excludes any such additional factor.

The lack of any creaturely parallel to creation from nothing makes the phrase open to various forms of misunderstanding. In addition to the risk that the grammar of the prepositional phrase "from nothing" may suggest false analogies with the various ways one entity can be made from (i.e., out of) another, the radically privative character of the doctrine constitutes a serious impediment to positive descriptions of God's creative work: rather than illustrating what it means to say that God creates, the doctrine functions mainly to rule out the possibility of providing any such illustration. In order to forestall errors in interpretation rooted in the peculiar logic of the term "nothing," I will explore the meaning of "from nothing" in terms of three interpretive paraphrases: (1) that creation is grounded in *nothing but God*, (2) that the doctrine of creation implies the existence of *nothing apart from God*, and (3) that in creation *nothing limits God*. It is my contention that together these three paraphrases help to show how the language of creation from nothing clarifies identity and activity of God as Creator.

NOTHING BUT GOD

To say that God creates the world *from nothing* is in the first instance to say that the existence of the world is to be ascribed to *nothing but God*. To critics of creation from nothing, virtually all the problems with the doctrine are encapsulated in this claim, which they see as casting the Creator in the role of an "immutable, unilateral All-Power," whose creation instantiates "a template of omnipotent—total—order" rooted in a dualistic logic of domination and exclusion.[3] But to

---

3. Catherine Keller, *Face of the Deep: A Theology of Becoming* (New York: Routledge, 2003), 16, 21; cf. 10, where Keller uses the equivalence of "from nothing" with "nothing but" to help diagnose what she sees as the theological problems with *ex nihilo*.

say that God is the only cause of creation affirms neither despotism nor dualism; indeed, I argue that neither charge is consistent with the Christian doctrine of creation from nothing.[4] To make this case, it is important to frame the doctrine biblically. As I already suggested in chapter 1, the decisive passage in this regard is neither Genesis 1 nor those New Testament verses (Rom. 4:17; Heb. 11:3; cf. 2 Macc. 7:28) that are often cited as proof texts for creation from nothing, but rather John 1.

John does not speak explicitly of creation from nothing any more than does Genesis, but the evangelist does offer a rescript of Genesis 1 that points toward a theological resolution of its grammatical and ontological ambiguities in much the same way that the New Testament identification of Jesus as the image of God (2 Cor. 4:4; Col. 1:15; cf. Heb. 1:3) gives definite content to Genesis's suggestive but undefined category of the divine image.[5] Where Genesis includes a variety of terms (viz., "darkness," "the deep," "waters") whose relation to God and God's creative work is unclear, in John there is quite simply *nothing but God*. And yet over against the worry that the result is invariably a suffocating and totalizing vision of God, who finally can leave room for nothing else, what emerges is rather different: "In the beginning was the Word, and the Word was with God, and the Word was God. He was in the beginning with God" (John 1:1–2). Significantly, the Gospel does *not* read, "In the beginning was God," as though "nothing but God" rendered the use of any word other than "God" impossible and as though "God" were all that could be said. There is indeed nothing but God in the beginning, but because of who God is, "nothing but God" does not mean that "God" is all there is to say. No, "in the beginning was the *Word*."

To be sure, "the Word was God," and this specification is vital; but that is not the first thing the evangelist says about the Word; if it were, then "the Word" would simply be a synonym for "God"—a term of sheer equivalence that would render the verbal difference theologically nugatory. Instead, the affirmation of

4. In specifying the *Christian* doctrine of creation here, I do not mean to imply that the charge of divine despotism is any more justified when applied to Jewish or Muslim accounts of creation, but only to recognize that my counterarguments are conducted on specifically Christian (viz., Trinitarian) grounds.

5. Needless to say, the legitimacy of these New Testament interpretations is a theological question tied to a commitment to the unity of the Christian biblical canon and therefore cannot be decided on purely historical-critical grounds. Defending their legitimacy certainly does not entail any claim that the human author(s) of Genesis had identical intentions with any of the New Testament writers. Rather (and following Thomas Aquinas, *Summa theologiae* [hereafter *ST*] 1.1.10, in Blackfriars ed., 61 vols. [London: Eyre & Spottiswood, 1964–81]), it is born of the conviction that since it is God who seeks to communicate to us through Scripture, there is no conceptual obstacle to the idea of God giving a specific text meaning that exceeds the intentions of its human author and can only be identified with hindsight (cf. Gen. 50:20). In this context, Francis Watson helpfully suggests that New Testament rereadings of Old Testament texts be understood as instances of *critical* rather than *literal* exegesis, so that one may assess any given instance as follows: "Can the text be read in this way? Retrospectively, in light of the Christ-event, it can and must be." While Watson is here speaking specifically of the interpretation of Ps. 8:3–8 found in Heb. 2:5–9, the principle is capable of general application (Francis Watson, *Text and Truth: Redefining Biblical Theology* [Edinburgh: T&T Clark, 1997], 297).

the Word's identity with God follows on, and is therefore to be interpreted in light of, a further statement highlighting their distinction: "The Word was *with* God." In light of this clause, it is clear that identifying the Word as God does not mean collapsing the Word into God or reducing the Word to a divine attribute. Rather, the Word *is* God as the One who stands *with* (or *in the presence of*) God.[6] Indeed, as if to emphasize the point, the theme of mutual presence is repeated in verse 2: "He was in the beginning with God."[7] There is nothing but God in the beginning (since the Word is God), but God is not alone (since the Word was with God).

Before exploring this point further, it is necessary to reckon with a fact that at first glance would seem to constitute a significant problem for any attempt to use John in support of creation from nothing: quite simply, there is no reference to "nothing" in John 1. In chapter 1 (above) I observed that even those biblical passages that seem to speak of creation from nothing cannot plausibly be taken as evidence for that doctrine.[8] It may therefore seem doubtful that creation ex nihilo can receive meaningful exegetical support from a passage like John 1 that fails even to use the term. Yet while John 1:1–2 certainly cannot serve as a proof text for creation from nothing (any more than Matt. 28:19 can prove the Trinity), the absence of the word "nothing" in these verses is not fatal to citing them in support of the doctrine. Indeed, that absence provides an occasion for helping to clarify the doctrine's meaning. Specifically, the Johannine depiction of "the beginning" as including nothing *but* God is not equivalent to a state of affairs that could equally well be described as including God *and* nothing, as though the "nothing" in "creation from nothing" were some sort of shadowy power (i.e., some *thing*) to be conceived beside, over against, or in contrast to God.[9] If Genesis 1 is at least open to interpretation along the lines of "God in the beginning was confronted by preexisting entities of some sort," for John there is only God and the Word (who is God). In this way, the absence of "nothing" from the Gospel's opening verses does not undermine their significance for the doctrine: precisely because apart from God there is nothing to mention, there is no need to mention "nothing" in describing how things were "in the beginning."

The lack of explicit reference to "nothing" at the start for the Fourth Gospel also provides an occasion for clarifying the meaning of creation from nothing in another sense that speaks more directly to the charge that the phrase *ex nihilo* implies divine arbitrariness. The fact that creation has no presupposition other than God does not mean that it comes from nowhere. In this context, Anselm

---

6. The Greek of John 1:1b is *pros ton theon*, which means, literally, "toward God" or (more idiomatically) "in God's presence."

7. Cf. John 1:18 RSV, where the Word is described as dwelling "in the bosom of the Father." The NRSV's "close to the Father's heart" is infelicitous since it loses the spatial and physical connotations of the Greek *eis ton kolpon*.

8. See pp. 4–5 above.

9. For a critique of Karl Barth's postulate of "nothingness" (*das Nichtige*) as a kind of metaphysical counterweight to God's good creation, see the first section of chapter 5 below.

offers an important qualification of what it means to say that creatures are made "from nothing":

> But I seem to see something that forces me to distinguish carefully the sense in which the things that were made can be said to have been nothing before they were made. After all, there is no way anyone could make something rationally unless something like a pattern (or to put it more suitably, a form or likeness or rule) of the thing to be made in the reason of the maker. And so it is clear that what they were going to be, and what sorts of things, and how they were going to be, was in the reason of the supreme nature before all things were made.
>
> Therefore, it is clear that the things that were made were nothing before they were made, in the sense that they were not what they are now and there was not anything from which they were made. Nevertheless, they were not nothing with respect to the reason of their maker, through which and in accordance with which they were made.[10]

In short, while it is true that prior to the act of creation, a creature is "nothing" considered as an entity that can be said to exist outside of or apart from God, it is *not* "nothing" with respect to God. For Anselm, the work of creation is not an arbitrary piece of action with no other root than divine whim, but an expression of who God is, and therefore a work of reason.[11] In this context the invocation of the Word in John 1 is significant just because it points to difference within the divine life in a way that blocks the temptation to reduce God to sheer will. The fact that this difference is named *Logos* (a term that can equally be translated as "reason") indicates specifically that for God to be God is precisely to be characterized by *order*: not an order that is higher than God and thus constrains God in any way (for the Word *is* God), but an order that is intrinsic to God's own life and immediately expressive of that life.[12] Thus, while creation from nothing rules out any ontological *continuity* between God and creatures (so that creation is not in any sense divine), it affirms the ontological *grounding* of creatures in the inexhaustible richness God's own life (so that, in line with Maximus's theology of the *logoi*, creation is a reflection of the divine).[13]

Paraphrasing *creation from nothing* as the claim that in the beginning there was *nothing but God* would at first blush seem only to accentuate the profoundly privative character of the doctrine to questionable effect. The enormous diversity

---

10. Anselm, *Monologion* 9 (in his *Monologion and Proslogion*, 22). Cf. Karl Barth, *CD* III/2:155: "As there stands behind [creation] God and His Word, it is not *ex nihilo* but very much *ex aliquo*."

11. Anselm develops this position in the subsequent chapters of the *Monologion*, arguing that the form of reason in God is God's speech (chap. 10), and that the simplicity of God dictates that God's speech be identical with God's essence (chap. 12).

12. "To let this subject give content and definition to the concept of power means concretely that the power of God is never to be understood as simply a physical possibility, a *potentia*. It must at the same time be understood as a moral and legal possibility, a *potestas*. God's might never at any place precedes right, but is always and everywhere associated with it" (Karl Barth, *CD* II/1:526).

13. "What creatures get from God pre-exists in God in exemplary fashion, and therefore when they participate in God in virtue of their creation creatures also image God." Kathryn Tanner, *Christ the Key* (Cambridge: Cambridge University Press, 2010), 9.

of creation is collapsed back to a single point: the inscrutable and irresistible divine fiat. But when derived from the opening verses of John, "nothing but God" draws attention to the identity of the Creator in a way that checks the worry that creation from nothing reduces God to sheer, overpowering will. Directed to the beginning, the eyes of faith are confronted not with an unfathomable and terrifying Almightiness, but with the Word: a God (for the Word *is* God) whose own life takes the form of self-communication that is realized as the sharing of life (so that the Word is God as the One who is *with* God). In short, the confession "By the word of the LORD the heavens were made, and all their host by the breath of his mouth" (Ps. 33:6) is rooted in the fact that God is already Word and breath (Spirit) in God's self.[14] Because God's life as Word is in itself simply the intradivine expression of God's own infinite goodness, in God even that which has not yet been created is not nothing, since (as Anselm argued) it is held from eternity in the divine Word. Seen from this perspective, the act of creation is not the arbitrary decree of a windowless divine monad, but the extradivine expression of an inexhaustible richness that is already fully present and real in God. In this way, although "nothing but God" does affirm that the Creator is without any rival or competitor, the point is not that God will not tolerate any other existent, but that God has already anticipated and blessed every other existent in God's own life. For this reason, talk of any reality alongside God "in the beginning" simply fails to reckon with who God is, since anything that might be imagined "outside" God would, precisely as a *thing*, necessarily have its ground "inside" the Word.

NOTHING APART FROM GOD

With the first two verses of John's Gospel, we have not yet arrived at creation. Whatever the ambiguities of the Hebrew text may imply for the interpretation of the opening verses of Genesis, there can be no doubt that John does not begin in medias res. The "beginning" of John 1:1 specifies the preconditions of the world's coming into being.[15] Only after this ontological background is established does the evangelist go on to speak of God's work of creation: "All things came into being through him [viz., the Word], and without him not one thing came into being. What has come into being in him was life, and the life was the light of all people" (John 1:3–4; cf. v. 10). If in the beginning there is

14. While the Spirit is not mentioned in John 1, the Fourth Gospel develops the interdependence of Word and Spirit well beyond what is found in the Synoptics. In addition to resting on Jesus from the start of his ministry (John 1:32; cf. Matt. 3:16; Mark 1:10; Luke 3:22), the Spirit is "another Advocate" (John 14:16) who will testify on Jesus' behalf (15:26; cf. Luke 12:12), and whom Jesus himself breathes forth on the disciples on Easter (John 20:22).

15. "This is not, as in Genesis, the beginning of creation, for creation comes in vs. 3. Rather the 'beginning' refers to the period before creation and is a designation, more qualitative than temporal, of the sphere of God." Raymond E. Brown, SS, *The Gospel according to John (i–xii)*, Anchor Bible 29 (Garden City, NY: Doubleday, 1966), 4.

"nothing but God," it follows that anything other than God exists only because God brings it into being. That God should do so is a matter of grace, since there is neither any power external to God nor any deficiency internal to God that could render creation necessary to God. At the same time, creation is not arbitrary because it is grounded in the expressive character of God's own life in and as the Word, so that the graciousness of creation itself is a reflection of the gracious character of God's own triune existence as loving and unstinting gift of being.[16] As the recipient of this gift within the Godhead, the Word is both the intradivine form and instrument of creation: "All things came into being through him, and without him not one thing came into being" (1:3; cf. Col. 1:15–16; Heb. 1:2).

The account of creation given in John 1:3 marks the transition from an account of existents that includes "nothing but God" to one that encompasses "God and other things." Creatures are not God. They are, to be sure, most intimately related to God. God is the only presupposition of creation, and even prior to their being created, creatures are not absolutely "nothing," because they are held in the Word as objects of God's intention; but when they are created, the being of creatures is different than God's being. Within the Trinity, God expresses God's self *as* the Word in a way that is God once again, the eternal realization of God's own divinity in a manner that is itself fully divine; in creation God expresses God's self *through* the Word to bring into being that which is not God. Expressed in other terms, if God (as absolutely transcendent and therefore incapable of being circumscribed) is infinite, then creatures, by virtue of being other than God, are finite. This distinction brings out another dimension of the doctrine of creation from nothing: just as the confession that the Word is God is the basis for affirming that *nothing but God* conditions creation, so the claim that all things came into being through the Word grounds the claim that in creation there is *nothing apart from God*.

At first glance this summary phrase may seem to say far too much. Thanks to the ambiguity of the English adverb, the claim that in creation there is "nothing apart from God" could be taken to mean that "God is all there is" (i.e., only God exists), thereby undermining the very distinction between Creator and creation that the doctrine of creation from nothing is supposed to protect in favor of a pantheism that simply equates the world with God.[17] In the face of

---

16. God's desire for creatures "is *groundless*, in the sense that nothing other than God causes it, but it is not *arbitrary*, because there is no extraneous or random element within God's own being." Rowan Williams, *On Christian Theology* (Oxford: Blackwell, 2000), 73.

17. Austin Farrer noted that a pantheism of this sort results when the relation between the infinite God and finite creatures is constructed along occasionalistic lines, such that creation is "simply a manifold of neutral stuff . . . directly and solely dependent on God, who is a real and inner necessity for the existence of every element in it; while no element is . . . necessary to the existence of any other." Austin Farrer, *Finite and Infinite: A Philosophical Essay* (New York: Seabury Press, 1979), 19. On the following page he goes on to note that, in such a scheme, talk about God becomes logically problematic: whereas meaningful discourse about God depends on analogical application to the infinite God of terms that apply properly to finite creatures, here finite substances are an illusion, so that "the possibility of our speaking truth [about God] depends upon our being victims of error."

this risk of misinterpretation, it might seem preferable to follow the standard translations of John 1:3 and speak of there being "nothing *without* God." Yet if "nothing apart from God" runs the risk of saying too much by collapsing the distinction between God and the world, "nothing without God" arguably says too little.[18] After all, the principle that no creature comes into being without God implies no more than that God contributes in some respect to its being—a rather limited claim that seems unavoidable for any ontology that treats "God" as a meaningful concept. While this position is certainly consistent with creation from nothing, it is equally compatible with doctrines of creation constructed along very different lines. It is, for example, also consistent with a theology that identifies God as the Creator of a world that subsists on its own—and thus apart from God—once it has been created. Though often identified with deism,[19] this model of creation is at least suggested by biblical descriptions of God as creating through manufacture (most famously in Gen. 2:7, but see also the imagery of God as potter in Isa. 29:16; 45:9; 64:8; Jer. 18:6; Rom. 9:21; cf. Ps. 139:13), and it is an effective way of stressing both the substantiality of creatures and their distinction from God (since a pot is both real and different from the potter who made it). When promoted without qualification, however, such imagery suggests that the reality of creatures entails their ontological independence of God, as though created being could subsist apart from God, however necessary God may be to its coming into existence in the first place.[20] In comparison with this idea of creatures subsisting by virtue of their own ontological inertia, process theology offers a much stronger interpretation of "nothing without God." Because in process metaphysics enduring individuals subsist only through God's continually relating to them at every moment of their individual existence, there can indeed be "no-*thing*" apart from God.[21] Nevertheless, process theologians reject the principle that creatures are *absolutely* nothing apart from God, on the grounds that any entity whose being depends on God without any qualification

18. Both "without" and "apart from" are legitimate translations of *chōris*, the Greek preposition in John 1:3, but the fact that the preposition is used elsewhere by John to speak of the disciples' total dependence on Jesus ("apart from [*chôris*] me you can do nothing," in John 15:5) suggests that "apart from" is more in keeping with the theological perspective of the evangelist.

19. The idea of God as an absentee landlord who made the world and then left it to run on its own is a caricature of the beliefs of seventeenth- and eighteenth-century deists. In fact, deist convictions regarding God's benevolence toward creatures implied a strong doctrine of providence, albeit one in which God's relationship with the world was understood in terms of maintaining the natural order (i.e., what would in traditional theological language be termed "general" rather than "special" providence). See Peter Byrne, *Natural Religion and the Nature of Religion: The Legacy of Deism* (London: Routledge, 1989), 53–61; cf. S. G. Hefelbower, *The Relation of John Locke to English Deism* (Chicago: University of Chicago Press, 1918), 90–93.

20. "There is no statement of theism that can dispense with this analogy [of manufacture]; yet there is no more vulgar and trivial statement of theism than one which relies upon it principally." Farrer, *Finite and Infinite*, 24.

21. See John B. Cobb and David Ray Griffin, *Process Theology: An Introductory Exposition* (Louisville, KY: Westminster John Knox Press, 1976), 66.

whatsoever lacks sufficient integrity to be in genuine relation with God.[22] Creation from nothing goes beyond this treatment of the relationship between creatures and Creator in insisting that creatures are ontologically distinct from God and yet have no ground of existence other than God.

In short, if the doctrine of creation from nothing means (as argued in the first section of this chapter) that even prior to being created, creatures are not absolutely nothing insofar as they are grounded in the Word, it also implies that creatures, as created, *are* absolutely nothing *apart from God*. The richness of divinity not only lies behind creation's diversity as its presupposition (*nothing but God*), but also is an active presence that underlies and sustains every feature of that diversity at every moment of its existence (*nothing apart from God*). Nor can this perspective be charged with compromising the integrity of creatures' relationship with God, as though that which has absolutely no existence apart from God is reduced to the status of a puppet. Once again, the Trinitarian framework of the Christian doctrine of creation is crucial here, since the existence of creatures is rooted in the Word, whose very being establishes, within the divine life itself, a set of relationships whose constituent terms (viz., Father, Son, and Holy Spirit) also have no existence apart from God. From this perspective, the idea that ontological independence from God is a necessary condition of genuine relationship (and more particularly, of love) fails to reckon with the character of God's own being as relationship.

The upshot of all this is that "nothing apart from God" is not justified as an independent metaphysical principle, but as a corollary of the Johannine claim that all things were made through the Word. The claim that *creation from nothing* means *nothing*—absolutely nothing—*apart from God* is certainly an affirmation of divine omnipotence, but once again, it need not imply a tyrannical or arbitrary deity. In the face of that charge, it is vital to remember that because God is radically transcendent, the content of any divine attribute can only be determined on the basis of the faithful exposition of God's identity (so that, conversely, it is only appropriate to predicate any given attribute of God insofar as so doing aids in that faithful exposition). In this context, the first thing that needs to be said about a specifically Christian doctrine of divine omnipotence is that it is not equivalent to the claim that only God has power. This becomes clear when the doctrine is explicated in its properly creedal context, where the property of being omnipotent (or, in the traditional English rendering of both the Apostles' and Nicene Creeds, "almighty") is ascribed specifically to the *Father*.[23]

---

22. The doctrine of creation from nothing is seen as "part and parcel of the doctrine of God as absolute controller" (ibid., 65).

23. The Apostles' Creed begins, "I believe in God, the Father almighty [*omnipotentem*], creator of heaven and earth." Underlying the Latin is the Greek *pantokratōr* (literally, "all-ruler"), which is drawn from the biblical book of Revelation (1:8; 4:8; 11:17; and *passim*) and early on became a standard feature of Christian creeds. It is preferable to either "almighty" or "omnipotent" because it points specifically to God's concrete lordship over all that is rather than suggesting a divinity who is simply identified with power in the abstract.

The significance of this point for the character of divine power should not be underestimated. Most obviously, the use of this personal term distinguishes the Creator from any understanding of deity as power in the abstract, so that while it is true and necessary to confess that God is almighty, it does not follow that "the Almighty" is God.[24] Furthermore, the fact that "Father" is a relational term signals that divinity, precisely in its omnipotence, is not to be understood as a monad. God is Father in that God begets the Son (who is nothing less than God's own Word) in the power of the Holy Spirit. Correspondingly, to ascribe almightiness to the Father in particular is to identify divine omnipotence in the first instance with the eternal begetting of the Son rather than with reference to creation. The resulting image of divine power gives no support whatsoever to the image of a tyrannical or controlling deity:

> Jesus said to them, "Very truly, I tell you, the Son can do nothing on his own, but only what he sees the Father doing; for whatever the Father does, the Son does likewise. The Father loves the Son and shows him all that he himself is doing; and he will show him greater works than these, so that you will be astonished. Indeed, just as the Father raises the dead and gives them life, so also the Son gives life to whomever he wishes. The Father judges no one, but has given all judgment to the Son, so that all may honor the Son just as they honor the Father. . . . For just as the Father has life in himself, so he has granted the Son also to have life in himself." (John 5:19–23a, 26)

The Father's power takes the form of *giving* power to another: because the Son receives *everything* from the Father, he "can do nothing on his own"; but precisely because the Father gives the Son *everything*, it is also true that "whatever the Father does, the Son does likewise," to the extent that "just as the Father has life in himself, so he has granted the Son also to have life in himself." Viewed in its Trinitarian context, divine power is not a quantity that needs to be hoarded or guarded against encroachment by others, because its exercise does not result in its diminishment. By placing "all things" into the hand of the Son (John 3:35; 13:3), the Father does not become any less almighty; on the contrary, God's almightiness is realized just as the Father eternally gives the fullness of the Father's own being to the Son. In this act the Father, far from incurring any loss, is glorified (see John 14:13; cf. 12:28; Phil. 2:11).[25]

If divine power is in its essence nothing else than the Father's eternal empowering of the Son through the Spirit, then the Johannine claim that all things came into being through the Son follows naturally, since for the Father to have

---

24. "The man who calls 'the Almighty' God misses God in the most terrible way. For the 'Almighty' is bad, as 'power in itself' is bad. The 'Almighty' means Chaos, Evil, the Devil. We could not better describe and define the Devil than by trying to think this idea of a self-based, free, sovereign ability." Karl Barth, *Dogmatics in Outline*, trans. G. T. Thompson (New York: Harper & Row, 1959), 48.

25. If one adopts the pneumatological language of the Spirit proceeding from the Father and eternally resting on the Son, one can view the Spirit's eternal sealing of the Son as precisely the Son of the Father as a further act of bearing witness to the undiminished character of the Father's power.

created anything apart from the Son would indicate that the Father had with-held something from the Son, making the Word something less than the full expression of the Father's being. But this is just what is ruled out by the doctrine of the Trinity, according to which the Son is "of one substance" (*homoousios* in Greek) with the Father and so has everything the Father has (John 16:15). In this way, creation from nothing is fundamentally a Trinitarian doctrine, since *nothing apart from God* is equivalent to the claim that not one thing came into being apart from the Word. And since the identity of the Word (and thus of the Father and the Spirit through and with whom the Word is the Word) is revealed only as the Word takes flesh in Jesus Christ (in whom "all things in heaven and on earth were created," according to Col. 1:16), it follows that creation from nothing is also a christological doctrine.

To be sure, the creeds appropriate the work of creation to the Father, but this in no way compromises the christological focus of creation, since the Father is Father only in relation to the Son and so (precisely *as* Father) creates through the Son, who is incarnate in and as Jesus. As the opening verses of John suggest, for the Father to create *from* nothing is precisely to create *through* the Word. Once again, creation from nothing does not reduce creation to a divine whim that lacks any rational ground, but rather grounds creation explicitly in the structure of God's own life. Far from an arbitrary divine decree, as the product of God's Word, it is a faithful expression of God's own being.

Of course, creation does not express the Word in the same way the Word expresses the Father. Because the Word is God, the Word has everything the Father has. Creation, by contrast, is not God. The *logoi* of all creatures subsist in and reflect the one divine *Logos*, but even taken all together, they are not the same as that *Logos*—which is why to see the Word (indeed, the Word made flesh) is to see the Father (John 14:9), but to see creatures is not the same as to see the Word.[26] Nevertheless, there is real parallelism between, on one hand, the internal (or "immanent") expression of divine power in the Father's begetting of the Son in the power of the Spirit; and on the other hand, its external (or "economic") expression in the Father's creating the world through the Son in the power of the Spirit. Within the Trinity the expression of the Father's power is the giving of power to the other divine persons, and so, analogously, creation too is the giving of power—although now this giving extends outside the God-head to bring into being that which is not God. And just as the Son, by virtue of the Father's gift, does nothing without the Father and yet is by the same token empowered to do everything the Father does, so creatures that have everything from the Son are thereby empowered to do everything they can. Once again, divine power is not something that needs to be taken or hoarded, which is how

---

26. Jesus is not a creature: even though his human nature is created, according to the christologi-cal Definition of Chalcedon it (partly) specifies *what* he is (viz., truly human), not *who* he is (viz., the uncreated Son of God). While we see created stuff (eyes, skin, hair, etc.) when we look at Jesus, to see him as Jesus (i.e., as the particular person he is) is precisely to see the Son of God—and thus not a creature. See pp. 172–73 below.

we fallen and finite creatures tend to conceive of power; rather, it is exercised in giving. *God is supremely powerful as the one who bestows power.* This bestowal happens within God in the generation of the divine persons and outside of God in God's bringing into existence creatures who have their own, nondivine spheres of power.[27]

Creatures' reception of power is of a different and lower order than that which obtains within the Trinity. Like the Son, creatures receive everything they have from outside themselves. But because the "everything" that the Son receives from the Father includes everything the Father has, the Son is "the exact imprint of God's very being" and for that reason "sustains all things by his powerful word" (Heb. 1:3). By contrast, because the "everything" that creatures receive does not include everything the Son has to give, the life of creatures, whether considered individually or collectively, is just a very partial image of the divine that falls infinitely short of divinity. Importantly, however, this is not a function of divine stinginess, as though God could have given more but out of avarice, fear, or jealousy chose not to. If God were to give everything to the creature in the way that the Father gives everything to the Son, they would no longer be creatures, but God. This "repetition" of divinity is already characteristic of God's life in and as the Trinity. The point of creation is to do something different: to share the blessing of being with that which is *not* God. Since whatever is not God, who is infinite, must by definition be finite or limited, creatures are finite. It follows that in creation the fullness of divine being is dispersed among many creatures, each of which reflects only a splintered fragment of the whole; but this is part of their own peculiar goodness as creatures rather than a defect.[28] It is an important corollary of the Christian doctrine of creation that goodness is not exhausted by divinity: God is the source of all goodness, but it is not necessary to be divine in order to be good. Creatures are good in *not* being God.

In the same way that creatures' finite goodness is no obstacle to their being fully and genuinely good, so their necessarily finite power is nevertheless genuine power. Just as the Father's empowering the Son is not rightly conceived in zero-sum terms (as though the integrity of the Son were threatened by dependence on

---

27. This point provides insight into the meaning of Phil. 2:6. What does it mean that Christ, "though he was in the form of God, did not regard equality with God as *something to be exploited*" (*harpagmon*; literally, something seized or snatched at), if not that he understood divinity as a matter of giving rather than taking? Following this line of interpretation, the "emptying" of the next verse is best understood not as referring to the act of incarnation itself (as though taking flesh were a giving up of divinity), but rather as referring to the character of the Son's earthly life precisely in virtue of his divinity. For a helpful review of exegetical and theological issues in this passage, see Sarah Coakley, "*Kenōsis* and Subversion: On the Repression of 'Vulnerability' in Christian Feminist Writing," in *Powers and Submissions: Spirituality, Philosophy and Gender* (Oxford, Blackwell Publishing, 2002), 3–39.

28. "Reality must, as it were, be translated into a medium of finitude to be anything distinct from God. So that limitation is positive for the fact of the existence of the creatures, but negative for their representation of the divine nature." Farrer, *Finite and Infinite*, 49; cf. 55: "The notion of God is the notion of richness without accident. Accident belongs to the finite, and to eliminate it would be to impoverish the finite, were such elimination in fact possible."

the Father, or contrariwise, the Son's coming into existence constituted a threat to the Father's divinity), neither does the absolute dependence of creatures on God render their power illusory. On the contrary, precisely because creation from nothing means that creatures are nothing apart from God, the worry that God might constitute a threat to their integrity simply fails to account for what it means to say that they are created. Even to speak of God as limiting creatures' power is fundamentally misleading, insofar as it suggests that God establishes boundaries to the exercise of creaturely power that creatures are forbidden to cross. Again, since whatever power creatures have comes from God, this picture just fails to take into account the logic of creation from nothing, according to which God makes creatures precisely so that they may exercise all the power they have (see John 10:10; cf. 1:12), in order to enter as far as they are able into fellowship with God. For God to seek to limit creatures' exercise of their power would therefore be in contradiction with the act of creation itself.[29] That there is *nothing apart from God* means that everything that is truly is from God; and, given who God is, this principle cannot meaningfully be interpreted as indicating any inherent poverty in created being, but rather as a statement of its inconceivable depth and fullness: "In him was life, and the life was the light of all people" (John 1:4 RSV alt.).[30]

NOTHING LIMITS GOD

If in the beginning there is *nothing but God*, then whatever exists continues to exist only by God's grace and thus through a definite act of divine will. This brings us to yet a third implication of creation from nothing: because there is *nothing apart from God*, it is also true that *nothing limits God*. Since God is the only condition of the existence for whatever exists other than God, the being of creatures is always the immediate and direct expression of God's will rather than any sort of constraint on its operation. This point, too, is reflected in the opening of John's Gospel: "The light shines in the darkness, and the darkness did not overcome it" (John 1:5). As will be explored in greater detail in the following chapters, it is an important implication of creation from nothing that even where creatures seek to thwart God's will, God's purposes remain undefeated, in

29. As will be explained in the following chapter, the evil perpetrated by creatures is not best understood as the exercise of their power, but as its subversion: the creature's act of undermining the conditions of its own existence in a way that disempowers it. From this perspective divine law is not an arbitrary set of limits on creatures' exercise of power, but the specification of conditions under which that power can be exercised to its absolute maximum in the face of temptations to act in ways that make its exercise impossible.

30. This is a modified form of the RSV translation. As quoted on p. 22 above, the NRSV, following most modern commentators, treats v. 4 as the continuation of a sentence begun in v. 3, as follows: "What has come into being in him was life, and the life was the light of all people." There is some evidence that this is the more ancient reading, but that it was ultimately rejected because it can be read as qualifying the presence of life in the Word and was thus susceptible to an Arian interpretation. For a discussion of the evidence, see Brown, *John (i–xii)*, 6.

line with Joseph's words to his brothers: "Even though you intended to do harm
to me, God intended it for good, in order to preserve a numerous people, as he
is doing today" (Gen. 50:20). Where there is *nothing apart from God*, there is no
possibility that any existent can escape the sovereign power of God so as to limit
the efficacy of the divine will.

This having been said, the persistence and enormity of creaturely suffering
seems to render such confidence in the irresistibility of God's will not only misplaced but also indicative of everything that is wrong with the doctrine of creation from nothing. Even leaving aside the myriad ways in which experience fails
to bear witness to the victory of good in the world, the implications of the claim
that *nothing limits God* appear profoundly unattractive: a totalitarian fantasy of
control ("the triumph of the will"), with creatures as the helpless, hapless victims
of God's inscrutable decrees. Furthermore, it seems doomed to collapse into
incoherence in the face of the contradictions that attend all fantasies of absolute
power (e.g., "Can God make a stone so heavy that even God could not lift it?").
In the face of such objections it is necessary to clarify exactly what it means to
say that *nothing limits God*.

As a first step in this process, the principle that *nothing limits God* needs to be
distinguished from the claim that there are no limits on what we can say about
God. As noted in chapter 2, all language about God is problematic because
language functions by means of categorization, and God cannot be categorized.
Theology gets off the ground by trusting that God is able to make use of human
words such that they genuinely communicate knowledge of God, even though
there is an inherent and ineradicable mismatch between the meaning of any
term as applied to creatures and as applied to God.[31] It follows that no words are
intrinsically suited to speak of God—or intrinsically disqualified from communicating knowledge of God. Nevertheless, theologians have typically affirmed
that theological speech is limited by the law of noncontradiction, so that it is ille-
gitimate to claim that God could, for example, make square circles or decree that
two and two equal five.[32] Crucially, however, this stipulation is not a constraint
upon *God*, but a condition of the possibility of meaningful discourse and thus
fundamentally a constraint upon the *theologian*. In any argument the meanings
of individual terms provide the bases for the work of deduction and inference.
Where a contradiction is allowed to stand, terms lack the stability to serve as

31. "The[ological] discourse is concerned with the manipulation of terms. Only thus is God
known, but to know Him is not to know the terms. Yet what we know in knowing Him cannot be
further stated [viz., apart from those terms]. Farrer, *Finite and Infinite*, 61.

32. Barth is often cited as an exception to this rule (see his *CD* I/1:8), but George Hunsinger
notes that for Barth "the law of noncontradiction is neither simply accepted nor simply rejected as
appropriate to the subject matter of theology. It can be accepted, Barth thinks, only in a qualified
sense. Theology, when true to its subject matter, will be unable to avoid making statements which
appear to be contradictory. It regards these 'contradictions' as apparent but unavoidable. They are
merely apparent, because their status is basically noetic rather than ontic. They pertain, that is, to
the state of our perceptions rather than to an actually existing state of affairs." George Hunsinger, "A
Response to William Werpehowski," *Theology Today* 43 (October 1986): 355n1.

points of conceptual leverage (since anything can be shown to follow from a contradiction), and discourse simply ceases to have any meaning.[33]

A similar point can be made about questions like "Can God make a stone so heavy as to be unable to lift it?," or, "Does God have the ability to cease to be omnipotent?" At one level, it is entirely proper to answer these kinds of questions negatively, but it is important to recognize that they are different from questions like "Is God made of wood?," or, "Is God impersonal?," even though for Christians these, too, should receive a negative response. For while the denial that God is wooden entails claims about the character of God's being, to deny that God has the power not to be powerful or the freedom not to be free is not to assert any property of the divine nature. To see how this is the case, consider that to answer such questions affirmatively would not be to offer a particular (though false) claim about God, but rather to render one's use of the term "God" incoherent by affirming a contradiction (viz., that "God is omnipotent" entails that "God may not be omnipotent"). In short, asserting God's "inability" to cease to be God is to make a *grammatical* point about the conditions of meaningful talk about God, not an *ontological* one about God's being.

Nor are these the only sort of apparent but ultimately illusory ways in which limitation may be ascribed to God. For example, Thomas Aquinas argued that it is impossible for God to create an omnipotent being on the grounds that a creature is by definition dependent on its Creator and therefore cannot be omnipotent.[34] Generalizing from this example, the claim that God cannot create divinity is, again, a purely logical point: it is simply impossible to create that which is by definition uncreated. The question of whether God can lie or commit any other sin falls into a slightly different category, since there seems to be nothing inherently contradictory in imagining God as breaking a promise (that is, it is not simply inconceivable in the way that a four-sided triangle is). Yet here too, it would be wrong to understand the impossibility of divine sin as a limitation in the sense of an internally fixed or externally imposed constraint on God's activity. The apparent difficulty here turns on the character of divine freedom. If freedom is simply the ability to do anything that does not entail a logical contradiction, then the ability to tell lies or break promises is a manifestation of freedom (one thinks again of the whim of a despot). If, however, freedom is defined as the ability to effect one's will, and if God's will is inherently good,

---

33. Similar objections can be made to the claim that all terms are predicated of God analogously, on the grounds that in the absence of a commitment to univocal predication, theological discourse lacks sufficient stability to allow meaningful argument. It is impossible to reject this objection out of hand (though Thomas Aquinas makes an interesting argument to the effect that all univocal predication is based on the analogical predication of being; see *ST* 1.136.1; cf. his *Commentary on the Sentences of Peter Lombard* 2.34.1.1); the meaningfulness of theological discourse cannot be guaranteed from within, but only on the basis of God's providential guidance. The gambit of the theologian is that she deploys her words in a manner that is both faithful to God and attentive enough to the requirements of logic to avoid the kind of flat-out incoherence that would render theological discourse the kind of scandal that Jesus warns against (Matt. 18:6–7 and pars.; cf. 1 Pet. 3:15). It is in service of the latter criterion that the law of noncontradiction plays a necessary role in theology.

34. Thomas Aquinas, *De potentia Dei* 3.4.5, in *On Creation*, 32.

then divine sin would amount to a diminishing of God's freedom and not its manifestation.[35]

A more trenchant—and specifically Christian—example of divine limitation would seem to be the incarnation. After all, if the Word's identity with God is crucial to explicating the claims that in the beginning there was nothing but God, so that there is created nothing apart from God, then the confession that Christ "emptied himself, taking the form of a slave, being born in human likeness" (Phil. 2:7) would seem to constitute a decisive counterexample to the principle that nothing limits God. More detailed reflection, however, shows that it is not a counterexample, at least according to the Christology of the Council of Chalcedon.[36] According to the Chalcedonian Definition, in Christ the divine and human natures are united "without confusion or change," such that "the character proper to each of the two natures was preserved as they came together."[37] In other words, the claim that "the Word became flesh and lived among us" (John 1:14) does not entail that the Word's divinity was in any way diminished in assuming a human nature and living a human life. That it might be thought to do so depends on a failure to appreciate both the doctrine of the Trinity and God's status as Creator. If the incarnation is conceived as the act of God leaving heaven in order to take up residence on earth, then it would be reasonable to conclude that this act must entail at least the temporary suspension of some aspects of divinity; but that is a misunderstanding of the incarnation. Within a Chalcedonian framework the incarnation is not something that happens "outside" of God, because in taking flesh God is not "doing" anything to creation other or more than God is always doing in sustaining creation. What changes (as will be explained further below) is the *mode* in which God relates to creatures.[38]

35. To the objection that specifying God's will as good itself amounts to limiting God, it may be countered that because the good is that which is inherently desirable, God, as the source and end of all being, is the ultimate good. Thus, for God to desire the good is simply for God to desire God; and since by the doctrine of the Trinity, this desire takes precisely the form of the mutual fidelity of the three divine persons (so that, e.g., the Father desires the life of the Son, and the Son desires the glory of the Father), for God to be false would be for God to be less—and therefore other—than God (cf. 2 Tim. 2:13).

36. Some Christologies, including that of W. F. Gess and other "kenotic" theologians in the nineteenth century and certain versions of "death of God" theology in the twentieth, do interpret the incarnation as the Son's giving up of the attributes of the divine nature, but, eo ipso, such theologies do not subscribe to the principles of Chalcedon.

37. DS 302 (see n. 6 in chap. 2 above), as cited in *The Christian Faith in the Doctrinal Documents of the Catholic Church*, ed. J. Neuner, SJ, and J. Dupuis, SJ, rev. ed. (New York: Alba House, 1982), 154–55.

38. This point has been made by Herbert McCabe, who argued that the intra-Trinitarian roles of the Son and the Spirit are "reflected (I prefer the word 'projected'—as on a cinema screen) in our history in the external missions of the Son and the Spirit by which we are taken up into the life of the Godhead. . . . It is not therefore adequate to speak of God's redemptive act as an *opus ad extra*. It is precisely the act by which we cease to be *extra* to God and come within his own life" (In his "Aquinas on the Trinity," in *Silence and the Word: Negative Theology and Incarnation*, ed. Oliver Davies and Denys Turner [Cambridge: Cambridge University Press, 2002], 92–93). While McCabe is right to see that the work of redemption blurs the distinction between "internal" and "external" acts of the Trinity, one could argue that it nevertheless preserves the principle that the external works of the

It is in this way that the incarnation, though quite distinct from the work of creation, plays an important role in explicating the latter by helping to illuminate the specifically Christian meaning of the claim that *nothing limits God.*

To see how this is the case, it is helpful to begin by remembering that the doctrine of creation from nothing posits God as the sole antecedent condition of all that is. It follows that all creatures exist only insofar as God actively sustains them in existence, since, absent God, there is just nothing else available to do so. Now, if this point is granted, it cannot be accepted that the incarnation involves any sort of quantitative intensification or increase of divine presence in the person of Jesus, as would be the case if the incarnation were conceived of as the self-insertion into the created order of a God who is otherwise outside of or removed from the world. This is because creation from nothing implies that God is *already* maximally "inside" the world: since God's sustaining presence is the one necessary and sufficient condition of every creature's existence at every moment of its existence, any degree of divine absence would result in the total and instantaneous dissolution of created being (see Ps. 104:29). As argued in the preceding section of this chapter, creation from nothing rules out talk of any creature existing apart from or at any distance from God. It follows that God is and cannot be *more* present in Jesus than in you or me or the lowliest sea slug.

So what happened in the incarnation, if it was not a matter of God entering the world from outside? A human being, Jesus of Nazareth, was born. In itself this is a perfectly ordinary, inner-worldly occurrence (see Gal. 4:4): as Creator, God is no more or less the cause of Jesus' birth than of anyone else's. To be sure, it is a traditional feature of Christian belief that the circumstances surrounding Jesus birth were miraculous, in that he was conceived without a human father and born without damaging the physical tokens of his mother's virginity; but the confession of Jesus as the Word of God incarnate is logically independent of these miracles. There is no reason why God could not have become incarnate in a human being conceived and born normally, and the discovery of other instances of human parthenogenesis would in itself carry no theological implications.[39] Jesus' status as the Word made flesh is absolutely independent of any aspect of his human nature. No analysis of his created existence, including any aspect of his physical or his psychological makeup, could isolate any feature that would mark him as more or other than a human being: that is the central point of Chalcedon's insistence that he is "truly man composed of rational soul and

---

Trinity are undivided, since redemption, like creation, is effected "through the Word": as part of a fully Trinitarian act in which all three persons are fully and inseparably, though by virtue of the incarnation not indistinguishably, active.

39. The claim that Jesus' divine status is a matter of ontology rather than biology is outlined in Joseph Ratzinger, *Introduction to Christianity* (London: Burns & Oates, 1969), 208. Insofar as Jesus' birth was miraculous, it can be said that the *mode* of God's activity in it differs from that in other human births, but again, his miraculous conception and parturition are not what secures Jesus' identity as Son of God—though they are not for that reason any less true and remain for Ratzinger obligatory features of Christian belief.

body" and "one in being with us as to the humanity."[40] What makes Jesus to be *adoptionism?*
God incarnate is not any modification of his humanity, but just that God identifies this particular human life as God's own.[41]

On the most practical level, this divine identification with Jesus means that
"the Son" (or "Word" or "second person of the Trinity") and "Jesus of Nazareth" are fully convertible terms: whatever can be predicated of the one applies
equally to the other. For example, if it is true to say that "Jesus was born of the
Virgin Mary," then it is true to say that "the Son of God was born of the Virgin
Mary."[42] Likewise, the claim "All things were created through the Word" (see
John 1:3) may be reformulated as "All things were created through Jesus" (see
Heb. 1:2). Importantly, this identification cannot be reduced to a matter of linguistic convention, as in the kind of legal fiction according to which an ambassa-
dor speaks in the name of a queen, who therefore is understood to be the object
of any insults directed at her envoy. Christologically, that would amount to a
kind of adoptionism. The upshot of Chalcedonian Christology (viz., that the
two natures of Christ are united under the single divine hypostasis of the Word)
is not that God commandeers a human life for God's own purposes in the way
that God might claim the life of a prophet (see, e.g., Jer. 1:4–10), but that Jesus'
identity just *is* the second person of the Trinity. In the technical language of
Christology, the Word "enhypostatizes" human nature in Jesus, such that Jesus
has no identity as a particular person (viz., hypostasis) apart from the Word.

This specifying of the hypostasis as the locus of unity between God and
humanity in the incarnation obviates some of the more typical problems associated with the idea that Jesus was God incarnate, including, for example,
the question of his apparent deficiencies with respect to divine properties like
omniscience (Matt. 24:36 and par.). Because human nature is finite, it does
not follow that Jesus' human nature acquires any special powers in virtue of its
enhypostatization by the Word. Insofar as human beings naturally grow, learn,
and are subject to various other sorts of limitation, so it is with the incarnate
Word (Luke 2:52; John 4:7; 11:35; cf. Matt. 26:38 and pars.).[43] Capacities are
a function of nature, not hypostasis. Consequently, a person's identity (i.e., who

---

40. DS 301, as cited in Neuner and Dupuis, *The Christian Faith*, 154. The claim that Christ's
likeness to us did not include sin (DS 301; cf. Heb. 4:15) does not affect his consubstantiality with
other human beings, since sinlessness is not an exclusive property of divinity (cf. the widespread
Christian belief that the Virgin Mary was without sin from the moment of her conception, or the
sinlessness of the angels in heaven).

41. Because it was the second person of the Trinity who becomes incarnate, this self-identifica-
tion with the life of Jesus, while common to the three divine persons, is differentiated among them
according to their eternal relations, so that in the New Testament the Father identifies Jesus as "my
Son" (Matt. 3:17; 17:5 and pars.), the Spirit who rests upon Jesus in witness to the Father's love
identifies Jesus as the Father's Son (John 15:26; cf. 1 John 4:13–15; 1 Cor. 12:3), and Jesus identifies
himself as the Son of God (John 10:36; cf. Matt. 11:27; 27:63–64 and pars.).

42. Thus comes the vindication of the acclamation of Mary as *Theotokos* ("God-bearer"), at the
Council of Ephesus in 431.

43. Jesus does perform miracles, but they are no more a proof of his identity as Son of God than
is his miraculous conception. After all, Jesus himself is recorded as saying that his disciples will do
greater miracles than he does (John 14:12; cf. Matt. 10:8).

they are) cannot be determined on the basis of possessing any given set of capacities, since the latter change over the course of a lifetime, as particular abilities are acquired—and lost—with varying degrees of permanence and rapidity. To be sure, personal identity is exhibited in and to some extent defined by one's acts, in the sense that it is natural to identify a person by referring to what she or he has done or typically does (e.g., "Mary is the teacher who rides the red bike to work"). Jesus is no exception to this rule, and both he (Matt. 11:4–6 and par.; John 5:20, 36; 10:25, 37–38; 14:10–12) and his disciples (Acts 2:22–24; cf. Matt. 7:28–29; John 3:2; 7:31) view what he says and does as marks of his status; but it is significant that the Gospels close with a (double!) recognition that all such accounts of his identity are inherently incomplete (John 20:30–31; 21:25). Thus, although reference to what Jesus says and does is necessary for identifying him as the particular human being he is, the claim that this human being is the Son of God cannot be deduced from Jesus' actions; it can be known only by grace (John 6:44–45; cf. Matt. 16:17).

In this way, the incarnation does not mean that God becomes other or less than God, but just that God lives as a creature in addition to living as God. And yet it may still appear that there is something artificial or distant about the incarnation when it is understood in this way as the Word's identification with the human being Jesus. Even if trumped up by using the technical jargon of enhypostatization, the idea that "becoming flesh" simply means "identifying" with the life of Jesus—that idea can make incarnation seem both weak and arbitrary, as though the Word might just as easily have become incarnate in someone else. At one level this appearance is accurate enough: if the incarnation is considered in purely ontological terms, there is no conceptual difficulty with the idea of God having become incarnate as a Paleolithic European man or a nineteenth-century African woman—or indeed, with the possibility of multiple incarnations.[44] At another level, however, this sort of worry trades on a misunderstanding of the incarnation, as though the Word's identifying Jesus' life as God's own were equivalent to my "identifying" myself with my children, my dog, or my car. Here again, it is vital to keep in view the character of the relationship between Creator and creatures implied by creation from nothing. However much I may project my identity onto someone or something else, such projection is ultimately a fiction (albeit one with potentially very damaging effects on both myself and the object of my identification): whatever my desires or intentions, my life is not and cannot be that of my daughter, for the simple if obvious reason that I am a different person than she is, so that she exists independently of whether or not I choose to identify myself with her. By contrast,

---

44. Thomas Aquinas explicitly affirms that there is no ontological barrier to the Son assuming other individual human natures in addition to that of Jesus (*ST* 3.3.7); but it does not follow for him that multiple incarnations are to be expected, since God's actions are to be evaluated according to their fittingness and not only according to what is possible for God. Along the same lines, he argues that while any of the three persons of the Trinity could have become incarnate (*ST* 3.3.5), it was fitting that only the Son should have done so (*ST* 3.3.8).

the Christian claim is precisely that Jesus has no existence independent of the Word; rather, the Word simply *is* Jesus (in the same way that I am Ian, not Magdalena or Olivia). Nor does this identification of the Word with Jesus require God to "do" anything extra (viz., an external work) beyond what God is always already doing as Creator: God is maximally involved in sustaining and enabling Jesus' existence, just as God is maximally involved in sustaining and enabling *every* creature's existence. The only difference is that in this one case the life of the creature whose existence is being enabled is the Word's own life.

Because the incarnation does not mean that God is doing anything more or different in Jesus than in any other creature, the confession that in Jesus the Word "became flesh and lived among us" does not imply that God has undergone any change in becoming incarnate, whether in terms of the properties of the divine nature or the relations among the three persons. And it is on these specific grounds that the incarnation exemplifies the principle that *nothing limits God*. Obviously, if creation from nothing implies that in the beginning there is *nothing but God* and thus *nothing apart from God*, then it follows that there are no external limits on God's power; but there might still be internal constraints on what God can accomplish. It is, for example, a feature of certain metaphysical systems that divine simplicity precludes God's immediate creation of (or unmediated engagement with) a multiplicity of beings. In such systems God's transcendence over the world precludes God's immanence in it, so that God's very nature constitutes a limit to God's ability to interact with creation.[45] Transcendence and immanence do not stand in this sort of zero-sum relationship in the Christian doctrine of creation from nothing, because the nature of God's difference from creatures—precisely as the One who transcends all categories—cannot be defined in terms of the categorical differences of kind (viz., *this* rather than *that*) by which creatures are distinguished from one another.[46] By virtue of these contrasts, creatures are limited by their natures: for them to be is precisely to be one kind of thing rather than another, and so to be restricted in their range of possible activities by the kind of thing they are.[47] But the divine nature

45. The basic assumption underlying these metaphysical proposals is that God's unity as first cause necessarily precludes the immediate production of any but a single effect (viz., the intelligence by which God understands God's self). Thomas Aquinas attributes this opinion to Avicenna in *De potentia Dei* 3.16, in *On Creation*, 148; it is also a feature of the Neoplatonic ontology of Plotinus (see *Enneads* 6.9, in *Greek and Roman Philosophy after Aristotle*, ed. Jason L. Saunders [New York: The Free Press, 1966], 261–70).

46. Kathryn Tanner describes this as a "non-contrastive" model of divine transcendence, on the grounds that "a God who transcends the world must also . . . transcend the distinctions by contrast appropriate there," so that right speaking of God will "avoid both a simple univocal attribution of predicates to God and the world and a simple contrast of divine and non-divine predicates." Kathryn Tanner, *God and Creation in Christian Theology: Tyranny or Empowerment?* (Oxford: Basil Blackwell, 1988), 46–47.

47. Of course, the Christian doctrine of creation precludes the interpretation of such limitation as any sort of defect in creatures (see the comments by Farrer in note 28 above); but it does mean that each creature "has [its] act confined to one genus and species" so that "each acts as a particular being confined to this or that species," in distinction from God, whose transcendence means that the scope of divine action is not so restricted (Thomas Aquinas, *De potentia Dei* 3.1, in *On Creation*, 8).

does not define God as a particular kind of thing. <u>Rather than limiting God</u>, <u>the divine nature is the expression of God's freedom as Father, Son, and Holy</u> <u>Spirit</u>. While (as argued above) it is a corollary of this freedom that God cannot cease to be God, the fact that God, in God's transcendence, is (to cite again the expression of Nicholas of Cusa) "not other" than creatures means that *God can also be other than God without thereby ceasing to be God*. That is the meaning of the incarnation: the Word, while remaining always fully God, assumes a human nature and is therefore also truly a human being.

In this way, the <u>claim that *nothing limits God* is at the furthest possible remove from a fantasy of absolute power</u>. Creatures are limited: while different creatures can do many different things, their various possibilities are all constrained by their finite natures, not least in the inability of any creature to secure the life of another. The God who creates from nothing is not so limited, and this lack of limitation takes form precisely as the power to secure the life of the other. Within the Godhead this power takes the form of the infinitely and inexhaustibly generous sharing of life as the Father begets the Son in the power of the Holy Spirit; but the God who in this way is for the other within the Trinity is free also to be for the other who is not divine, not only bringing it into and sustaining it in existence but also making the very being of the creature God's own. Interpreted christologically, the claim that nothing limits God is not primarily a claim about God's power over the creature and still less about God's independence from creation. On the contrary, its focus is God's freedom to enter into creation in order to bind created life to God from within by making it nothing less than God's own life. In this freedom—which allows God, all the while remaining God, at the same time and without reservation to be also other than divine—lies the ultimate significance of the biblical claim that "nothing will be impossible with God" (Luke 1:37; cf. Matt. 19:26 and par.).

Interpreting creation *from nothing* as meaning that in the beginning there is *nothing but God*, that there is created *nothing apart from God*, and that in creating *nothing limits God*—this interpretation in the first instance suggests very traditional views of divine self-sufficiency, omnicausality, and sovereignty, respectively. Read within the specifically christological framework suggested by the opening verses of John's Gospel, however, these forbidding-sounding attributes acquire a rather different spin: *Nothing but God* points to the fact that divine self-sufficiency takes the form of love that is realized in the mutual communion of the Father with the Son in the power of the Spirit. *Nothing apart from God* proposes a vision of divine omnicausality as the extension outside of God of the sharing of being that constitutes God's own triune life. *Nothing limits God* means that divine sovereignty is perfected in God's making the life of a creature to be God's own, as a means of ensuring creation's flourishing. Viewed in this threefold, christological mode, the point of creation from nothing is not, as the doctrine's critics fear, to affirm God's ultimate indifference to creatures but rather God's total and unrestricted dedication to them.

In this way the doctrine of the incarnation, as the definitive exemplification of the principle that nothing limits God, is arguably the key to a specifically Christian understanding of creation from nothing. And yet if incarnation is the event through which God's identity as the One who creates from nothing is revealed, the incarnation is not itself part of the doctrine of creation. Creation is the work by which God establishes and sustains the existence of beings that are other than God. The incarnation effects the further divine work of redemption and glorification, whereby God, having established created life as other than (though at every point dependent on) God, goes on to enable the creature to participate directly in God's own triune life through the Son and in the power of the Spirit. In this way (and as David Kelsey has pointed out), both redemption and glorification presuppose creation but are logically distinct from it, such that the belief that God has created the world does not entail the further beliefs that God will redeem and glorify it.[48] This should not be seen as a novel claim. It is simply another way of stating the traditional Christian conviction that redemption and glorification are not the outworking of creatures' own capacities, but gifts of divine grace added to rather than demanded by the grace of creation.

At the same time, it is part of Christian belief that redemption and glorification, while not entailed by creation, in their own distinct ways bring creation to perfection in ways consistent with the movement intrinsic to creaturely existence. God intends creatures to flourish, but even within the context of creation alone, this flourishing is not instantaneous. For nonangelic beings at least, the goodness of created life includes growth in time—from acorn to oak tree, spore to mushroom, infant to adult—quite apart from the hope of eschatological consummation. This latter hope reflects the further belief that a movement of grace supervenes upon the movement of nature in order to effect a return to God, in which creatures' existence is not only continually sustained by God *objectively* but also continually experienced *subjectively* as communion with God. While the story of this return takes us beyond the doctrine of creation, it is rooted there, since it is the same world created in the beginning that is to be glorified in the end. The task of part 2 of this book is to explore the context within which creation, having arisen from the love of God, is drawn to perfection in that love by showing how the ways in which creatures both flourish and fail to flourish in the present shape Christian hope for the fulfillment of created life in glory.

48. See David H. Kelsey, *Eccentric Existence: A Theological Anthropology*, 2 vols. (Louisville, KY: Westminster John Knox Press, 2009), 1:120–31 and passim.

PART 2
REDITUS

5

Evil

In the preceding chapter the explication of creation *from nothing* culminated with the claim that *nothing limits God*, interpreted through the lens of the incarnation and as a corollary of the biblical affirmation that "The light shines in the darkness, and the darkness did not overcome it" (John 1:5). Left unaddressed was the status of this "darkness" that threatens, however unsuccessfully, to overcome the divine light. Here as elsewhere in the opening verses of John, the author echoes Genesis, where God separates the light from the darkness (Gen. 1:4). In Genesis the darkness is not described as hostile to the light, with which it is simply juxtaposed as night to day (1:5). At the same time, the darkness was not created along with light but was already on the scene when the world was yet formless and empty (1:2). So while the darkness is not depicted in Genesis as limiting God, it does appear to be something God desires to limit—to the extent that at the other end of the Bible, it is promised that when God's will for creation is finally fulfilled, "there will be no more night" (Rev. 22:5).

The ambiguity of the biblical language about darkness points to what theologians and philosophers typically call (in what can only be described as a sustained commitment to understatement) the "problem" of evil. In Genesis, God repeatedly judges the creation "good" (Gen. 1:4, 10, 12, 18, 21, 31), yet human

111

beings do not consistently experience it as good, and in the face of the multitudes of those whose lives are marked from birth by want, violence, pain, and fear, the claim that creation is essentially good can seem not just "problematic" but also outrageous. Nor is this dissonance simply a matter of conflict between the biblical depiction of creation and the hard realities of human experience: the Bible itself testifies that human life is "of few days and full of trouble" (Job 14:1), and Isaiah reports God saying, "I form light and create darkness, I make weal and create woe; I the LORD do all these things" (Isa. 45:7).[1] How can this be?

Traditionally, Christians pointed to the first humans' transgression of God's command and consequent expulsion from the garden of Eden (Gen. 3; cf. Rom. 5) as the source of this dissonance between the goodness of creation as originally established by God and our experience of creaturely existence afflicted by evil, but contemporary scientific knowledge has undermined the credibility of this approach. Humans have existed for only a tiny fraction of the hundreds of millions of years during which multicellular organisms have populated the earth, and all the evidence indicates that the suffering and death produced by natural disasters (e.g., floods, landslides, volcanic eruptions, bolide impacts), predation, and disease have characterized terrestrial life from the beginning. Nor is there any reason to suppose that things would be different for life elsewhere in the universe. These facts raise serious problems for a defense of creation from nothing. How can it be that in a universe where all that exists depends for its existence at every moment and in every respect on the divine will, any state of affairs can come about that contradicts God's will for the flourishing of all creatures? Since the seventeenth century the attempt to answer this question has been described as *theodicy*, or the justification of God's ways with creatures.

The challenge of theodicy takes classic form in the so-called Epicurean trilemma, according to which the seeming incompatibility of the propositions that God is *omnipotent*, that God is unqualifiedly *good*, and that evil (understood here specifically as whatever counters God's will for the flourishing of creatures) is *real*—this incompatibility demands that one of them be denied as the price of theological coherence.[2] Among Christians the preferred option has generally been to qualify (though not to deny) the reality of evil. Though it has been developed by some of the church's leading theologians with great ingenuity and sophistication, at bottom this strategy can be seen as the result of a process of

---

1. There is considerable variation in modern English translations of the second clause of Isa. 45:7: alongside the archaic "weal" and "woe" of the RSV and NRSV, the NIV offers "prosperity" and "disaster," the NJB "well-being" and "disaster," and the CEB "prosperity" and "doom." Since the Hebrew *shālôm* and *rāʿ* are clearly in synonymous parallelism with the "light" and "darkness" of the verse's first clause, it makes sense to construct some kind of semantically balanced antinomy of the sort reflected in these versions; at the same time, there is something to be said for the harshness of the KJV's "I make peace, and create evil."

2. The trilemma is attributed to Epicurus by the fourth-century Christian writer Lactantius (though in a "tetralemmal" form that includes a fourth option of denying both God's goodness and God's power simultaneously), but it seems more likely to have its origins among the skeptics. See Reinhold Glei, "*Et invidus et inbecillus*: Das angebliche Epikurfragment bei Laktanz, *De ira Dei* 13,20–21," *Vigiliae christianae* 42 (1988): 47–58.

elimination. After all, questioning the goodness of God undermines the whole point of theodicy (which is precisely to vindicate divine goodness) and seems flatly inconsistent with the most basic principles of Christian faith (for which God is the highest and most appropriate object of human love).[3] And the doctrine of creation from nothing emphasizes divine power in a way that raises similar problems for the idea that God lacks the power to prevent evil, though in recent times process theologians have embraced this strategy in concert with their rejection of creation ex nihilo.[4]

Be that as it may, in this chapter I will not make a choice among the three options defined by the Epicurean trilemma. Instead, I will explore the question of evil through an extended engagement with three biblical books—Proverbs, Job, and Ecclesiastes—that with particular intensity both reflect on the fact that creatures do not invariably flourish and seek in very different (and arguably irreconcilable) ways to account for it. I do not claim that these three books exhaust the biblical witness on the "problem" of evil. Although I do find it interesting that their respective approaches to evil correspond roughly to the horns of the Epicurean trilemma, the fact that none of them directly engages the biblical accounts of God's response to human sin and suffering, which in many ways structures the shape of the biblical canon from the primordial history of Genesis through the drama of Revelation, can make them appear in significant respects as marginal to the main line of biblical engagement with evil. And yet precisely because of their distance from the story of God's work in the history of salvation, these three books are particularly well suited to exploring the place of evil within the context of the doctrine of creation, apart from the logically distinct topics of creatures' redemption and glorification. Indeed, all three can, in their own ways, be read as meditations on creation, and it is in that context that their witness to the character of evil is particularly compelling.[5]

<hr>

3. Notwithstanding these difficulties, this approach has been developed with considerable moral power by Jewish theologians attempting to wrestle with the theological implications of the Holocaust. See, e.g., Arthur A. Cohen, *The Tremendum: A Theological Interpretation of the Holocaust* (New York: Crossroad, 1981); and Richard L. Rubenstein, *After Auschwitz: History, Theology, and Contemporary Judaism* (Baltimore: Johns Hopkins University Press, 1992).

4. It is important to recognize that process theologians do not claim that their denial of divine omnipotence simply "solves" the problem of evil, since God enables the emergence of complex entities capable of choosing evil and therefore remains "in an important sense responsible for much of the world's evil." Because God never wills evil and is incapable of preventing other entities from willing it, however, God is not indictable for evil within process thought. David Ray Griffin, *God, Power, and Evil: A Process Theodicy* (1976; repr., Louisville, KY: Westminster John Knox Press, 2004), 276; cf. 292–97.

5. David Kelsey uses the biblical Wisdom literature as the basis for exploring the doctrine of creation in his *Eccentric Existence: A Theological Anthropology*, 2 vols. (Louisville: Westminster John Knox Press, 2010), esp. chaps. 4–11. I am further indebted for this choice of texts to my colleague Carol Newsom, whose emphasis on the mutual incompatibility of the perspectives on evil found in Proverbs, Job, and Ecclesiastes in her paper "The Conversation about Evil (and Good) in Israelite Wisdom Literature" (presented at the 2010 Annual Meeting of the Society of Biblical Literature), served as the stimulus for my choice of these biblical books as the framework for my discussion of evil in this chapter.

IS EVIL NOTHING?

It is possible to dismiss evil as an illusion. For example, one might argue that everything humans call evil is actually a manifestation of divine love and therefore not really evil at all. According to this view, God uses pain and suffering to help perfect creatures, whether by correcting faults or encouraging good behavior.[6] This view is not without biblical warrant (see, e.g., Deut. 28:58–59; Rom. 5:3–4; Heb. 12:6), and a good case can be made that some forms of suffering do further spiritual growth (e.g., it does seem that virtues like courage and generosity can only be cultivated where pain and loss are real possibilities); but to try to account for every human experience of evil on these terms seems inconsistent with the many biblical depictions of suffering as contrary to God's will for creatures (see, e.g., Exod. 3:7–8; Luke 13:10–16). Consequently, a more nuanced approach to qualifying the reality of evil begins by defining evil as that which is contrary to God's will. Within the context of creation from nothing, because anything that exists other than God is by definition a product of divine willing and therefore good, it follows that evil, as that which God does *not* will, is a lack (or privation) of being. Evil can therefore be said to "exist" only in an improper sense: it has no genuine being of its own but is instead parasitic upon that which does exist, in the way that the evil of rot is dependent on the goodness of an apple. From this perspective, the moment evil reduces a creature to nonexistence, it too ceases to "exist" (e.g., as soon as an apple is completely dissolved by rot, the rot vanishes along with the apple). As Augustine put it, "Nothing evil exists *in itself*, but only as an evil aspect of some actual entity."[7]

Speaking of evil as nothing in itself seems like a good option in that it distinguishes evil from God and from creation, both of which can be said to exist in themselves, albeit in the radically different ways proper to the Creator on the one hand, and the creature on the other. Thus, if creation is that which is not God but nevertheless is from God, evil may be defined as that which is neither God nor from God. Indeed, it is precisely because it is neither Creator nor creature that evil can be characterized as "nothing" (i.e., no *thing*). At the same time, the grammar of the word "nothing" creates its own set of theological challenges. Like God, "nothing" is not subject to conceptual categorization: strictly speaking, it is not possible to say anything about it. The difference is that while God eludes categorization by an excess of being (i.e., transcendence), nothing does so because of a complete lack of being, since to speak of "nothing" is precisely to deny the existence of an entity of which something might be said.

---

6. The most influential and comprehensive defense of this "soul-making" theodicy is John Hick's *Evil and the God of Love* (1966), 2nd ed. (New York: Palgrave Macmillan, 2007).

7. Augustine, *Enchiridion* 4.13, in *Confessions and Enchiridion*, ed. and trans. Albert Cook Outler (Philadelphia: Westminster Press, 1955), 344. Cf. Thomas Aquinas, *Quaestiones disputatae de potentia Dei* 3.6, in *On Creation*, trans. S. C. Selner-Wright (Washington, DC: Catholic University of America Press, 2011); and still more extensively, *On Evil* 1.1, in *On Evil*, ed. Richard Regan, trans. Brian Davies (New York: Oxford University Press, 2003).

This grammatical feature of "nothing" can easily drive privative accounts of evil into metaphysically murky waters. After all, even when evil is understood as the privation of being, it still seems both natural and necessary to ask how it comes to be—or at least (given that it is a category mistake to say that "nothing" exists) how it happens that anything God has called into being and sustains in existence should suffer any sort of declension from existence that contravenes God's will that it exist. A frequent temptation here is to invoke the doctrine of creation from nothing itself, as though creatures, having been made from nothing, were for this reason ontologically close to nothing and so constitutionally liable to fall back into it.[8] While there is a certain rhetorical attraction to this way of talking, it cannot be justified by appeal to *creatio ex nihilo*, since it fails to honor the purely adverbial character of the phrase "from nothing" and instead falls into the trap of treating "nothing" as *something*—a reality that somehow serves as the backdrop or ground of creation and to which it may revert.[9] If "creation from nothing" means simply that God is the sole antecedent condition of creation, then the characterization of "nothing" as a hostile force that stands at the gates ready to overwhelm creaturely existence can only be viewed as an ill-advised bit of mythologizing. If talk of evil as nothing is to be theologically defensible, it needs to be constructed on other grounds.

Such an alternative framework is suggested by the biblical book of Proverbs. It is certainly not true that this text provides a metaphysically elaborate account of evil. On the contrary, its (implicit) theodicy is easily dismissed as an intolerably naive, based on a rather mechanistic vision of the relationship between behavior and reward that is belied by worldly experience, and correspondingly in need of supplementation by the more sober perspectives of Job and Ecclesiastes.[10] Yet while it is true that these books do supplement the vision of Proverbs

---

8. This approach can take a number of different forms. In the work of Jürgen Moltmann (esp. *God in Creation: A New Theology of Creation and the Spirit of God*, trans. Margaret Kohl [1985; repr., New York: Harper & Row, 1991], 86–93), God first needs to withdraw the divine being in order for God to make a place for creation. In this way, nothing is directly caused by God and is indeed a precondition of creation—though in its inherent godforsakenness it also constitutes an ongoing threat to it. Karl Barth does not view nothing (or, following his own terminology, "nothingness") as inherent to creation in this way, but he nevertheless envisions nothingness as caused by God indirectly, since in electing creation God simultaneously rejects chaos and nonbeing—and in so doing gives nothingness a sort of shadow existence that threatens creation from its frontier (*Church Dogmatics*, III/3, ed. and trans. G. W. Bromiley and T. F. Torrance [Edinburgh: T&T Clark, 1960], §50). Even Thomas Aquinas, who is much less inclined to speculative elaboration than Barth or Moltmann, ascribes the presence of evil (viz., imperfection or deficiency) among creatures to the fact that they are created from nothing (see esp. *On Creation* 1.1.14; cf. *On Evil* 1.2 and 1.3.9).

9. There is no parallel to be drawn between these accounts of the corrosive power of nothing and the "You are dust, and to dust you shall return" of Gen. 3:19. Aside from the obvious fact that "dust" is not "nothing," the point of the Genesis passage is that God (and God alone) disposes over human destiny—a claim that clearly rules out any attempt to ascribe the dissolution of human life to some occult power of nonbeing.

10. This is a long-standing judgment, reflected in the tradition that Proverbs was written by Solomon in the vigor of manhood, while Ecclesiastes reflects the less enthusiastic realism of his old age.

in the canon, they do not replace it.[11] Nor is it appropriate to view them as unqualified advances on Proverbs. As already stated, it is my contention that all three texts give important and unsubstitutable (if not clearly reconcilable) accounts of evil, without which any Christian theological discussion is necessarily incomplete. And if Proverbs in its alleged naivety can be shown to correspond with what is generally taken to be more theologically sophisticated accounts of evil as privation of the good, that may perhaps serve as some indication of its enduring value.

But can Proverbs really be read in this way? There is certainly plenty of talk about evil in Proverbs (the English word is used as a substantive over two dozen times in the NRSV), but it is always spoken of in resolutely practical terms as types of actions or dispositions to be avoided.[12] The following passage is typical:

> It [wisdom] will save you from the way of evil,
>   from those who speak perversely,
> who forsake the paths of uprightness
>   to walk in the ways of darkness,
> who rejoice in doing evil
>   and delight in the perverseness of evil;
> those whose paths are crooked,
>   and who are devious in their ways.
>   (Prov. 2:12–15)

Evil is never subject to abstract definition but is identified primarily in terms of its destructive consequences (see esp. Prov. 2:22; 5:22–23; 6:12–15; 10:27–31; 11:5–6; 12:21; 13:6; 14:11, 32; 21:7; 24:19–20; 28:18). It is the product of human actions, or more fundamentally, of a particular type of human being. The wise person fears God (9:10; cf. 1:7; 15:33), and this fear entails the rejection of evil (3:7; 8:13; 16:6). By contrast, evil is committed by the fool (13:19; 14:16; cf. 24:9; 30:32).[13] This antithesis between the wise and the foolish person is central to Proverbs (see, e.g., 3:35; 10:8; 12:15; 14:3, 24; 15:2; 29:11) and the key to understanding the way in which Proverbs offers a privative account of evil; for the fool's folly lies in his failure to realize that he undermines the conditions of his own existence when, whether by action (7:23) or inaction (13:4), he embraces—and thereby reduces himself to—nothing.

---

11. Although Proverbs contains ancient material, it may not have assumed its final form until the Hellenistic period, long after Job was written and roughly contemporary with Ecclesiastes. See James L. Crenshaw, *Old Testament Wisdom: An Introduction* (1981), 3rd ed. (Louisville, KY: Westminster John Knox Press, 2010), 5.

12. "Evil" is normally used to translate the Hebrew nouns *raʿ/rāʿâ* (Prov. 1:16, 33; 2:12, 14; 3:7, 29; 4:27; 6:14, 18; 8:13; 11:19, 27; 13:19; 14:16, 22; 16:6, 17, 27, 30; 17:13; 20:8, 22, 30; 21:10), though it is also used for *zimmâ/mĕzimmâ* (Prov. 12:2; 24:8; 30:32) and *rāšʿâ* (Prov. 16:12).

13. Crenshaw reports that Proverbs contains a number of terms for "fool" (he lists eight), each with its own set of connotations (*Old Testament Wisdom*, 68), but in the vast majority of cases the English "fool" renders either *ʾĕwîl* or *kĕsîl* (and "folly," correspondingly, translates the cognates *ʾiwwelet* and *kĕsîlût*, though the latter occurs only in Prov. 9:13).

To defend this association of Proverbs with a privative account of evil, it is necessary to explore the book's contrast between wisdom and folly in greater depth. On the one hand, Proverbs treats wisdom as a concrete, practical skill set, something one can and should "get" for oneself: "The beginning of wisdom is this: Get wisdom, and whatever else you get, get insight" (4:7; cf. 1:2; 3:13; 4:5). The point of acquiring wisdom is simple: it helps one prosper, both by increasing one's wealth and by enhancing one's social status (1:33; 3:16; 4:21–24; 8:21; 24:3–4). And the reason it gives success is that it connects one deeply with the order of things, since the same wisdom through which humans prosper is that by which God "founded the earth" and "established the heavens" (3:19). Viewed from this perspective, wisdom is not simply a set of precepts or skills, but a living being who calls to human beings in the street (1:20; 8:1–3; cf. 9:1–6), and whose words demand attention because she was with God in the beginning as the work of creation unfolded (8:22–31). To seek wisdom is thus to seek life in harmony with the power that sustains the world. Wisdom "works" because it instantiates a basic correspondence between the individual and creation as a whole (15:24).

If heeding wisdom brings life, ignoring it leads to death (Prov. 8:35–36; 11:19). That is the road of folly, and the fool takes it. Yet folly is less a way with its own integrity than a failure to follow the one, true way of wisdom, which, again, is a power rooted in the very structure of creation in a way that folly is not.[14] Consequently, however seductive the voice that lures the fool toward destruction, the calamity that invariably strikes him is rooted in a culpable (and ultimately inexplicable) failure to heed the ever-present call of wisdom (1:22–27; cf. 8:1). The fool suffers from a fundamental misapprehension of the way things are, and death is the result (14:12; 16:25). He does not flourish because he fails to reckon with the dynamics of the created order, in much the same way that a driver who does not grasp the rules of the road will inevitably crash. In this way, the destruction that afflicts the fool is not so much a matter of retributive punishment as the natural outworking of a life lived against the grain of the world:

> Because they hated knowledge
> and did not choose the fear of the LORD,
> . . . .
> therefore they shall eat the fruit of their way
> and be sated with their own devices.
> For waywardness kills the simple,
> and the complacency of fools destroys them.
>   (Prov. 1:29, 31–32)

14. This is not to deny that Proverbs can speak of the "way" of evil or folly (see, e.g., 2:12; 4:14; 8:13; 12:26; 21:8; 22:5), only that it is understood negatively, as a departure from the "way" of wisdom or the good.

Within this framework the ruin of the fool lies on his own head. Indeed, the inherent foolishness of the wicked arguably lies in their failure to understand that their violent deeds invariably recoil on themselves (Prov. 1:18; 5:22–23; 11:5–6, 17). This is not to say that the destructive consequences of evil action operate independently of God (i.e., automatically) in a manner analogous to the law of karma in Hindu and Buddhist teaching. Given that Proverbs contains a strong doctrine of providence (see, e.g., 5:21; 16:1, 9, 33; 19:21; 20:24; 21:31), there is little basis for supposing that the author has any interest in insulating God from direct involvement in human suffering. Indeed, at one point readers are encouraged not only to accept their suffering, but also to interpret it as inflicted by God as a mark of divine favor, since "the LORD reproves the one he loves" (3:12). The problem with fools is precisely that they fail to heed such reproof (1:25, 30; cf. 12:1; 13:18; 17:10), with the result that God hands them over to the disorder and destruction intrinsic to their actions (cf. Paul's account of divine punishment in Rom. 1:24, 26, 28). In short, while it is God who governs the way of things, for the fool to blame God for his misfortune is simply a further instance of his chronic misapprehension of the nature of things (Prov. 19:3; cf. 5:12–14).

So in Proverbs, evil is not from God (the chastisements God visits upon human beings may be painful, but nowhere in this book are they described as evil), nor is evil characterized as some sort of independent force or in its own right.[15] In this sense evil is nothing, but it is certainly not an illusion: Proverbs does not "solve" the problem of evil by arguing that it is merely a matter of faulty perception. On the contrary, the reality of evil is evident in its effects: violence (10:6; 11:30; 21:7), bloodshed (1:16; 6:17), want (5:10; 6:11; 13:18; 23:21; 24:34), disgrace (3:35; 6:33; 11:2; 18:3), and untimely death (2:18; 5:5; 7:27; 28:17).[16] But as real as these effects are, they are not intrinsic or natural to the created order. Creation itself, in both its human and nonhuman dimensions, is purely an object of delight (8:31), in which evil has neither ontological ground nor any proper place. Evil names those states of affairs that arise when human beings fail to see and honor this basic fact, but for that very reason it is a surd that cannot be explained by reference to any feature of divine or created

---

15. It might seem that folly has this sort of independent status, even if evil does not. Especially in Prov. 9 the parallelism between vv. 1–6 and vv. 13–18 prompts some contemporary translations to name the character in v. 13 "Woman Folly" (CEB), or even just "Folly" (NIV), corresponding to "Wisdom" in v. 1, but the Hebrew of the two verses is not quite parallel: v. 13 speaks periphrastically of "a woman of folly" (*'ēset kĕsîlût*; cf. LXX *gynē aphrōn*), while in v. 1 the personification of Wisdom is unambiguous (*ḥokmâ*). Moreover, while "Wisdom" is consistently personified throughout Prov. 1–9 (1:20; 8:1), "folly" is not: the opponent of Wisdom in these chapters is not another quasi-divine figure, but the "loose woman" (2:16; 5:3; 7:5), clearly conceived as a person of flesh and blood. So while Crenshaw invokes Prov. 9 to argue for Folly as the counterpart of Wisdom, he concedes that there is no parallel to this personified dualism anywhere else in the surviving corpus of Israelite Wisdom literature (see *Old Testament Wisdom*, 87).

16. The qualifier "untimely" is important, for "the book of Proverbs never utters so much as a sigh over the prospect of natural death." Crenshaw, *Old Testament Wisdom*, 72.

being. Proverbs ascribes evil to a combination of ignorance (7:6–21), stupidity (6:6–11), and malice (2:12–15), but this does not explain it.

> Does not wisdom call,
> and does not understanding raise her voice?
> On the heights, beside the way,
>   at the crossroads she takes her stand;
> beside the gates in front of the town,
>   at the entrance of the portals she cries out.
> (Prov. 8:1–3)

What basis is there, then, for ignorance, stupidity, or malice? Evidently, there is none. The public availability of wisdom renders evil inexplicable, and those who perpetrate it are correspondingly without excuse (Prov. 1:24–31; cf. Rom. 1:20).[17]

In this context it is important to recognize that Proverbs neither states nor (so far as I can see) implies that all human experience of evil can be explained away either as just deserts from God or as part of a divine training regimen. "Evil" is not used in Proverbs for divine chastisement; the logic of the book suggests that the two categories are radically opposed to one another: while the chastisement comes from God, evil is a function of human resistance to God and God's ways. To be sure, Proverbs teaches that some sorts of suffering can be beneficial (3:11; 5:23; 6:23; 12:1; 13:1; 20:30; 22:15; 23:14; 25:12; 29:15), but it does not follow that all suffering is either deserved or helpful, and in the book there is no suggestion that those who suffer from the violence of the wicked either merit their pain or gain any benefit from it. Indeed, it seems to be the utter irrationality, uselessness, and futility of such suffering that qualifies it as evil. If the account of evil in Proverbs is to be faulted, it cannot therefore be on the grounds of simple naïveté, as though the author lacked an appreciation of the horror or gravity of evil. The problem is rather that Proverbs' treatment of evil is limited to the moral sphere, and all evil does not seem to be the product of (human) moral activity. The suffering caused by fire, famine, flood, and the like are not part of the scope of reflection in Proverbs, but if they, too, are evil, then there needs to be some qualification of Proverbs' vision of creation, considered apart from human wickedness, as an unambiguous object of delight.

IS GOD EVIL?

If there is evil that cannot be attributed to human activity, then whence does it come? One might conjecture that it is caused by other, nonhuman creatures

---

17. "Perversity is both utterly inexplicable, and perfectly simple. It is inexplicable, because it is perverse; how can you rationalize sheer unreason? It is . . . simple with the simplicity of idiocy, or of the mind which refuses to think." Austin Farrer, *Love Almighty and Ills Unlimited: An Essay on Providence and Evil* (London: Collins, 1962), 140–41.

(viz., fallen angels), and this idea is not without biblical basis, given the many references in the Gospels to afflictions caused by "unclean spirits."[18] Such a solution could in principle be developed within the framework of Proverbs: evil remains nothing, in the sense that it arises through inexplicable creaturely rejection of God and thus lacks any ontological ground. Unable to be accounted for as a natural result of either divine or creaturely existence, it can only be described as a failure of being: the creature (whether human or angelic) failing to be what it properly is.

As already noted, although this kind of privative account of evil has been popular in the Christian tradition, the logic of creation from nothing makes it difficult to rest content with any attempt to explain evil entirely as a matter of creaturely defection from the good. If God is the sole condition of every creature at every point and in every aspect of its existence, then it seems doubtful that responsibility for evil can really be pushed off onto the creature in such a way as to leave God in the clear. In this context (quite apart from passages like Isa. 45:7), Proverbs itself includes the enigmatic claim that God made "everything for its purpose, even the wicked for a day of trouble" (16:4).

In this context, it is significant that while another wisdom text, the book of Job, does attribute natural evils (specifically, firestorm, hurricane, and disease) to an angelic being, it also teaches that such activity is only possible as approved by God (see 1:12, 16, 18–19; 2:6–7).[19] In such a narrative all evil cannot be viewed as resistance to God's will for the creature, since it is precisely God who is portrayed as willing that evil befall the creature. That the calamities afflicting Job are evil and not the beneficial "discipline" (let alone the deserved rebuke) of Proverbs is stressed in the narrative: since Job is—in God's own words!—"a blameless and upright man who fears God and turns away from evil" (1:8), there can be no punitive or pedagogical point to his suffering. In this way, and although Job's friends will later argue otherwise, the prologue alerts the reader that Job is right when he insists on the meaninglessness of the suffering he endures.[20] By framing the discourse between Job, his companions, and God in

---

18. One might also cite biblical accounts of the devil (esp. Rev. 12:7–17), as well as the ancient fragment known as the "Watcher legend" (Gen. 6:1–4), as examples of malevolent angelic activity; but in neither case is it clear that the beings mentioned are understood as the cause of natural evils; their role in the narrative seems rather to be that of prompting human beings to commit moral evil, in analogy with the role of the serpent in Gen. 3 (cf. 1 Pet. 5:8). For a contemporary explanation of so-called "natural evil" in terms of supernatural agency, see Alvin Plantinga, *The Nature of Necessity* (Oxford: Oxford University Press, 1974), 192.

19. In Job 2:3 God explicitly assumes responsibility for the loss of Job's property when he says to Satan, "You incited me against him, to destroy him for no reason."

20. A remarkable feature of many modern commentaries on Job is their reluctance to take the prose prologue (chaps. 1–2) and epilogue (42:7–17) as integral parts of the book. Granted the truth of the historical-critical judgment that elements of an ancient folktale (cf. Ezek. 14:14, 20; Jas. 5:11) are deployed in these passages to provide the framework for a more elaborate, poetic dialogue between Job and his friends, it does not follow that the prose sections can be ignored (see, for a typical example, Crenshaw's dismissal of the epilogue in *Old Testament Wisdom*, 97). Such judgments fail to reckon with the fact that the biblical writer evidently did not think this material dispensable.

this way, the book of Job addresses directly the question of whether the presence of evil in the world is not best accounted for by positing evil in God.

There are several further points to note in the way the prologue sets up the rest of the book. First is Satan's initial challenge to God, "Does Job fear God for nothing?" (1:9). These words suggest that the central question of the book is less the problem of innocent suffering than the grounds of human religious devotion.[21] In context, their force is rhetorical, since Satan's point is precisely that Job's prosperity gives him ample reason to honor God. From the standpoint of the doctrine of creation, however, there is no reason to suppose that the disinterested piety Satan implicitly holds up as an ideal is either possible or what God desires, since everything human beings have, including their lives, is owed to God (see Luke 17:10; 1 Cor. 4:7). In both Testaments, worship is essentially thanksgiving, motivated precisely by gratitude for what God has given.[22] It seems to follow that proper worship is not marked by the absence of any motive, but rather by the acknowledgment that whatever one has is owed to God. Job makes this very point in responding to the disasters that wipe out his family and property: "Naked I came from my mother's womb, and naked shall I return there; the LORD gave, and the LORD has taken away; blessed be the name of the LORD" (Job 1:21). Whether it be much or little, whatever one has is a gift, so thanks is always appropriate.

Especially when viewed from the perspective of creation from nothing, this perspective is logically impeccable: because whatever one receives from God is good, the quantity of goods received is not relevant to piety, since anything, however small or seemingly insignificant, is a gain. One might prefer to find a roll of twenty-dollar bills on the sidewalk rather than just one such bill, but even one is likely to be received with pleasure. And yet Job's dilemma is not simply a matter of his receiving less, but of the sudden and inexplicable withdrawal of what he had. Such actions may be within God's rights, but insofar as they clearly diminish Job's ability to flourish (not to mention that of the animals and people who are killed through Satan's machinations), they do not seem consistent with God's aim in bringing creatures into being in the first place. As Job himself implies in passages like 10:8–9, if God did not want them to flourish, best to leave them uncreated! In this context, God's actions do not seem to be good, and significantly, Job does not claim that they are. Instead, he asks his

---

For a study that quite deliberately refuses to marginalize the prose portions of the book, see Carol A. Newsom, *The Book of Job: A Contest of Moral Imagination* (New York: Oxford University Press, 2003).

21. "The initial question of the book is whether truly disinterested piety exists." Carol A. Newsom, "Job," in *Women's Bible Commentary*, ed. Carol A. Newsom and Sharon H. Ringe (Louisville, KY: Westminster John Knox Press, 1998), 139.

22. So, e.g., the three major festivals of ancient Israelite religion—Passover, Pentecost, and Booths—all originally seem to have been harvest festivals of thanksgiving, with the first and second eventually taking on additional significance as expressions of gratitude for deliverance from slavery and for the giving of the law, respectively. And it is likewise no accident that the quintessential act of Christian worship is commonly called Eucharist, which means "thanksgiving."

wife, "Shall we receive the good at the hands of God, and not receive the bad?" (2:10). So, in a striking departure from Proverbs, Job openly (already even in the prologue) makes God the author of at least some evil. And lest the reader be tempted to think that the protagonist is overstepping the bounds of theological propriety, the narrator immediately adds, "In all this Job did not sin with his lips" (Job 2:10).

Whether or not this last statement continues to hold true as the story develops is the central question in the rest of the book. Certainly Job's three friends view his complaints as evidence of his failure to honor God properly. They emphasize God's righteousness, encouraging Job to see (and ultimately condemning him for refusing to see) his affliction either as deserved punishment or as helpful reproof, but disallowing any suggestion that Job's experience calls God's goodness into question. The opening words of Bildad summarize the position of all Job's human opponents (including the latecomer Elihu in chaps. 32–37): "Does God pervert justice? Or does the Almighty pervert the right?" (8:3).[23] Job's position is more complicated. He rejects the view that God gives the righteous and the wicked their just deserts (see 9:22–24; 21:7–34; 24:1–25; though cf. 27:7–23), but the bulk of his discourse is not given over to this kind of theoretical reflection on God's ways. Instead, it is a direct expression of his own suffering (7:11; 10:1) that begins and ends with imprecations, moving from a curse on his own life (3:3–26) to a series of oaths calling down calamity on himself if he has committed any injustice (31:5–40). But as much as he insists on his own integrity in the face of his friends' accusations (27:5–6), the point of his speeches is less to accuse God of having done wrong (indeed, in 19:6 he complains that "God has put *me* in the wrong"), than to make God confront him and provide an explanation for what has happened to him.

If this is a correct reading of what Job desires, half his wish is fulfilled: God does confront him, but without providing any rationale for what Job has suffered. Indeed, far from offering information of any sort, God's address is resolutely interrogative: "I will question you, and you shall declare to me" (38:3; 40:7). Moreover, most of the questions God asks have nothing whatever to do with issues of human justice or, indeed, with human beings at all.[24] Theological evaluation of God's speech is correspondingly difficult. Given Job's initial response to the divine barrage of questions (40:4–5), it is easy to conclude that their purpose is simply to overwhelm him and thereby drive him to silence. And yet if God's point is simply to shock and awe, it seems to be a supremely unnecessary effort since there is no reason to think that God's awesomeness was ever in doubt. The debate between Job and his companions is an empirical one over

---

23. For further examples of this theme in the speeches of Job's friends, see Job 4:7–9; 15:20–32; 18:5–21; 20:4–29 (Elihu stakes out the same position in 34:21–30). Once again we emphasize that their viewpoint is *not* the same as that of Proverbs, which at no point suggests either that all human suffering is justified or that it all comes from God.

24. The chief exception is Job 40:10–14 (cf. 38:15), where God challenges Job to constrain the proud and wicked.

whether there is in fact any difference between God's treatment of the righteous and the wicked. No one questions God's transcendence of human moral categories. Eliphaz asks, "Can mortals be righteous before God? Can human beings be pure before their Maker?" (4:17; cf. 22:2; 25:4–6); the same question also appears on Job's lips just a few chapters later (9:2; cf. v. 20). And when Zophar highlights the unsearchability of God's ways (11:7–9; cf. 36:22–23), Job has no interest in contesting the point ("Who does not know such things as these?," 12:3; cf. 26:14; 28:20–21). Indeed, long before his climactic encounter with the whirlwind, Job himself not only cites some of the very same examples of divine power that God will later bring up (cf. 9:4–10 and 38:4–5, 12–13, 16, 31–32), but even anticipates his own inability to offer any response to God:

> How then can I answer him,
>   choosing my words with him?
> Though I am innocent, I cannot answer him;
>   I must appeal for mercy to my accuser.
> . . . .
> If it is a contest of strength, he is the strong one!
>   If it is a matter of justice, who can summon him?
> Though I am innocent, my own mouth would condemn me;
>   Though I am blameless, he would prove me perverse.
>   (Job 9:14–15, 19–20)

And on the other side of the debate, although Elihu closes his speech by assailing Job with the same sorts of questions God later poses (cf. 37:14–18 and 38:19–30), no sooner has he finished speaking then God dismisses him with the words, "Who is this that darkens counsel by words without knowledge?" (38:2).[25] But if acknowledgment of God's transcendent majesty is not at stake, then what is?

If Job's silence were all that God desired, then the battle would have been won after the first divine speech, to which Job responds precisely by eschewing any further talk (40:5); but God does not accept this surrender. Instead, God repeats his initial summons ("Gird up your loins like a man; I will question you, and you declare to me"; 40:7) and proceeds with a further set of questions that ups the ante, confronting Job with the legendary monsters Behemoth and Leviathan instead of more run-of-the-mill creatures like mountain goats and wild donkeys. This second time around, Job's response is less straightforward. Even as God has not directly addressed Job's questions about justice in human affairs, so Job does not speak directly to God's invocation of the wonders of

25. It is a matter of critical consensus (acknowledged even by Newsom, who is otherwise reluctant to interpret change in genre as evidence of textual interpolation) that Elihu's speech is a later addition to the text. If so, 38:1 would originally have immediately followed 31:40, which would explain why 38:1 speaks of God as answering *Job* out of the whirlwind (cf. 42:3), as well as why Elihu is ignored when God passes judgment on the theology of the other characters in 42:7–8. But the fact remains that in the book's present form God's opening rebuke in chap. 38 falls immediately on Elihu.

nature. Instead his response focuses on the opening words of God's first speech, which he quotes (albeit in paraphrase; cf. 38:1):

> "Who is this that hides counsel without knowledge?"
> Therefore I have uttered what I did not understand,
>   things too wonderful for me, which I did not know.
> "Hear, and I will speak;
>   I will question you, and you declare to me."
> I had heard of you by the hearing of the ear,
>   but now my eye sees you;
> therefore I despise myself,
>   and repent in dust and ashes.
>
> (Job 42:3–6)

Significantly, Job does not admit to having spoken wrongly about God (in the very next verse, God confirms that he has not done so). Rather, he confesses that he did not understand what he said. It is therefore not true that God's speeches have given him new data that would lead him to modify the content of his claims. In this final passage the contrast is not between what Job had heard before and what God had just told him (as though the text read, "I had heard *x* of you, but now I know that *y* is true"), but between hearing and seeing ("I had heard of you by the hearing of the ear, but now my eye sees you;" cf. 19:26–27). It is on the basis of this contrast that Job repents; but on its own terms this repentance takes nothing away from the truth of his previous statements regarding the frequent prosperity of the wicked or the unjust suffering of the innocent. In any case, if Job's repentance is the goal of the theophany, it seems that what God wants is not silence (since repentance is not a refusal to speak) but recognition—and in this way God is like Job himself, whose fundamental desire throughout has been for God to acknowledge him. But all this provides no rationale for Job's suffering. There is no claim that it accomplished anything (contrast the conclusion of the Joseph story in Gen. 50:20). God's "answer" to Job is simply God's presence.[26]

So is God evil? Job nowhere says so. Even as he insists that he is innocent of any concrete act of injustice or impiety and demands that God face him, he concedes that he cannot claim any righteousness before God. Yet though he does

---

26. While modern commentators rightly stress the tension between the "naive" piety of the prose sections and the theological parrying in the speeches, to my mind the message of the book of Job (and, *pace* Newsom, I think a unitary reading of the text need not be purchased at the price of ignoring the book's "polyphonic" character) is the same as that of the folktale that seems to have served as the occasion for its composition: Job is a pious person, and God, being righteous, ultimately rewards him for his piety. What the canonical book of Job challenges is not this basic plotline, but the way its key concepts—human piety, divine righteousness, and eschatological reward—are to be understood. What does it mean to be pious if piety is a quality of Job in chaps. 3–31 no less than chaps. 1–2? How can the portrait of God in the prologue as well as the speeches from the whirlwind be understood to exemplify divine righteousness? And what does it mean to speak of Job as rewarded in the end (42:10–17), if we take seriously God's claim (42:7) that it is Job and not his friends who have spoken rightly of God over the course of the book (i.e., is this "reward" more plausibly interpreted as a matter of works or of grace?)?

not call God evil, from the very beginning he allows that evil (*hārāᶜ*) comes from God's hand (2:10). And even in the middle of the book's happy ending, the narrator reenforces the point by reminding us that "all the evil" (*kol-hārāᶜâ*) Job experienced came from God (42:11). In these verses the book of Job explicitly ascribes to God responsibility for evil, as Proverbs does not.[27] Nevertheless, it does not seem to teach that God *is* evil. Here the epilogue of the book is worth bearing in mind as more than a dispensable appendage. Again, it does not paper over divine responsibility for Job's suffering (in fact, explicit statements that evil comes from God are found *only* in the prologue and epilogue), but it does serve to illustrate God's goodness. By contemporary lights, the idea that God's goodness is vindicated by the "replacement" of lost children as well as of lost goods may seem crudely materialistic, but the point remains that the final message of the book is that God not only speaks to Job, but also cares for him. This does not amount to a theodicy in the modern sense, for no claim is made that the book's happy ending justifies Job's suffering. How God's care for Job can be reconciled with the evil with which God afflicted him remains unexplained. As with Proverbs, for Job the reality of evil is a surd; but in Job its inexplicability is a function of divine transcendence rather than of human perversity.[28]

No less than is the case in Proverbs, however, the picture of evil in Job is incomplete. Job certainly provides a different and important perspective: while in Proverbs evil is understood as human violation of God's will, Job ascribes to God a causal role in human experience of evil (even when that evil is mediated through human and other created agents). As portrayed in Job, evil is a function of deliberate (though not, it seems, malevolent) divine action: if the reasons why God should bring it about that an innocent person like Job should suffer while the wicked prosper remain mysterious, the presupposition remains that it is none other than God who makes it so. So while no explanation is given for evil, it is assumed that the afflicted person stands directly under the hand of God. But though Job reckons with the suffering caused by nonhuman forces as Proverbs does not, the cause of evil remains fundamentally *personal*: the act of an identifiable agent, whether divine or human. In this way both texts leave out what might be called systemic forms of evil (e.g., predation, climatic cycles, aging, and death) that do not, like the violence of the wicked in Proverbs or the calamities that befall Job, erupt mysteriously in the midst of the otherwise ordered fabric of creation, but rather seem to be intrinsic to creation's everyday patterns of operation. The suffering caused by these phenomena suggests the need for a further perspective on the place of evil within the created order.

27. Again, while Proverbs allows that various kinds of suffering are sent by God, it reserves the term "evil" for human wickedness.

28. This is certainly not to say that Job has no appreciation for human wickedness as a cause of evil, since a major topic of reflection in the book is precisely how God deals (or fails to deal) with the wicked. The point remains, however, that the focus in Job is on divine sovereignty, as evident from the beginning in the fact that the depredations of the Sabeans and Chaldeans against Job (1:15, 17) are viewed as no less under divine control than the ("natural") evils of fire and storm (1:16, 19).

IS EVIL A CREATURE?

In much the same way that the gaps in Proverbs' account of evil could be filled by appeal to the agency of supernatural creatures, these objections to Job's account can also be met, within the book's narrative framework, by arguing that while certain dimensions of evil appear to be natural features of the created order that recur automatically, they are in fact the result of deliberate divine action. After all, since the doctrine of creation from nothing implies that God immediately causes every created event, there seems to be good reason to want to avoid the suggestion that any wordly happening stands at some remove from God. At the same time, to the extent that Christians want to affirm that creatures genuinely have being, they will want to affirm creatures' capacity to cause events in space and time. The theological issues raised by this simultaneous insistence on divine sovereignty and creaturely integrity are important and will be examined in greater detail in the next chapter. For now it is sufficient simply to recognize that within biblical Wisdom literature, Ecclesiastes provides a third perspective on evil, a view that lodges it much more firmly in the structures of creaturely existence. The difference from Proverbs could not be starker. Far from being seen as fundamentally delightful, creation in Ecclesiastes is viewed as fundamentally disappointing and futile: "All things are wearisome; more than one can express" (Eccl. 1.8; cf. v. 14). Here evil does not intrude upon creation from without, but infects it from within.

Like Job, the book of Ecclesiastes does not restrict its understanding of evil to human resistance to God's will (though, as in Job, the author's understanding of evil also includes human wickedness; see, e.g., Eccl. 5:1; 8:11; cf. 7:20, 29). Unlike Job, however, the reflections of Ecclesiastes do not include the kind of challenge to God that prompts consideration of divine malevolence as a possible source of evil.[29] This is not to say that the author denies God's involvement in the world. He characterizes the basic features of everyday life, in both their joy and their routine, as coming from God's hand (Eccl. 2:24; cf. 3:10; 5:19), emphasizing that God "has appointed a time for every matter (3:17; cf. vv. 1–8). Yet true as it is that God "makes everything" (11:5; cf. 7:14), the shape of this divine work seems at once inaccessible to human understanding (8:17)

---

29. The author of the text identifies himself as *qohelet*, the feminine participle of a verb meaning "to assemble" (hence the English title "Ecclesiastes," from the Greek word for "assembly"). This Hebrew word has been interpreted as a name, an acronym, and a title. Since the book's author is clearly, if anachronistically, identified with Solomon (Eccl. 1:1, 12, 16; 2:9; cf. 1 Kgs. 2:12; 4:29–30; 10:23; see 1 Kgs. 8:1, where Solomon "assembles" [*yaqhēl*] the elders and other leaders of Israel), it does not seem appropriate to treat the term as a proper name (as is suggested when the transliteration Qoheleth is used). Given the way the text associates the author with the sages who pursued wisdom (Eccl. 1:17; 12:9–10), as well as its use in combination with the definite article in 12:8–10, the NRSV's "Teacher" seems fair enough (though "Compiler" may accord better with the Hebrew root). I will stick with "Ecclesiastes" in order to avoid the need to distinguish between the book and its author. For a summary of the philological issues surrounding the Hebrew term, see James L. Crenshaw, *Urgent Advice and Probing Questions: Collected Writings on Old Testament Wisdom* (Macon, GA: Mercer University Press, 1995), 500–501.

and predetermined (9:7), as though God has long since finished appointing the times for things, and what we experience is simply the working through of a fixed—and essentially repetitive—sequence of events (3:14–15; cf. 1:9–10). It is not that God is absent ("for apart from him who can eat or who can have enjoyment?"; 2:25; cf. 5:20), but God's engagement with the world is not such as to prompt humans to address the Divinity directly, whether in praise or lament. Correspondingly, the form of evil that preoccupies Ecclesiastes is neither individual wickedness (as in Proverbs) nor sudden and unexpected calamities (as in Job), but the numbing regularity of the everyday: "What do mortals get from all the toil and strain with which they toil under the sun? For all their days are full of pain, and their work is a vexation; even at night their minds do not rest" (Eccl. 2:22–23). Or, still more bluntly: "This is an evil in all that happens under the sun: the same fate comes to everyone" (9:3).[30] In contrast to the logic of both Proverbs and Job, evil in Ecclesiastes is not a surd that disrupts creation's order, but apparently is intrinsic to that order itself.

To be sure, the pessimism of Ecclesiastes is not completely unqualified. Repeatedly the author commends enjoyment of food, drink, work, and companionship (3:12–13, 22; 5:18; 8:15; 9:7–10); but such amusements are just a temporary distraction from the essential futility of a world where "all is vanity and a chasing after wind" (1:14; 2:11, 17). Proverbs is rooted in the belief that disciplined behavior can secure human flourishing; Job at least allows the possibility that God may be appealed to in order to redress the world's injustices; but Ecclesiastes appears to offer little more than bleak resignation in the face of creation's inexorable and pitiless laws. At the same time, the writer does not seem inclined to blame God for this state of affairs: God is depicted as inscrutable rather than hostile (though see 3:18).[31] Nor is creation judged to be evil as a whole or in every respect, for God "has made everything beautiful in its time" (3:11 RSV). Nevertheless, Ecclesiastes' vision of life as ultimately "an unhappy business" (1:13), which finds "the dead . . . more fortunate than the living" (4:2), raises the question of whether he understands evil as *part* of creation—not simply a relative lack of goodness, but some *thing* that distorts and degrades created being.

In one respect this possibility may not seem particularly strange. After all, one way of speaking of evil as a creature is to identify a particular creature as the source of evil, and in Christian tradition the devil has served this function. But Christians have not wanted to claim that the devil is inherently evil because

---

30. At some points, this "evil" is described in terms virtually identical to the situations that call forth Job's protests: the prosperous are unable to enjoy their wealth (Eccl. 2:21; 6:1–2), or fools prosper while the deserving languish (8:14; 10:5–7); but for Ecclesiastes these are less occasions for moral outrage than further evidence of the general futility of things.

31. In the final form of the book, the insistence that prosperity is not proportional to merit (9:11) is combined with repeated exhortations to fear God that are justified precisely on the grounds of divine justice (7:18; 8:12–13; cf. 1:1–17; 12:1). A further consequence of this latter perspective is that in the same verse that the writer commends enjoyment, he warns that it too is subject to divine judgment (11:9).

that would deny the inherent goodness of everything made by God as affirmed in Genesis 1:31. In any case, the devil plays no role whatsoever in Ecclesiastes, where evil is associated with insubstantiality: "vanity" (*hebel*, from a root meaning "breath") and "chasing after wind" (*rĕʿût rûaḥ*, with the verb carrying connotations of herding or even eating; Eccl. 1:14, 17; etc.). This language suggests that evil is not properly understood as one kind of creature (even a supersubtle one) alongside others; rather, the insubstantiality refers precisely to a basic characteristic of all created being: pleasure (2:1), toil (2:11, 19; 4:4, 8), wisdom (2:26), wealth (5:10; 6:2), and youth (11:10) are all "vanity" because they pass away: "the dust returns to the earth as it was, and the breath [*rûaḥ*] returns to God who gave it" (12:7). The "problem" of evil in Ecclesiastes is this stubborn, inexorable fact of creatures' transience.

In summary, from the perspective of Ecclesiastes, evil is not a characteristic of any creature considered in itself (i.e., in abstraction from its relationships with other creatures), but refers to the ephemeral character of created being as it subsists concretely in time and space: everything is good in its time, but that time passes, and there is neither permanence (some inextinguishable core that remains stable amid the flux of change) nor progress (evolutionary movement toward a higher, richer, or more harmonious state) in creaturely affairs. Significantly, Ecclesiastes does not claim to have received these insights through revelation. He reports them instead as the consequence of sober empirical research: he "applied" his mind to seek wisdom (1:13, 16–17; 8:16), "searched" (2:3), "considered" (2:11), "perceived" (2:14), "saw" (3:16; 4:1; 5:13, 18; 6:1; 7:15; 8:10; 9:11), "tested" (7:23), and "found" (7:29)—all this though an extended program of "examining" (9:1), "weighing," and "studying" (12:9). It follows that if Ecclesiastes' inclusion in the biblical canon is taken as evidence that its content is divinely inspired, the book's own language implies that in this case inspiration is a matter of God underwriting the conclusions of a purely secular analysis, the sum of which is that the world, considered on its own terms, gives no evidence of meaning or purpose.

Of course, Ecclesiastes is not all there is to the canon. The teaching of other biblical books goes beyond what can be derived from the observation of worldly phenomena, including especially the communication of God's promise to redeem creaturely existence from the futility and injustice observed so acutely by Ecclesiastes. Even allowing for this broader canonical context, however, Ecclesiastes' assessment of creation remains theologically troubling, because it appears to correlate evil with the basic conditions of creaturely existence, not simply with its perversion or corruption. Every creature may be good "in its time," but the interactions of creatures with one another inevitably lead to their demise:

> Everything that confronts them is vanity, since the same fate comes to all, to the righteous and the wicked, to the good and the evil, to the clean and the unclean, to those who sacrifice and those who do not sacrifice. As are

the good, so are the sinners; those who swear are like those who shun an oath. This is an evil in all that happens under the sun, that the same fate comes to everyone. (Eccl. 9:1–3)

No creature, whatever its merits, escapes dissolution. And if dissolution is rightly characterized as an evil, then it seems difficult to view creation as good, since creatures' transience seems to be a function of their most basic characteristic as creatures: their finitude as entities located in a particular place (that is subject to encroachment by other creatures) and at a particular time (that inexorably passes away). Indeed, Ecclesiastes raises serious questions for Christian confession of creation's unity under God, since unity implies an integration of creaturely being that allows their mutual flourishing, whereas Ecclesiastes highlights the ways in which the flourishing of any one creature comes at the expense of others. Granted that the interactions that lead to the destruction of an individual creature are often part of a wider context that make possible the existence of the species (e.g., hunting down the zebra not only sustains the lion but also enhances the overall fitness of the zebra herd by removing the old and infirm), but the evident impossibility of the simultaneous flourishing of all creatures under the conditions of time and space leads quite naturally to the conclusion that (in the words of Austin Farrer) "the world is not a system, it is an interaction of systems innumerable."[32]

To be sure, even on the most sober scientific grounds, it is possible to affirm that creation is a "unity" in the sense that all creatures are made of a common material substrate, are subject to the same physical laws, and share a common origin; but not in the sense that their mutual interactions reveal a common goal. In the face of this challenge, the first point to make is that creation's unity (like its contingency) is a matter of faith. Indeed, the presence of Ecclesiastes in the Bible serves as a useful reminder that belief in the fundamental unity of creation is a corollary of belief in one God who creates from nothing rather than an empirical judgment. Given this belief, it is appropriate to characterize the apparently pointless destruction of creatures identified by Ecclesiastes as evil—a deviation from God's will for their mutual flourishing. But the question of why this evil should afflict creation persists, given that the evil lamented by Ecclesiastes is not an intrusion (whether owing to creaturely perversion or divine whim) into the otherwise smooth operation of the created order; it is a constitutive feature of the created order itself. Within the framework of creation from nothing, evil thus appears to be a direct result of God's decision to create finite beings.

In chapter 3 I made the claim that living creatures' temporal finitude, whether on the level of the individual or of the species, need not be seen as an evil, since the claim that a creature has its time (and no more than that time) is simply part

---

32. Farrer, *Love Almighty and Ills Unlimited*, 51.; cf. 52: "It would sound better if we called it a society of systems; but the term would suggest a mutual regard and peaceful coexistence scarcely to be found."

of what it means for it to be a creature.[33] Time, moreover, is connected with other defining features of creaturely existence, like movement and place. The encroachment of creatures on one another is a function of their natural movement, and thus in each case is part of an individual creature's goodness as the kind of creature it is.[34] The "evil" lamented by Ecclesiastes is a result of the fact that these various manifestations of goodness are mutually incompatible, in the sense that creatures' interference with one another precludes that they all have their "time" at once.

The evident impossibility of all creatures' having their time simultaneously does not speak against creatures' goodness, because goodness is not the same as perfection. Every creature is good insofar as it exists, but the fact that its goodness includes certain patterns of movement (i.e., change) is an index of the fact that it is incomplete.[35] Indeed, the same movements that cause some creatures to block the flourishing of others are precisely the means by which creatures come to realize their own various forms of perfection. In making creatures, it is God's concern that they realize their several perfections.[36] Given that the interactions accompanying existence in time and space prevent any creature's perfection from being realized fully in time, it follows that God's intentions for creation can be achieved only through a fundamental transformation of the conditions of created existence:

> For the creation waits with eager longing for the revealing of the children of God; for the creation was subjected to futility, not of its own will but by the will of the one who subjected it in hope that the creation itself will be set free from its bondage to decay and will obtain the freedom of the glory of the children of God. We know that the whole creation has been groaning

33. See pp. 77–78 above.

34. It seems to follow that purely spiritual creatures could avoid such mutual interference (see Farrer, *Love Almighty and Ills Unlimited*, 58), but even though Thomas holds that angels are nonmaterial, he denies that several of them can simultaneously occupy the same place on the grounds that an angel's location is defined by the exercise of causal power and it is logically impossible that multiple secondary causes should have the same causal relation to a given effect. See Thomas Aquinas, *Summa theologiae* [*ST*] 1.52.3.

35. "Man is reckoned to be a fallen creature; his precarious condition has been lowered by his own perversity. But his needing to be saved is not the mere effect of his fall; it is the consequence of his animal nature. Man is not first an immortal soul; he is an animal on whom the capacity for everlasting life has been conferred" (Farrer, *Love Almighty and Ills Unlimited*, 107). While one might question the appropriateness of the word "saved" in this context (since it might be taken to imply that earthly existence is evil rather than simply incomplete), the quotation nevertheless highlights this distinction between our present state and our promised end.

36. "[God] is concerned with everything in so far as it exists, or rather, it exists in so far as He is concerned with it. It is not even proper to say that He is concerned with one thing more than another, except in the sense that there is more in one thing than another for Him to be concerned with. . . . God's concern with several things cannot conflict in Him; but only in the finite sphere where in virtue of their own finitude they run against one another. If God wills the survival of the boy rather than of the sparrows when the boy shoots the sparrows for food, then only does His concern with one take precedence of His concern with the other. But in the concerns that make up the divine life as it is in itself apart from all creatures, not even such a conflict can arise." Austin Farrer, *Finite and Infinite: A Philosophical Essay* (1943), 2nd ed. (1959; repr., New York: Seabury Press, 1979), 59.

in labor pains until now, and not only the creation, but we ourselves, who have the first fruits of the Spirit, groan inwardly while we wait for adoption, the redemption of our bodies. For in hope we were saved. Now hope that is seen is not hope. For who hopes for what is seen? But if we hope for what we do not see, we wait for it in patience. (Rom. 8:19–25)

No less than Ecclesiastes, Paul recognizes the vanity of created existence as we now see it (the Greek word rendered "futility" in Rom. 8:20 is *mataiotēs*, which the Septuagint also uses for the key Hebrew term *hebel* in Eccl. 1:2, 14; etc.), but Paul also believes in an order beyond what can be seen.[37] Paul's belief that creation will ultimately be freed from the "bondage to decay" characteristic of life in time and space is a result of his having received "the first fruits of the Spirit." That belief is just not accessible to Ecclesiastes, who lays no claim to such special revelation. Nevertheless, in highlighting the intractability of evil under conditions of material, finite existence, Ecclesiastes raises the question of theodicy with a sharpness that even Job can scarcely match: why did not God make a world in which there were no structural impediments to creatures realizing their several perfections?

IN PLACE OF A THEODICY

A proper conclusion to this chapter would offer an answer to this last question, but the nature of the topic precludes a conclusion of that sort. Proposed "solutions" to the "problem" of evil invariably run afoul of the basic logic of creation from nothing by assigning evil a place in creation as an experience that is either inevitable or justifiable. But if evil is that which God does not will, and nothing is created except that which is willed by God, then evil can have no place in creation, and any attempt to argue otherwise is false either to the essential character of evil or to the sovereignty of God. In this respect, Christians do well to avoid every attempt to explain evil.

It does not follow, however, that evil's inexplicability in the context of a doctrine of creation from nothing means that we should not talk about it, any more than the impossibility of our grasping God dispenses us from proclaiming the gospel. After all, it is only as we name and seek to understand particular instances of evil that we are able to resist them; but such naming must always be coupled with an understanding that our efforts to make sense of evil (efforts

---

37. While consideration of the broader context of Paul's argument certainly does not justify interpreting Rom. 8:19–23 as evidence for an expansive theology of nature, neither is it plausible to limit the passage's significance entirely to the human sphere, as John Reumann does in *Creation and New Creation: The Past, Present, and Future of God's Creative Activity* (Minneapolis: Augsburg Publishing House, 1973), 98–99, 101. For a more balanced assessment, which acknowledges that "nature plays a very small role for the apostle," while also recognizing that for Paul, "life always has a cosmic dimension, since it is always integrated in creation," see Ernst Käsemann, *Commentary on Romans*, trans. and ed. Geoffrey W. Bromiley (Grand Rapids: Wm. B. Eerdmans Publishing Co., 1980), 233.

we can never wholly avoid if we are to counter its power) are always false to the extent that they invariably try to find a place for that which has no place. To worship God truly entails the realization that God can be assigned no place in creation, because God claims every place; by contrast, to reckon with evil is to recognize that it deceives us (and thereby leads us to deceive both others and ourselves) precisely when it would have us give it a place that it cannot rightly claim as its own. God resists containment; but evil craves it, because while containment constitutes a denial of God's freedom, it provides evil a springboard to exercise a freedom to which it has no right. The recognition that evil "doesn't fit" thus serves as a salutary reminder that the temptation to explain evil is the first step to empowering it. The divergent perspectives on evil in the three Wisdom books are a felicitous sign within Scripture itself that no one account of evil, however accurate or perceptive it may be, will do.[38]

Yet it is not possible to dispense with the question posed at the end of the last section quite so easily. After all, while the perspectives of the three canonical Wisdom texts, while clearly divergent, are not utterly dissimilar. Most obviously, insofar as Proverbs, Job, and Ecclesiastes all acknowledge the power of evil to thwart human flourishing and do not posit any limits to divine power, they seem to support the idea that God permits evil, and that claim can certainly seem theologically problematic. Yet there are resources in the Christian tradition to help us avoid some especially problematic ways of understanding what divine "permission" might mean in this context. Properly speaking, the claim that God permits evil is designed to make just three points: (1) evil is not an illusion (i.e., to "permit" something is to acknowledge that it has power and real effects); (2) God does not commit evil (i.e., to "permit" is not to "enact"); and (3) evil is subject to God (i.e., it has only as much power as God "permits"). Beyond these three points, analogies with human permission are likely to lead astray. For example, it would be profoundly mistaken to suppose that God permits evil in the way that I might, say, permit my daughter to play with matches or to bully other children, for such a picture presupposes that creatures have some capacity to go about their business independently of God. But this possibility is logically incompatible with the doctrine of creation from nothing, according to which creatures are always both totally and immediately dependent on God for their being and actions. Nor can talk of divine permission be understood as God giving evil some sort of autonomy, as though it were a power independent of

---

38. I recognize that my own presentation effectively gives a certain prominence to the view of evil found in Ecclesiastes, as the final example. In response I can only plead that sequential ordering of material is unavoidable in any comparative analysis, and that the privileging of Ecclesiastes in the present account is defensible insofar as a focus on evil as bound up with the conditions of physical existence is both natural and appropriate in a study of creation. If my subject were redemption, I would be much more inclined to conclude my analysis with Proverbs' emphasis on human perversity. Similarly, Job's face-to-face encounter with God would have particular salience in a book on Christian eschatology, where examination of the proximate causes of evil in creatures' movements (whether "moral" or "natural") gives way to the question of its ultimate relation to the will of the Creator.

God, toward which God maintains an attitude of toleration. That claim would violate the principle that in the beginning there is nothing but God—and thus no reality with which God has to reckon that is not itself the immediate product of God's agency.

In short, the claim that God permits evil cannot be interpreted to mean that God has conceded evil a place within creation. Evil is not a power that God more or less grudgingly allows some sway (however limited) in the present, with the promise of its eradication at some point in the future. If evil were conceived in these terms, then the question of why God did not make creation otherwise would be perfectly appropriate. But if evil refers to a lack of correspondence between God's will for creation and creation's present state, then there is no basis for viewing it as an object of divine indulgence, as though it had some purpose or rationale within the wider economy of creation. Considered from the perspective of their finitude, creatures inexorably suffer evil; but evil has no part in God's will for them. Because evil by definition does not accord with God's will for creation, it can have no positive purpose: it does not serve either to educate or to punish, nor is it rightly conceived as the condition for the possibility of some other desirable feature of created existence (e.g., freedom). As that to which God is absolutely opposed, it can be said to exist only as that which God continually and without qualification works to eradicate by bringing creation to the end envisioned by Paul in Romans 8. Considered in the context of the doctrine of creation from nothing, the experience of evil is simply evidence that creation has not yet attained God's goal for it.

It remains true that there would be no evil if God had not created the world. But it does not follow that God "permits" evil as a necessary condition of finite existence, as though God weighed (and thus implicitly enjoins us to weigh) the good of created existence against the exposure to evil that it entails. Such a calculus makes sense only if creation is conceived as a means to some end, in the way one might imagine assessing whether the benefits of a proposed invention were likely to prove greater than its potential for abuse. But the existence of creatures is not a means to an end in this way: God's intention in creating is simply that creatures should exist. The goodness of creatures thus consists entirely in the fact that they are, not in some further effect that may or may not follow from their existence. To be sure, God intends that each creature exist in its own proper perfection, and in line with the conviction that movement is intrinsic to created existence, this perfection is not realized from the beginning. That the realization of creaturely perfection is a movement, however, should not be interpreted as some sort of a defect, as though God might have made creatures perfect but chose for some reason not to do so. After all, if movement is an intrinsic feature of created being, then part of creatures' inherent goodness, and what it means for them to flourish, is to undergo the kinds of changes associated (in the case of living beings) with growth and maturation. From this perspective, evil is in no way a matter of divine concession, or a possibility that God allows in order to realize some greater good. On the contrary, evil is properly understood as that which God is always in the process of disallowing by the very act of holding creatures in being. It is what God from the beginning rejects and refuses, what God is always countering and encouraging us to counter. God remains free to draw good from evil (Gen. 50:20), but evil in itself does not help us on our way to perfection; it is always a limit, an impediment. If God achieves God's purposes by drawing good out of evil, it does not follow that evil is "really" good (as though our sins were other than sinful), but only that it cannot finally defeat God's will for creatures' flourishing.

How that will is realized in the face of the futility of the present age is, as Paul insists, a matter of hope rather than sight, and thus finally of eschatology rather than of creation. Nevertheless, insofar as God even now holds creation in being in spite of the threat posed by evil, the realization of God's will for creaturely flourishing cannot be restricted to the future and therefore has a place in the doctrine of creation, too. Even in the present, God resists evil by preserving, empowering, and coordinating the various forms of created being. The next chapter explores this ongoing dimension of God's work with creatures through an exposition of the doctrine of providence.

6

Providence

Creation is inherently *good* because it is the product of God's will, but creation is not (yet) *perfect* because the flourishing of creatures that God wills is in the present partial, competitive, and transient—a series of qualifications that can be overcome only in a state of communion with God to be realized beyond the constraints of life in time and space. As argued in the preceding chapter, this gap between creation's goodness and its perfection is the locus of evil: that which thwarts God's will for creatures' flourishing. Now, to identify this gap as the locus where evil appears is not to say that the gap is evil in itself. On the contrary, because the movement by which creatures come to perfection is (as argued in chap. 3 above) part of the inherent goodness of created being, evil properly refers to that which blocks creatures from completing that movement. The claim that creatures are not yet perfect does not, therefore, imply any qualification of their present goodness, as though (e.g.) a baby ought to be considered less than good because she is not being a fully grown—let alone an eschatologically glorified—human being. Nevertheless, it remains central to God's will for human beings that earthly growth and eschatological glorification take place.[1]

---

1. "The ultimate happiness of human beings consists in their highest activity, which is the

As the term itself suggests, providence refers to the ways in which God *provides* for human (and other) creatures to achieve their proper ends in the face of the threat posed by evil.[2] Christian theologians commonly distinguish between *nature* and *grace* as distinct modes of this work of divine provision. Within this framework, "nature" refers to the innate capacities specific to a particular kind of creature (e.g., human nature includes bipedalism, speech, growth from infancy to adulthood), and "grace" refers to features that God freely adds to these natural capacities (e.g., the putting on of immortality described by Paul in 1 Cor. 15:53). In principle, there is nothing wrong with this distinction, which simply reflects well-established Christian sensibilities regarding the difference between, say, the ability to see on the one hand, and the ability to have faith on the other: both are God's gifts, but they are given differently.[3] Yet as noted in the preface (above), the distinction becomes problematic when natures are thought to function independently of God, as though creatures were provided with natures in the way that the players at the start of a game of Monopoly are provided with money that can be spent without any input from the banker.[4] Creation from nothing means that every aspect of a creature's nature is no less immediately, directly, and totally dependent on God than any gift of grace. It follows that what distinguishes nature and grace is not the degree of dependence on God each entails but rather the mode of that dependence. God provides the gifts of nature anonymously (so to speak); but one cannot receive a gift of grace without knowing it, because grace involve God directly addressing, and being

---

exercise of his mind. If therefore the created mind were never to see the essence of God, either it would never attain happiness or its happiness would consist in something other than God. This is contrary to faith, for the ultimate perfection of the rational creature lies in that which is the source of its being." Thomas Aquinas, *Summa theologiae* (hereafter *ST*) 1.12.1, in Blackfriars ed., 61 vols. (London: Eyre & Spottiswood, 1964–81). Note that if the final clause is taken seriously, there is no reason for limiting the scope of this argument to rational creatures. Even if happiness is understood as an intellectual activity (and so not a possible goal for nonrational beings; see *ST* 1/2.3.4), it would still seem to follow that the perfection of every creature would consist in "rising" to God—though it would obviously be necessary to maintain a healthy dose of agnosticism about what this would mean for the nonhuman realm.

2. As Thomas Aquinas puts it, "The function of providence is to arrange things to an end" (*ST* 1.23.1). The further specification of providence as the doctrine of God's provision for creaturely flourishing *in the face of evil* is illustrated not only by Joseph's laconic observation to his brothers (Gen. 50:20), but also by the story of Abraham and Isaac on Mount Moriah. With Isaac seemingly about to be slain, there seems no possibility that Abraham's descendants will flourish as God has promised, and yet (in line with Abraham's own prediction in Gen. 22:8), the story concludes with God providing a ram in Isaac's place, "So Abraham called that place 'The LORD will provide'; as it is said to this day, 'On the mount of the LORD it shall be provided" (Gen. 22:14).

3. To claim that a capacity belongs to a particular nature is not to claim that it is possessed by every creature with that nature: there are human beings who cannot walk, who are unable to speak, who are blind, and so forth, and such people are no less human for any of these reasons. Indeed, insofar as human nature is perfected—and thus fully revealed—only in glory, which includes the profound transformation of that described by Paul in 1 Cor. 15, it is a serious error to *define* human nature in terms of presently observed capacities.

4. Cf. the analogies offered in Augustine in his *The Literal Meaning of Genesis* 8.25–26, in Augustine, *On Genesis*, trans. Edmund Hill, OP, ed. John E. Rotelle, OSA (Hyde Park, NY: New City Press, 2002), 361–62.

acknowledged by, the recipient.[5] To put it in concrete terms, while an atheist's disregard of God is no impediment to her walking or talking, one cannot be an atheist and have faith in Jesus or be raised to glory.[6]

While there is ample space within Christian dogmatics to emphasize the distinction between nature and grace (most especially in connection with the doctrine of redemption, with its focus on the incarnation as an irruption of divine grace in history that is utterly discontinuous with the capacities of created nature), the doctrine of providence stresses the gracious character of created nature. After all, if creation from nothing means that God is the sole antecedent condition of creatures' existence, then God's bringing creatures into existence, sustaining them in being, and guiding their movements are equivalent in their common affirmation of the Creator's role as necessary, sufficient, active, free, and gracious cause on the one hand, and the creature's status as dependent, fragile, contingent, and utterly passive effect on the other. Nevertheless, it remains possible to differentiate among various aspects of creatures' dependence on God's providential care. For although all of God's providential activity originates completely and unconditionally in God, its impact on creatures can be analyzed in terms of several discrete processes. The old scholastic distinctions between God's conservatio (preservation), concursus (accompaniment), and gubernatio (direction) of creation helpfully name these processes and will provide the framework for this chapter's analysis of providence.[7]

CONSERVATIO AND THE PROBLEM OF OCCASIONALISM

Because creation refers to God's relation to what is not God, it includes the relationship of origination. But because the origin and end of creatures are not identical (because movement is characteristic of created being), the doctrine of

5. The language of address-and-acknowledgment again raises the question posed in note 1 above regarding the coherence of the idea that nonrational creatures might be glorified. And once again it seems to me that a healthy agnosticism is in order. Certainly we have no inkling as to what glory would mean for a fruit fly or a toadstool, but given how little we understand of what glory means for us, this point cannot be allowed to carry much weight—especially given that in Scripture the glorification of human existence is not separate from the promise of the renewal of the whole creation.

6. The point is not that the atheist is immune to grace, but simply that the faith by definition precludes atheism, so that anyone who comes to faith will by that very fact cease to be an atheist. Similarly, insofar as life in glory is precisely communion with God in Christ, it too is incompatible with atheism. In this sense, the question "Can someone be saved without faith in Jesus?" reflects a basic misunderstanding of the Christian meaning of salvation (as though one were to ask whether it is possible to construct a triangle with only two sides). At the same time, there is every reason to beware of a facile equation of "faith in Jesus" with membership in a specific church or subscription to a particular creed.

7. The threefold framework of conservatio, concursus, and gubernatio seems to have been introduced by Johann Friedrich König in his Theologia positiva acroamatica (Rostock, 1664). It was adopted by the Lutheran Johann Andreas Quenstedt and thereafter became a standard feature of Protestant scholasticism, though some Reformed writers continued with the older, twofold scheme, which did not include concursus as a separate category. See Charles M. Wood, The Question of Providence (Louisville, KY: Westminster John Knox Press, 2008), 27; cf. 78n10.

creation cannot be limited to origins. Yet while God's relating to what is not God includes matters of divine provision for creaturely well-being that are logically distinct from questions of origin, the idea of creation from nothing rules out any sort of sharp division between God's bringing creatures into existence on the one hand, and providing for their continued existence on the other. After all, if God is the only condition of creaturely existence, God's power is no less crucial to the sustaining of created being once it has been made than to the act of bringing it into existence in the first place. For this reason, it is both possible and necessary to describe the work of creation as continuous, so that (in the words of Thomas Aquinas, who in turn cites Augustine), "it would not be unfitting to say that, just as air is being illuminated by the sun as long as it is light, so is the creature being made by God as long as it has being."[8]

One difficulty with this idea of continuous creation (*creatio continua*), however, is that it can seem to qualify the reality of created being by raising the specter of occasionalism. A theory of causation given perhaps its most complete theoretical articulation by the seventeenth-century French philosopher-theologian Nicolas Malebranche, occasionalism teaches that all causal efficacy is properly ascribed to God alone. Therefore, when a creature appears to cause a particular effect (e.g., the earth pulling an apple from a tree, a bat striking a ball, water reviving a wilted plant), that appearance is an illusion; the putative creaturely cause in fact simply serves as the "occasion" for God's action, which is the sole necessary and sufficient cause of the observed effect. According to the occasionalist, to argue otherwise undermines the claim of total creaturely dependence on God demanded by the doctrine of creation from nothing. To be sure, one may allow (as Malebranche did) that God generally acts in a regular, predictable fashion, so that any given sequence of created effects may be open to the kind of law-like, mathematical descriptions provided by the natural sciences; but the occasionalist insists that when a person is asked to identify the cause of any given event, the only correct answer is "God." From this perspective creation is continuous in the very specific sense that it is not in any respect finished or complete (contrast Gen. 2:1–3). Instead, whatever exists at any instant of time does so because the Creator God has brought it into being in that instant.

In its insistence on the continuous and all-encompassing character of creation's dependence on God, occasionalism can be contrasted with deism, according to which the world, though created by God "in the beginning," thereafter subsists largely on its own, in much the same way that a table continues to exist independently of the carpenter who constructed it. For the deist, there is no reason to speak of continuous creation because once the world has been called

<hr/>

8. Thomas Aquinas, *Quaestiones disputatae de potentia Dei* 3.3.6, in *On Creation*, trans. S. C. Selner-Wright (Washington, DC: Catholic University of America Press, 2011), 22 (citing Augustine, *The Literal Interpretation of Genesis* 8.26). Cf. Bernhard W. Anderson, *From Creation to New Creation: Old Testament Perspectives* (Minneapolis: Fortress Press, 1994), 89: "Creation is not just an event that occurred in the beginning, at the foundation of the earth, but is God's continuing activity of sustaining creatures and holding everything in being."

into being, it stays in existence on its own. Given belief in creation from nothing, occasionalism seems preferable to deism, since the deist position is built on a false analogy with human ways of making. The table is able to subsist apart from any carpenter because the material of which it is made preexists (and thus is ontologically independent of) the craftsperson, but creation from nothing is founded on the explicit rejection of the idea that matter exists prior to or apart from God.[9] Deism thus fails to honor divine transcendence.

Further consideration, however, shows that occasionalism, too, is based on an assimilation of divine to creaturely activity that fails to respect God's transcendence. Occasionalism is correct insofar as it entails the rejection of the claim that created being has any "ontological inertia"—that is, insofar as it denies that any creature has the intrinsic capacity to continue in existence on its own, apart from God. For it is indeed an implication of the doctrine of creation from nothing that the existence of anything other than God is at every point in its existence dependent for its existence on the activity of the Creator. That dependence, however, does not mean that the persistence of individual creatures over time is an illusion, as though the doctrine of creation ex nihilo entailed the continuous re-creation of the world at every moment. It is perfectly consistent with creation from nothing to allow that the Creator endows creatures with certain properties, including the capacity to subsist over time. That creatures should be able to exhibit these properties is at every moment due to God's creative power rather than to any inherent capacity of created being as such—but that does not make such properties any less real. In other words, God *might* have chosen to make the sort of world the occasionalist imagines, but God is not *required* to do so as a condition of creation from nothing, as the occasionalist believes. Ironically, the occasionalist ends up limiting divine power no less than does the deist by failing to acknowledge that God's power includes the capacity to create beings with their own causal efficacy. As a result, occasionalism, like deism, winds up identifying creation with origination, though "origination" is no longer restricted to a single event "in the beginning" but turns out to be a permanent state of affairs. Interpreted within an occasionalist framework, continuous creation is equivalent perpetual re-creation that leaves no space for the belief that creatures are or indeed can be preserved.

The doctrine of divine preservation (*conservatio*) amounts to a denial that the alternatives of deism and occasionalism exhaust the possibilities for thinking about God's way of relating to the world. For deism, preservation is superfluous (since creatures, once brought into being, subsist by their own ontological

9. "Divine preservation is an act not merely *negative or indirect*, for it does not consist in the fact that God does not wish to destroy or annihilate the things He has framed, but to leave to them their strength, so long as they can flourish from the energy given to them by creation; but it is a *positive and direct act*, by which God . . . enters in a general way into the efficient causes of the objects that are to be preserved, so that . . . they continue and remain." David Hollaz, *Examen theologicum acroamaticum* (Stargard, 1707), 441; cited in Heinrich Schmid, *Doctrinal Theology of the Evangelical Lutheran Church*, trans. Charles A. Hay and Henry E. Jacobs, 3rd ed. (Minneapolis, MN: Augsburg Publishing House, 1899), 179.

inertia); for occasionalism, preservation is impossible (since the subsistence of creatures over time is inconsistent with God's status as sole cause). The possibility of a third option can be explored by reexamining Thomas's analogy between God's preserving creatures and the way in which the continuous shining of a light source is necessary to keep air illuminated. This analogy is clearly opposed the deist idea of creatures being able to subsist on their own apart from the ongoing commitment and activity of God, but it also counters the occasionalist vision of discrete acts of re-creation by depicting preservation as both continuous with and distinct from origination (since it is possible to distinguish the ongoing illumination of the air from the moment that it is first illumined). And in distinction from both deist and occasionalist models, preservation is not merely the sustaining of the status quo (whether by the deist's God's passive letting be or by occasionalist's God's repetition of previous creative acts), but a productive act that continues and extends the work by which God brings creatures into being.

In short, preservation is that dimension of providence through which God provides for creatures by actively sustaining their existence. With its evocation of the opening chapters of Genesis and John, Maximus the Confessor's image of creatures as distinct *logoi* spoken through (and as partial reflections of) the one divine *Logos* can be helpful here.[10] According to this model, a creature comes to be when God speaks its *logos* (cf. Ps. 33:9), but there is no reason to understand this work—whether in relation to any existing creature or to creation as a whole—as an event located exclusively in the past. Instead, if a creature is the effect of a divinely uttered *logos*, one may posit that it subsists so long as that *logos* continues to be spoken. In this context, it is useful to remember that *logos* can mean not only "word" but also "statement" or even "discourse," and thus *logos* can maintain a distinct identity even when it assumes temporally extended form. Consider a clearly defined piece of discourse like the Gettysburg Address. It begins, "Four score and seven years ago . . ." (so that with the speaking of these syllables, one can truly say, "That's the Gettysburg Address"), and remains through the final, ". . . shall not perish from the earth." Although 272 words are uttered, it is just one thing, the Gettysburg Address, that is spoken throughout. So by analogy any creature may be conceived as a *logos* that is brought into being ("created") at a particular time yet continues (and so is "preserved") so long as God continues speaking it.

This analogy has two merits. First, it maintains a clear distinction between creation and preservation: just as to begin a discourse is not the same thing as to continue it, so God's bringing a creature into being is not the same as God's keeping it in being. Admittedly, God is producing the creature both in creating and in preserving it; moreover, the work of preservation is just

10. See pp. 81–83 above. Maximus tends to identify a creature's *logos* with its nature or essence, but there seems to be no conceptual barrier to understanding each individual creature as having its own distinct *logos*, even as the medieval theologian John Duns Scotus invoked the idea of *haecceitas* ("thisness") to ascribe to every entity something like an individual nature.

the continuation of the work of creation. It is not as though the difference between creation and preservation means that God stops doing one thing and undertakes something different, as in the transition a human being might make from, say, playing the piano to mopping the floor, or even between more naturally related activities like baking and eating a cake. Nor is it a case of repeating the same action, as in the occasionalist account of the appearance of creatures' persistence over time. Although God is doing the same thing in creating and preserving (viz., producing a creature), there remains a real difference between the two based on the perspective from which it is seen (viz., whether as the act of originating a creature's being or of maintaining in existence the being of a creature already originated).

The second merit of interpreting the relationship between origination and preservation in this way is that it depicts them as sequential aspects of a single divine project: the flourishing of creatures. This project is rooted in God's own Trinitarian being. God is the flourishing of diverse persons within the divine life eternally, and God wills the flourishing of nondivine beings in time, so that the subsistence of created *logoi* is an external reflection of the subsistence of the Father's *Logos* in the power of the Spirit. Whereas perfection is intrinsic to the divine life, however, the finitude of created being is such that creaturely perfection must be acquired and is in fact threatened by evil. God's ongoing provision is therefore necessary to enable created beings to resist the corrosive power of evil in the course of their movement toward perfection. Preservation is the first dimension of such provision: in order that evil should not subvert God's will that beings other than God should subsist, it is necessary that creatures already brought into being should continue in being.

The duration of God's preserving activity is variable. Some creatures' existence is very brief (the life span of some adult mayflies is less than an hour), others endure for millennia (the bristlecone pine, for example), and angels are held to subsist eternally once brought into being. This inequality across creaturely types poses no theological difficulties in itself: it is no more surprising that creatures, all good in themselves, should differ in duration than that they should differ in physical dimensions like height or weight. Even within a given species, variations in duration are in principle no more problematic than other individuating features. Questions do arise, however, in the face of the fact that the vast majority of terrestrial organisms do not live to adulthood, and still fewer die "old and full of days." And the difficulties become only more pronounced in light of the disparities in the quality of preservation from individual to individual, such that some have an abundance of resources available to enhance their existence, while others' days are marked by pain and want.

There are no easy answers to these questions. It is possible to redescribe the facts in a way that highlights divine generosity rather than creaturely transience. For example, arguing that it is part of the peculiar goodness of the dandelion that it should put forth hundreds of seeds, or of the octopus that it produces tens of thousands of eggs, places the focus on God's provision for the species rather than for the individual.[11] But there are limits to this strategy, since the flourishing of the population is no remedy for the death of the individual. Interpreting *conservatio* as God's continued production of every creature therefore does not explain how any particular creature's failure to flourish is consistent with God's will for the flourishing of all. The evident vulnerability of all creatures to destruction does, however, bring into relief their common and absolute dependence on God in order to exist. In this way, the doctrine of creation from nothing serves as a reminder that it is not "natural" (in the sense of being automatic or inevitable) that creatures, once made, should continue in being. That they do so is the result of God's will that they should flourish, of which their continued existence is a necessary condition. Creatures' preservation, no less than their creation, is thus a matter of grace.[12]

CONCURSUS AND THE PROBLEM OF DETERMINISM

In his book on the doctrine of providence, Charles Wood rightly argues that *conservatio*, *concursus*, and *gubernatio* are properly conceived as simultaneously enacted dimensions of God's single work of provision rather than as three separate and sequential activities.[13] Failure to honor this principle has especially pernicious effects on theologies of *concursus*, which, when separated from *conservatio*, can easily give rise to the false image of God as a puppeteer who first produces creatures and then manipulates them so that they do one thing rather than another. But *concursus* is not a distinct act subsequent to the work of preservation; it is simply a means of highlighting that God's ongoing production of creatures includes their *activity*. Because God creates from nothing, sustaining

11. In this context, even species appear to have life spans that vary across taxa (so that, e.g., Cenozoic bivalve species survive for around ten million years, but Cenozoic mammalian species only one or two million years); but because species are characterized by morphological stasis (which is what defines them as species in the first place), these life spans are not marked by anything corresponding to the development of individual organisms from juvenile to adult forms. See David Raup and Steven M. Stanley, *Principles of Paleontology*, 2nd ed. (New York: W. H. Freeman, 1978), 318.

12. Lest this invocation of *conservatio* as divine grace be thought to license human indifference to the fate of other creatures, we add that insofar as human beings acknowledge *both* God's will that all creatures flourish *and* their own power to affect the conditions necessary for such flourishing, they bear the responsibility to do all they can to ensure the preservation of their fellow creatures under God (Gen. 2:15; Prov. 12:10). This does not imply a leveling of moral distinctions among creatures (e.g., affirming that the same efforts should be made on behalf of the malaria-causing protozoan *Plasmodium* as a human person). As explained in the preceding chapter, the conditions of material finitude preclude the possibility of *all* creatures flourishing simultaneously, so decisions giving preference to some creatures over others are unavoidable; but that still leaves room for a considerable degree of mutual coexistence benefiting a broad range of organisms: "We seek to ensure that every [human] person . . . has a roughly similar chance to live the life of her choosing, in company with others having a like chance. . . . The same system can be imagined for wider egalitarians: we should seek to act according to rules that allow all sorts of creatures a fair chance of living a life of their choosing." Stephen Clark, *How to Think about the Earth: Philosophical and Theological Models for Ecology* (London: Mowbray, 1993), 115; cited in Ruth Page, *God and the Web of Creation* (London: SCM Press, 1996), 145–46.

13. Wood, *Question of Providence*, 80.

creatures in being is not limited to maintaining their physical integrity: it also includes giving them movement. In short, that creatures *act* is every bit as much a product of God's direct and immediate willing as the fact that they *are*.[14]

Concursus is normally translated "concurrence" or (slightly less obscurely) "accompaniment." While the Latin word does literally mean "running together," nothing could be more misleading than imagining the divine *concursus* on the model of a parent running alongside a child taking her first turn on a bicycle, as though creaturely action were basically autonomous, with God merely over-seeing (and perhaps occasionally interfering with) creaturely efforts to accomplish particular ends. Within the context of creation from nothing, terms like "enabling" or "empowerment" better capture what God is doing in *concursus*, and yet such language raises questions of its own by stressing God's activity to such a degree that creatures no longer seem the true subjects of their actions. In this way, much as *conservatio* can seem to imply an occasionalism that denies creatures' genuine being, so *concursus* raises the specter of a determinism in which creatures lack any proper agency.

This specter draws its plausibility from an assumption of what may be called metaphysical continuity between God and creatures, meaning that both operate on the same metaphysical plane, even if God is understood to do so from a position of vastly greater knowledge and power than any other entity. Within such a framework, to describe x as the cause of a particular effect e is necessarily to qualify the degree to which y may also be named as e's cause. Specifically, where x is the cause of e, then either y is not the cause of e, or x and y are each only par-tial causes of e. Thus, where metaphysical continuity between Creator and crea-ture is affirmed, to name a creature as the cause of a particular effect (whether this cause is a physical principle like the electromagnetic charge of an electron or the free will of a human being) excludes characterizing God as its cause, except in the indirect sense that God is responsible for establishing the order of nature within which such created causes operate. In short, the positing of metaphysi-cal continuity between God and the world means that in order for creatures to be genuinely active as the cause of an effect, the Creator must in some degree refrain from acting as the cause of that effect.[15] It follows that divine *concursus* can be affirmed only (if at all) in an attenuated sense.

14. "One ought not to say of any creature that it acts with absolute independence, lest we intro-duce the senseless notion of an uncaused something apart from God; but, that it is naturally ener-gized to do what as energized its nature is capable of doing." Maximus the Confessor, *Ambiguum* 15, in PG 91:1221A–B; cited in Maximus the Confessor, *The Ascetic Life; The Four Centuries on Charity*, trans. Polycarp Sherwood (New York: Newman Press, 1955), 47.

15. Importantly, *metaphysical* continuity between divine and creaturely action does not imply (though it can include) *ontological* continuity between divine and created being (i.e., qualification of God's ontological distinctiveness over against creatures as, say, eternal and necessary versus temporal and contingent). Metaphysical continuity is simply a corollary of the conviction that in accounting for any created effect, the word "cause" must be used univocally, and that God must, correspond-ingly, be understood as one cause among others when accounting for such effects. Thus even propo-nents of process thought, who insist on affirming metaphysical continuity between God and other

In contrast to models of God's relationship to the world predicated on meta-physical continuity, Thomas Aquinas understood God's ontological unique-ness to imply metaphysical *discontinuity* between God and all that is not God. This discontinuity follows from a refusal to allow that any attribute (including "cause") can be predicated univocally of God and creatures. In line with the doctrine of creation from nothing, Thomas argues that the all-encompassing character of God's agency as Creator (viz., the sole antecedent condition of every aspect of every creature's existence) demands that divine causing be distin-guished sharply from the operation of created causes. A machine may continue to run long after its inventor has quit the scene. But the relationship between God and the world is such that (in line with Jesus' words in John 15:5) the crea-ture can do nothing without the Creator:

> God is the cause of the actions of all things inasmuch as he gives them power to act and preserves them and applies them to action and inasmuch as by his power every other power acts. And when we add that God is his own power and that he is within each thing, not as part of its essence, but as holding the thing in being, it follows that he operates immediately in every operation, without excluding the operation of the will and nature.[16]

In short, God is the power that enables every creature to undertake whatever actions—eating, growing, knowing, willing, and so forth—define it as the kind of entity it is. As such, God is the *immediate* (or in the language of Aristotle, "primary") cause of all creaturely being and doing, so that the whole creation may be considered as a single, complex *effect* of that cause.

At this point it may appear that our initial suspicion that *concursus* evacuates creatures of any agency of their own has been confirmed, but this conclusion can be forestalled by taking seriously the claim that creation, though rightly regarded as a single effect of God's creative activity, is complex. Thomas highlights this complexity when he insists (in the above quotation) that God's immediate activ-ity in every created event does not exclude "the operation of the will and nature" of creatures. Although creation is at every point preserved and empowered in its existence by God, it also includes within itself subsidiary relationships of cause and effect: one billiard ball causes another to move by striking against it, the sun's shining causes a flower to turn its face in a particular direction, one human being causes another to write a letter by making a suggestion. In other words, among the many created effects brought into being by God, some are *also* causes of other created effects. While God, as primary cause, is the immediate cause of *all* created effects, in some cases God brings a particular created effect about through the actions of one or more creatures, which are thereby constituted as created (or "secondary") causes of that effect. In cases where such secondary

---

entities, defend God's ontological distinctiveness (e.g., by affirming that for God, in contrast to all other entities, the "mental pole" is ontologically prior to the "physical pole").

16. Aquinas, *De potentia Dei* 3.7, in *On Creation*, 64.

causes are operative, a created effect (e.g., an apple's falling to the ground) may with equal justice be ascribed to God as primary cause or to the operative secondary cause (viz., the force of gravity, in the case of the falling apple).

This account of the relationship between divine and created causation is precisely that elaborated in classical accounts of divine *concursus*. The language of the Lutheran Johann Quenstedt is typical:

> God not only gives and preserves to second causes the power to act, but immediately influences the action and effect of the creature, so that the same effect is produced not by God alone, nor by the creature alone, nor partly by God and partly by the creature, but *at the same time by God and the creature*, as one and the same total efficiency, viz., by God as the universal and first cause, and by the creature as the particular and second cause.[17]

The possibility of naming either God or a creature as the cause of a natural phenomenon is, again, a function of the metaphysical discontinuity between Creator and creation. The possibility of explaining created effects in terms either of primary or of secondary causes reflects the claim that these two types of cause operate on different metaphysical levels, such that each provides a completely adequate causal explanation of the effect on its respective level. For example, viewed from *within* the realm of creation, the apple's fall is fully accounted for by reference to gravity; reference to God is not necessary to complete the explanation. But neither does reference to God displace explanation in terms of a natural cause like gravitational attraction. Instead, ascribing the apple's fall to God represents an equally true account, but on the level of primary causation. In short, to say that gravity caused the fall is not to exclude God; neither does referring the fall to divine action exclude the operation of gravity. One might draw a comparison here with explanation of action in a drama. If asked, "Why did Duncan die?," it would be equally correct to answer, "Because Shakespeare so willed it" (at the level of primary cause), or (at the level of secondary causes), "Because Macbeth murdered him." Neither response is in competition with the other, and each is entirely sufficient within its sphere. To attribute Duncan's death to Shakespeare is not in any sense to qualify or undermine Macbeth's responsibility for his actions; it is simply to make the obvious point that the being and actions of Macbeth are entirely dependent on Shakespeare. The

---

17. Johann Andreas Quenstedt, *Theologia didactico-polemica* (Wittenberg, 1685) 1.531; cited in Schmid, *Doctrinal Theology*, 180. This perspective is often described by using Austin Farrer's phrase "double agency" (see his *Faith and Speculation* [London: A&C Black, 1967]), but Wood argues that the idea of double agency is incoherent since "act description is at least implicitly always 'agent-involving,'" such that "your act of x-ing (singing, say) cannot simultaneously be my act of x-ing" (Wood, *Question of Providence*, 85–86). Because (except in the case of Jesus) Christians do not want to argue that agency with respect to any creaturely occurrence can be ascribed indifferently to God as primary cause or a creature as secondary cause (e.g., "I put on my glasses" cannot be rephrased as "God put on my glasses"), I think that Wood is correct to commend Quenstedt's language of God and creatures as causing the same *effect* rather than of performing the same *act*.

playwright is the (primary) cause on account of which Duncan perished; but he produces this effect through the (secondary or "created") cause of Macbeth.[18]

Applied to the topic of divine action in nature, a model of *concursus* working from the postulate of metaphysical discontinuity between God and the world provides a means of accounting for worldly phenomena that avoids any suggestion of competition between divine and created causes. Where God and creatures are seen as operating on different planes, affirming that a particular effect has a created cause neither excludes God's acting as cause nor casts God's activity as indirect (e.g., as nothing more than that of an agent who established the relevant law in the first place and ensures its stability over time). Furthermore, *concursus* makes it possible to affirm a range of secondary causes within creation, since there is no inherent limitation on the types of secondary causes God might produce, any more than there is any intrinsic limit on the range of different creatures God should bring into being. At least three different kinds of created effects may be identified here: those that are the products of impersonal physical forces, those that are the product of free decisions, and those that are matters of chance.[19]

Created effects produced by impersonal physical causes—an apple falling (not rising) from a tree, a lion giving birth to a cub (not a foal), water boiling (not freezing) when put over a fire—are associated with the operation of what are usually described as "natural laws." The latter phrase is metaphorical, and there is considerable debate within the philosophy of science over how the processes so named should be understood. By no means do all agree that "natural laws" describe the ontological determination of one state of affairs by another.[20] Despite such differences in interpretation, however, modern science rests on the confidence that all worldly events are patient of analysis in terms of lawlike interactions among their component parts. Specifically (and allowing for

---

18. The *appropriateness* of either response will vary with context: answering the question on the level of primary causation will not win high marks in a class on English literature, just as referring to the causative agency of God for falling apples will be deemed inappropriate when one is talking physics. Yet in each case the problem is not that the proffered explanation is false, but that it does not speak to the metaphysical level in terms of which the question was posed.

19. Cf. the tripartite division of created effects given in the Westminster Confession 5.2: "Although, in relation to the foreknowledge and decree of God, the first cause, all things come to pass immutably, and infallibly; yet, by the same providence, He ordereth them to fall out according to the nature of second causes, either necessarily, freely, or contingently" (Presbyterian Church (U.S.A.), *Book of Confessions: Study Edition* [Louisville, KY: Geneva Press, 1996], 179). We see two differences between the language of the Westminster divines and the present study: First, to say that something happens because of the operation of a physical cause should not without qualification be equated with its happening necessarily, since (as reported below) the necessitarian character of physical laws is a matter of ongoing debate within the philosophy of science. Second (also discussed further below), the Confession's "contingently" is not the equivalent of "chance" since the Westminster divines understood contingent events as the product of secondary causes rather than as evidence of their absence.

20. Instrumental interpretations, e.g., view natural laws as human conventions for categorizing the observed relations between natural phenomena in a maximally efficient manner. For a nice summary of the major alternatives in contemporary philosophy of science, see Nicholas Saunders, *Divine Action and Modern Science* (Cambridge: Cambridge University Press, 2002), 60–72.

variations in particulars across different subdisciplines), any physical system is capable of being described in mathematical terms (e.g., measurements of masses and forces at a specified point in time) that allow for the accurate prediction of its future states.[21] Even where the "laws" of nature are understood to be irreducibly probabilistic in character (so that a system's state at any given future time cannot be described exhaustively based on the present configuration of a system, but only a range of possible states with varying probabilities of being actualized), the twin criteria of quantifiability and predictability remain decisive for scientific explanation. Theologically, this class of created effects may be understood as the product of created causes that are intrinsic to material bodies and, as such, operate both automatically and with calculable regularity.

By contrast, created effects that fall in the second category—those produced through the free acts of conscious beings—are not open to calculation in this way. This does not mean that they are random, since one may predict with a very high degree of confidence that (e.g.) an honest person will tell the truth. But to affirm human freedom is to deny that a person's actions, however regular, are as automatic as the evaporation of water on a sunny day or the movements an animal acting by instinct.[22] Instead, to be free is to be responsible for one's actions, such that an adequate account of the effects one brings about necessarily includes reference to one's own agency.[23] For any deed I do, however much I may have been tempted or threatened or persuaded or put off or attracted or repulsed by outside factors, it remains true that *I* did it. This is not to say that free acts are ultimately inexplicable. Belief in my own freedom is perfectly consistent with offering an explanation of why I willed one course of action over another (e.g., "I wanted to impress my peers," "I was afraid I would be killed

21. This idealized account is much more directly applicable in physics, chemistry, and microbiology, where it is comparatively easy to establish conditions that allow for the repetition and testing of results, than in disciplines like astronomy, geology, or evolutionary biology, which deal with phenomena on scales of time and space that make controlled experimentation impossible. Nevertheless, quantification and predictability remain touchstones of these sciences as well, so that (e.g.) arguments between proponents of phyletic gradualism and punctuated equilibrium in evolutionary biology turn on statistical analyses of the changes in the physical dimensions of fossil species over time (quantification), in which the discovery of new fossils may either confirm or refute a particular account (predictability). While particular judgments about the viability of any particular theory are complex and rarely (if ever) decided by a single observation, both philosophers and practitioners of science still broadly agree that a theory not making empirically testable predictions is vacuous.

22. Materialists deny that there is such a thing as freedom in this sense. They hold that all effects, including those produced by conscious beings, are caused by the operation of natural laws, the operation of which in principle is subject to calculation. There are significant problems with this position (not the least of which is the apparent inconsistency involved in attempting to defend it through argument), but my aim here is not to defend the reality of freedom, but only to show that it is consistent with the principle of divine *concursus*.

23. Perhaps the most radical formulation of this principle is Maximus the Confessor's insistence that "nothing natural is involuntary in a rational nature" (see his *Disputatio cum Pyrrho*, in PG 91:296A). Maximus's point is not that all our actions are matters of choice (e.g., we do not choose to be hungry or to sweat), but that they are all part of who we are (*I* am the one who is hungry or sweats). For a nuanced discussion of the varying degrees to which human action may be considered voluntary, see Austin Farrer, *The Freedom of the Will* (New York: Charles Scribner's Sons, 1958), 109–15.

otherwise," "I was dissuaded by the following arguments," etc.); the point is simply that the free person will not claim that any such account displaces her agency. If I lie, I may offer a complex and morally compelling explanation for so doing, even arguing that it was impossible for me to have done otherwise under the circumstances—yet the lie remains something that *I* did and not something that happened apart from my willing it.

At first glance this account of freedom seems inconsistent with the idea that God is the primary (and thus direct) cause of every creaturely effect. Christians tend not to be discomfited by the claim that God caused the apple to fall or the lion to give birth to the cub, even while acknowledging that these same phenomena can be explained in terms of the operation of secondary causes in the form of natural laws. By contrast, the claim that God causes me to eat or to walk or to write a book seems much more problematic, because by ascribing direct causal efficacy to God, I appear to be qualifying my own responsibility in a way inconsistent with the affirmation of my freedom. In the face of this worry, it is necessary once again to follow the logic of divine transcendence. Affirming that God is the cause even of my own free acts is not a contradiction so long as one attends to the distinction between primary and secondary causation. For God to create free beings does not make God any less the Creator, and to be Creator is to be the primary (and thus immediate) cause of every created effect, including the acts of free creatures. But affirming God's role as primary cause does not make free actions unfree, any more than the assertion that God (as primary cause) made the apple to fall entails a denial of gravity. No inconsistency is involved in affirming that both sorts of events are equally dependent on God's will, just as there is no inconsistency in affirming that within a play certain effects (e.g., the wounded Duncan's bleeding to death) may be attributed to natural law, and others (e.g., Macbeth's decision to wound him) may be attributed to the free action of the characters, even though from the perspective of primary causation both are equally the decision of the playwright (who might just as easily have decided that Duncan's wounds miraculously heal, or that Macbeth resist the temptation of regicide).[24] In this way the doctrine of divine *concursus* serves as a reminder that freedom does not imply the creature's independence from God, but is rather a particular form of creaturely dependence on God (1 Cor. 15:10; cf. Gal. 2:20): God is the author and ground of freedom, just as God is the author and ground of natural laws.

24. In this context, John Polkinghorne's objection that the analogy between God's activity and that of an author or dramatist reduces the former to "the exercise of a naked power of disposal which seems to bear little relationship to the subtle relationships of God to a world to which he has given a large measure of creaturely freedom" (in his *Science and Providence: God's Interaction with the World* [1989], Templeton ed. [Philadelphia: Templeton Foundation Press, 2005], 16) seems peculiarly out of place. In a poor novel or play, the action can undoubtedly seem to be forced or artificial; yet surely one mark of great literature is that the development of the plot does *not* come across as an "exercise of naked power," but is rather characterized by just the sort of subtlety and respect for the integrity of the setting and characters that Polkinghorne ascribes to God's dealings with the world. Is there any reason to doubt that what is possible for a human author can be achieved to an infinitely greater degree by the Trinity?

In this way, worries over the consistency of crediting God's role as Creator alongside recognizing human freedom can be averted if one is careful to differentiate between the claim that God is *primary* cause of all created effects and the very different assertion (characteristic of theological occasionalism) that God is their *only* cause. Again, the distinction between primary and secondary causation secures this point by reminding us that the word "cause" cannot be applied univocally to Creator and creatures. Because God does not cause an effect in the same way that a creature does (since it is only as God wills it that a creature *can* cause an effect), there is nothing logically problematic about affirming that the apple falling and the person choosing to go for a walk are both equally produced by God (as primary cause), while also insisting that the former is the product of purely physical forces and the latter of free will (on the level of secondary cause). So it is part of the diversity of creation that God wills not only a variety of creatures, but also a variety of ways in which those creatures affect one another.

Having made this point, it may seem perverse to define the third category of created effects as precisely those that have no created cause and for which, therefore, God *is* the sole cause. To understand this possibility, recall that to speak of God as primary cause is simply to make a logical point about divine transcendence: as Creator, God by definition is the immediate cause of *every* created effect, analogously to the way in which Shakespeare, as author, is the immediate cause of every effect in *Macbeth*. As primary cause, God may (and, if our everyday experience is any guide, generally does) make use of created causes as means to bring about particular effects in the world, but there is no necessity for God to do so.[25] God, as Creator, is free to bring about particular created effects without the mediation of a secondary cause. When God does so, it follows that the effect in question has only a primary cause. Importantly, however, it is no *more true* to say, "God caused this event," in such cases than in the most routine examples of the operation of the laws of motion drawn from an elementary physics textbook. The claim that God causes an event without making use of a secondary cause does not imply any quantitative increase in divine involvement over events in which God does make use of a secondary cause, since divine involvement is always already at the maximum in a world created from nothing. The significance of created effects that lack a secondary cause is rather that *within the causal context of the created order* (i.e., the totality of natural, physical causes and the free actions of creatures), they have no identifiable "cause" at all. Scientifically speaking, they are uncaused.

What kind of created effect lacks a secondary cause? One category that has become significant in modern science is the truly random event. Such events are matters of chance in the strict sense: not simply because a created cause cannot be readily identified for them, but also because, according to the best scientific

---

25. Here too, the analogy with the dramatist holds: Shakespeare uses a mix of character and circumstance to bring about specific events in his plays, so that it is Macbeth who kills Duncan, and not the unmediated action of the dramatist intervening on the stage as a deus ex machina.

judgment, no such cause exists.[26] This definition excludes numerous phenomena colloquially described as "chance" or "random" occurrences. In a coin toss, for example, physical factors—in themselves well understood and in principle subject to precise mathematical description (viz., the dimensions of the coin, the linear and angular momentum imparted to it when flipped, the contours of the surface on which it lands, etc.)—determine whether the result is heads or tails. Similarly, the intersection of independent causal chains (e.g., a ball hit out of the park that strikes the hood of a passing car) is not truly a "chance" event if each of the chains is itself subject to the kind of mathematical description that would make it possible in principle to predict it. By contrast, when physicists describe the radioactive decay of a particular atom, or say the position and momentum of a specific electron are "random," they are claiming (at least according to the majority interpretation) that it is, strictly speaking, uncaused, so that our lack of an ability to identify a cause is not simply a matter of (perhaps insuperable) limits on our knowledge of antecedent physical conditions, but a feature of the natural order itself.

As with the idea of creaturely freedom, the genuine indeterminacy of quantum events like radioactive decay is not a matter of scientific consensus. If sustained, however, it does mean an enrichment of our understanding of divine *concursus*. If quantum indeterminacy should indeed prove theoretically irreducible, it follows that God has determined that some created effects should arise through the free decisions of created agents, others through the law-like operation of physical forces, and others without any created cause ("randomly"). All three processes are equally dependent upon God's omnipresent activity, but although they are in this way *theologically* reducible to their single divine source, they are *theoretically* irreducible to any one overarching scientific account. Part of the upshot is that we have no way of conceiving what it means for *any* of them to be effected by God as primary cause, since our experience and understanding are limited to the level of created causes: for us a free action is caused by a created will, a physical law of the properties intrinsic to certain creatures (e.g., mass, charge, etc.), while a truly random event is uncaused. To invoke God as primary cause in any of these cases neither adds to nor detracts from our experience of their (created) character as a free, physically calculable, or chance events. The insistence that God is also active in them is an implication of the Christian

---

26. Some define miracles in these terms (viz., as created effects that lack a created cause; see, e.g., Quenstedt, *Theologia didactico-polemica* 1.535; cited in Schmid, *Doctrinal Theology*, 193), but this is not a matter of consensus. Although, e.g., the process of establishing the authenticity of miracles in the Catholic procedure for canonizing saints requires that no natural cause can be identified for an effect of which the saint's intercession is claimed as the (miraculous) cause, the use of this epistemic criterion does not necessarily imply that a miracle is defined ontologically by the lack of a secondary cause. In this context, the discussion of miracles in the Catechism of the Catholic Church focuses entirely on their communicative significance in eliciting and strengthening faith and not on their metaphysical status (see Catholic Church, *Catechism of the Catholic Church*, 2nd ed. [New York: Doubleday, 1997], §§156, 515, 547–49, 1335).

confession of creation from nothing, not the conclusion of empirical investigation of events.

Einstein's famous claim that God does not play dice with the universe can help to clarify this metaphysical discontinuity between God's activity as primary cause and the various forms of secondary causation observed in the world.[27] From the perspective of the doctrine of *concursus*, the validity of Einstein's claim depends on whether it is interpreted in terms of a claim about primary or secondary causation. Considered *within the context of secondary causes*, it should be no more shocking that God "plays dice with the universe" (i.e., make the universe such that some created effects have no created cause) than that God should give some creatures freedom, or that God should determine that other events be subject to the predictable course of natural law. But when created effects are considered *from the perspective of God* as primary cause, they cannot be "random"—or "free" or "necessary"—since these adjectives imply a degree of ontological independence that cannot hold between any created reality and God, since according to the doctrine of creation from nothing, all created effects are the product of divine willing. Nor does this conclusion imply a limitation on divine power, as though it would constitute an enhancement of divine capabilities if God could, for example, make an event that were truly random even with respect to God's self (and thus in some sense independent of God's creative activity and intentions). It is just part of the logic of creation from nothing that God can't do anything behind God's back. As Scripture itself puts it, "The lot is cast into the lap, but the decision is the LORD's" (Prov. 16:33).[28]

Yet the fact that no created effect is random, free, or necessary *for God* does not mean that the difference between chance, freedom, and necessity are any less significant *for us* as genuine features of our experience of the world. Here again, the literary analogy holds: a character in a novel becomes sick after drinking too much; she devotes her life to the care of the sick; she dies when struck by a stray bullet while serving in a war zone. We can willingly acknowledge that each an event is equally—and entirely—the product of the author's will without that in any way impeding our ability to recognize, as we read the book, that there is a world of difference between the chain of physical causation by which alcohol makes the character ill, the freedom with which she chooses her career, and the chance character of her death. In the same way, there is no theological difficulty in affirming that natural law, creaturely freedom, and uncaused events

27. "God does not play dice with the universe" paraphrases a sentence from Einstein's letter of December 4, 1926, to Max Born. In it he wrote, "Quantum mechanics is certainly imposing. But an inner voice tells me that it is not yet the real thing. The theory says a lot. But it does not really bring us any closer to the secrets of the 'old one.' I, at any rate, am convinced that He is not playing at dice." Albert Einstein and Max Born, *The Born-Einstein Letters*, trans. Irene Born (New York: Macmillan., 1971), 91.

28. "*Fortune*, which is an accidental event, accompanying a result intended by a cause acting freely, does not exist with respect to the omniscient and most wise God (Wis. 14:3), but only with respect to ignorant man." Hollaz, *Examen theologicum acroamaticum*, 440; cited in Schmid, *Doctrinal Theology*, 189.

are genuine and irreducible aspects of the mystery of creation—and thus recognizing that God, already infinitely rich in God's self, can bring into existence a reality other than God, with its own richness.

GUBERNATIO AND THE PROBLEM OF MELIORISM

Gubernatio, or God's directing of creation to its proper end, is a corollary of the other two dimensions of God's provision for creatures. Through *conservatio* God maintains creatures in their diverse forms of being, and by *concursus* God causes their diverse forms of activity. For example, God sustains human beings in existence (*conservatio*) as creatures that act freely (*concursus*). In so doing, God acts, and an act—the product of agency—implies a purpose or goal: I run to catch the bus, sleep so that I might be refreshed, or make a promise in order to assure a friend.[29] So, too, to speak of God's providing for creatures entails some end, and *gubernatio* characterizes the divine work of provision in terms of its end.[30] How then is God's end in creating to be characterized?

In contrast to the acts of creatures, the end of God's acts in creation do not fill any lack in the agent, since whatever emerges from creation has its immediate cause in God and thus can add nothing to what God already is. Thus when we say (paraphrasing the language of the Westminster Shorter Catechism) that the end of creation is to glorify God, the point is not to suggest that creation augments God's glory in any way, since whatever glory creation might give to God comes from God in the first place. What is distinctive about creation is the *way* in which it displays God's glory. God is already, eternally, and unsurpassably glorious in the threefold act of giving that constitutes God's life as Trinity; but in creation God's glory is manifest outside of God's own life in an act of divine giving that brings into existence myriad beings that are not God. And if God's purpose in creating is in this way simply that creatures should be as the creatures God intends them to be, then *gubernatio* can be understood as the activity by which God brings it about that creatures flourish.

Because movement is a defining feature of created being, creaturely flourishing is a process, and divine *gubernatio* is, correspondingly, temporally extended. Examples of God's direction of creation include the processes by which bees pollinate apple trees, foals grow into horses, or a mother teaches her child to read. In each case *conservatio* and *concursus* are presupposed: it is only as apple trees, foals, and children are sustained in existence and enabled to exercise their powers that they can multiply, grow, and mature. But that they should do all

29. Colloquially it is common to apply purposive language to unconscious beings as well (e.g., "The lion killed in order to eat," or, "That tree grew at an angle in order to get more sun"), but such evidently anthropomorphic usage does not imply that the speaker ascribes conscious agency to the subjects of such sentences.

30. "Direction is an act of governing Providence, by which God so regulates the good actions of creatures, that they tend and are led to the object intended by God (Acts 4:28)." Quenstedt, *Theologia didactico-polemica* 1.534; cited in Schmid, *Doctrinal Theology*, 190.

these things (along with whatever else contributes to their flourishing) requires the confluence of many other creaturely effects over time: soil, sun, and rain for the apple tree; food, water, and the protection of the herd for the foal; and physical sustenance, shelter, and the love and care of others for a child. If the world is created from nothing, then this provision of the full range of conditions necessary for each creature's flourishing must be ascribed to God, and *gubernatio* refers precisely to God's causing the relevant created effects to come together in the right amount and at the right time so that bees, trees, horses, humans, and countless other creatures should all be able to flourish.

This way of characterizing *gubernatio* immediately raises the specter of meliorism, or the idea that creation naturally progresses to ever-better (in the sense of more harmonious) states. Although a naive faith in human progress has long been identified as a weakness of much nineteenth-century Protestant thought, a fully cosmological meliorism is relatively uncommon in the Christian tradition. The universalist theologies of Origen and Gregory of Nyssa arguably tend in this direction, but both writers' horizons are largely confined to rational (viz., human and angelic) creatures. More explicitly universal in scope is the work of the twentieth-century Jesuit Pierre Teilhard de Chardin, who, drawing on Darwinian theory as well as Christian eschatology, envisioned a process of cosmic evolution progressing from disorganized aggregates of inorganic matter to a state of fully integrated and universal consciousness that he called the "Omega Point."[31] Although less triumphalistically than Teilhard, process theologians, too, posit an overall progressive dynamic to God's providential activity: for them, God always seeks to elicit occasions of ever-greater complexity so as to enhance creatures' capacities for enjoyment.[32]

There are at least two significant problems shared by such proposals. The first is scientific: there is little empirical evidence that the creation is progressing toward any well-defined goal. While there is at present no consensus among cosmologists as to the future of the universe as a whole, none of the leading theories is consistent with the steady, progressive enrichment of creaturely possibilities. Perhaps the most prominent scenario is one in which the universe continues on a trajectory of unending expansion, gradually thinning and cooling until it reaches a state of maximally diffuse, low-energy equilibrium (the "Big Freeze"). The main alternative presents a more dramatic but no more hopeful version of events in which the expansion of the universe accelerates, eventually reaching the point where the universe tears itself apart, starting with large structures like galaxies and culminating with the smallest subatomic particles (the "Big Rip"). Nor is meliorism any more credible if one sticks to the more immediate context of life on earth. While there are scientific defenders of overall

31. See esp. Pierre Teilhard de Chardin, *The Phenomenon of Man*, trans. Bernard Wall (1955; repr., New York: Harper Colophon, 1975).
32. See, e.g., John B. Cobb Jr. and David Ray Griffin, *Process Theology: An Introductory Exposition* (Louisville, KY: Westminster John Knox Press, 1976), 52–62; cf. 16–18. Since process thinkers reject creation from nothing, they limit the work of *gubernatio* to divine persuasion.

evolutionary progress, the overwhelming dominance of bacteria in the terrestrial biosphere (in terms of diversity of types, range of environments colonized, and even sheer biomass) suggest that evolution has no inherent bias toward the complex. Instead, the appearance of increasingly complex entities over time appears to be epiphenomenal: since there is a lower limit to how simple a living organism can be but no upper limit to how complex they may become, complex life forms may be expected to emerge over time even if the evolutionary process itself is essentially isotropic, lacking any inherent directionality.[33] Even setting aside the lack of scientific evidence for steady evolutionary progress, biblical support for the idea that the sum of creaturely movements tends toward the gradual realization of God's purposes for creaturely flourishing seems ambiguous at best. Paul expresses confidence that "all things work together for good for those who love God" (Rom. 8:28), even as Joseph assures his brothers that God effected good out of what they intended for evil (Gen. 50:20); yet the preponderance of biblical evidence seems to envision the vindication of God's purposes as the result of the sudden and (at least from worldly perspective) unexpected reversal of historical expectation rather than the culmination of a smooth, upward trajectory. The Synoptics' record of Jesus' own teaching about the end time is especially striking in this regard. On the one hand, he draws a parallel between the coming of God's kingdom and natural processes: "From the fig tree learn its lesson: as soon as its branch becomes tender and puts forth its leaves, you know that summer is near. So also, when you see all these things, you know that [the Son of Man] is near, at the very gates" (Matt. 24:32–33 and pars.). So far, so good—except that "all these things" for which the disciples are instructed to keep watch are not imperfect-but-recognizable anticipations of the kingdom, but signs of creation's ever more radical deviation from the earthly realization of God's righteousness:

> For nation will rise against nation, and kingdom against kingdom, and there will be famines and earthquakes in various places: all this is but the beginning of the birth pangs. Then they will hand you over to be tortured and will put you to death, and you will be hated by all nations because of my name. Then many will fall away, and they will betray one another and hate one another. And many false prophets will arise and lead many astray. And because of the increase of lawlessness, the love of many will grow cold. . . . For at that time there will be great suffering, such as has not been from the beginning of the world until now, no, and never will be. . . . Immediately after the suffering of those days the sun will be darkened, and the moon will not give its light; the stars will fall from heaven, and the powers of heaven will be shaken. (Matt. 24:7–12, 21, 29)

Although God brings victory out of this concatenation of crises, it is evidently by working *against* the ways of the world rather than *through* them. Nor is this an isolated perspective. From the vision of the successive degenerations of

33. See Stephen Jay Gould, *Full House: The Spread of Excellence from Plato to Darwin* (New York: Three Rivers Press, 1997).

earthly kingdoms in Daniel (2:31–45; 7:2–9) to the beasts of Revelation (13:1–18), the eschatological realization of God's purposes seems less the culmination of worldly processes than their reversal. God remains sovereign, but that sovereignty is manifest more in the overturning of earthly arrangements than in their direction. What place has *gubernatio* in this picture?

In response to this combination of scientific and theological considerations, two points may be made. First, *gubernatio*—no less than *conservatio, concursus,* and the doctrine of creation from nothing from which all three derive—is a confession of faith rather than an induction based on observation. It is not a claim about the course of world history, but rather about God's relationship to the world. And as a corollary of the doctrine of creation from nothing, the idea that the plausibility of *gubernatio* depends on the evidence of historical teleology, whether in human culture or in nature considered more broadly, is a category mistake.[34] Only if God were an inner-worldly principle, interacting with creatures as one causal factor among others, would it make sense to try to validate *gubernatio* empirically.[35] By contrast, if God is radically transcendent, then there is no reason to suppose that divine *gubernatio* should have any particular phenomenal correlate (viz., that world history should have thus-and-such a shape or develop in any particular direction), beyond the basic logical requirement that divine direction presupposes the existence of creatures for God to direct. That it should be possible to induce God's purposes from even the most comprehensive examination of the sequence of created effects does not follow, precisely because the goal of creation, whether considered in whole or in part, is a matter of God's will and not of any inherent or autonomous creaturely capacity. From this perspective, if the fulfillment of God's purposes for creation should appear from any given creature's perspective as a sudden and radical reversal of creation's "natural" course, that poses no theological problem.

Insofar as Christians have traditionally taught that creatures' eschatological glorification, however understood in detail, is a sharing in the divine life that necessarily exceeds their own capacities (since creatures are by definition not divine), this recognition of discontinuity between the present form of creation and its future destiny is not surprising. If emphasized, however, it seems to evacuate *gubernatio* of any content. After all, if the fulfillment of God's will for the

---

34. Oliver O'Donovan rightly states that not all teleology is historical: the very idea of creaturely flourishing presupposes a natural teleology that allows one to confess, e.g., that an acorn flourishes in becoming an oak, a colt in becoming a stallion, and so forth (see his *Resurrection and the Moral Order: An Outline for Evangelical Ethics* [Grand Rapids: Wm. B. Eerdmans Publishing Co., 1986], 35). At the same time, Ruth Page warns that the equation of flourishing with the achievement of *any* outcome can subvert a creation theology's proper emphasis on God's joy in the sheer existence of creatures at any point in their development, leading her to insist that Christian theologians should adopt the principle of "teleology now!," in which "every moment becomes . . . an end in itself" (*God and the Web of Creation*, 63). In this section I am trying to strike an appropriate balance between both of these insights.

35. Insofar as process theologians view God in just these terms, it is both natural and appropriate that on scientific grounds they should argue for a teleological interpretation of natural history—and correspondingly problematic for them if such arguments cannot be sustained empirically.

creature is a matter of eschatological intervention that is as (if not more) plausibly viewed as the reversal than the fulfillment of creatures' own trajectories, then it is hard to see that much hangs on God's direction of creatures in time and space, beyond the minimal condition that creatures continue to exist in the world as possible objects of God's glorifying work. When stress is placed on the utterly gracious character of God's vindication of the creature, does that imply it makes no difference whether, for example, a particular human being suffers a painful, lingering death in infancy or ends her life "old and full of days"?

At one level it is both important and necessary to answer this last question in the affirmative, for the good news of Jesus is precisely that God can make a way out of no way, so that it is God alone and no humanly perceived significance or insignificance that saves any of us. Here indeed all that is required is that there should exist creatures to whom God may freely give grace, without any further need that the course of a creature's existence should follow any particular trajectory as a condition for this gift being given or received. At this point, *gubernatio* acquires its proper place, not as a theory about the end or goal of history, but simply as a basic condition of creaturely existence in time and space alongside *conservatio* and *concursus*. While these latter two dimensions of providence relate to creatures preserved and empowered by God individually, *gubernatio* speaks to God's provision as considered collectively and relationally. For while all creatures are objects of God's immediate attention and care as primary cause (so that no creature can continue to act or to be at any point of its existence apart from God's directly willing its act and being), normally God sustains creatures through other creatures as secondary causes. The direction of *gubernatio* is most appropriately understood in these terms: God sustains creatures in relationships of mutual interdependence, so the being of any one creature is bound up with the being of others.

The obvious problem with this splendid vision of God making a world in which creaturely flourishing is a cooperative enterprise is that in reality this "cooperation" is very far from the vision of the peaceable kingdom where the well-being of one is tied to the well-being of all (cf. Isa.11:6–9; 65:25). It is certainly true that many creatures can and do live in harmony, with some participating in symbiotic relationships in which the flourishing of one species is not only consistent with but also dependent upon the flourishing of another (bees and apple trees are one example, but still more striking are the lichens, which are essentially compound organisms formed from the symbiosis of fungi and algae). But there is no shortage of situations where a creature is so constituted that its flourishing can come only at the expense of another, most clearly when organisms are linked by relationships of predation or parasitism.

In such cases the flourishing of one creature seems to depend unavoidably on the destruction of another in ways that bring back into relief the theodicy questions raised in the preceding chapter. There it was proposed that God's response to that which diminishes creaturely flourishing is to work to overcome it, so that in the very act of holding creatures in being and providing for their continued existence, God is ever rejecting evil. And yet this response seems to strain against what appear to be systemic relations in which, for example, cheetahs live by killing gazelles, bark beetles by decimating pine trees, and malarial parasites by infecting human beings. It is, of course, possible to point out symbiosis even here: cheetahs could not subsist without gazelles, but it is also true that the predatory activity of cheetahs enhances the overall fitness of the gazelle population, as is generally the case when predator-prey (or parasite-host) populations have evolved together.[36] But this does not help the situation of any particular gazelle that happens to be eaten, nor of the human being struck down by a fatal disease. And there are still other natural events (volcanism, climate fluctuation, bolide impacts) that can provide a dramatic check to the flourishing of *all* living creatures in a particular area.[37]

To these concrete situations of creaturely suffering, there is no theological solution. As I have tried to stress, the confession of divine *gubernatio* does not imply that the circumstances of created existence show steady improvement. Even though natural history is characterized by repeated and extraordinary processes of diversification through the emergence of new life forms, individual species themselves seem to be remarkably stable, changing neither for the better nor for the worse, but simply living out their time (Eccl. 3:1).[38] Thus, while the players have changed, the basic patterns of symbiosis, predation, and parasitism seem to be unchanging features of life on earth, and there is no reason to suppose that they do not hold for life that may exist on other planets. In this context, it is crucial to recognize that *gubernatio* is neither a basis for optimism nor a denial of the tragic. Like *conservatio* and *concursus*, *gubernatio* entails no predictions, for the simple reason that the doctrine of providence is not intended as an explanation of why things happen the way they do. Indeed, it is not an *explanation* of anything, but rather serves as a reminder that creation is at bottom the product of grace: creatures exist because God continues to provide for their existence. In the case of *gubernatio*, the mode of provision takes the form of interdependence: God creates a world in which everything made continues to exist not only in absolute dependence on God, but also in relative but ongoing dependence on other creatures. This dependence ranges from the fundamental forces of physics that hold the diversity of creatures (both living and nonliving) together as distinct entities—and even to the complex ecological relationships between

36. Where there has been no coevolution, the sudden introduction of an exotic predator or parasite can wreak havoc on local populations, as shown by the disappearance of large mammals from Australia soon after the arrival of human beings, or the way in which chestnut blight (of Asian origin) came close to wiping out the entire population of American chestnut trees after its first appearance in North America in the early twentieth century.

37. Even here, one may point to long-term benefits. For example, the decimation of dinosaur populations as the result of the bolide impact at the end of the Cretaceous period provided the opportunity for the rapid diversification of mammals, which had to that point been a small and marginal part of the biosphere. On a more restricted scale, volcanism in Hawaii creates pockets of isolated habitat that allows for the rapid diversification of both plant and animal species.

38. For the scientific case for stasis in species over time, see Stephen Jay Gould, *The Structure of Evolutionary Theory* (Cambridge, MA: Belknap Press, 2002), 824–39; cf. 651–52, 875–76.

single-celled organisms, fungi, plants, and animals that sustain life on earth. In short, it is a function of divine *gubernatio* that there should exist not simply *creatures*, but also the *creation*: a discernible whole, in which each of the parts is bound up—albeit with widely varying degrees of immediacy—with every other. And if this whole does not appear to be progressing to any particular end, that it should exist at all is for Christians a matter of wonder and an occasion for praise.

But the Christian encounter with creation does not end with wonder and praise at its present state. It ends with hope: the sure and certain conviction that the future of creation includes a fullness of blessing for creatures beyond what is visible in the present. As Paul was keen to stress, this eschatological hope is characterized precisely by the fact that it is *not* seen (Rom. 8:24), and as already noted, in Scripture this future is depicted as the radical reversal or overturning of worldly processes. In short, the glory that is to come cannot be deduced from (or, as Paul also stresses, compared with) the present state of things. Nevertheless, because it is precisely the creation we see about us now that is the intended recipient of this glory, and because God wills that we should have this future glory as the object of our present hope, it is appropriate that even now the creation should contain intimations of what is to come. Those intimations are the subject of the next chapter.

7

Glory

A good case can be made that the topic of glory has no place in a book on the Christian doctrine of creation. As I have already had occasion to note, it is important to keep dogmatic accounts of creation and glorification (or eschatological consummation) distinct, because while consummation logically presupposes creation (since it is precisely what God has created that is glorified), creation does not imply consummation.[1] Consistent with this line of reasoning, the preceding chapter focused on how God provides for creation so that it may come to its intended eschatological goal, but it also emphasized that this provision does not in itself advance creatures toward glory. For while *conservatio*, *concursus*, and *gubernatio* are activities whereby God sustains, enables, and coordinates creatures' natural capacities, in glorification God transforms those capacities in a way that enables creatures to share in God's own life.[2] The Bible

---

1. See p. 107 above.

2. Because of humanity's fall into sin (i.e., opposition to and consequent alienation from God), a full account of the divine economy must include the topic of reconciliation as well as creation and glorification. The center of reconciliation is the incarnation, which I described in chap. 4 (above) as the breaking open of God's triune life to enable its participation by the creature. Insofar as such participation is here equated with glorified existence, it might seem to follow that the incarnation would have happened even apart from the fall, insofar as God's intention that creatures should come

describes this transformation in terms of a *new* creation (Isa. 65:17; 66:22; 2 Pet. 3:13; Rev. 21:1), and that fact alone suggests that the topic lies beyond the scope of the present study, which is concerned with creation as it exists in the here and now.

And yet precisely because of this focus on the present, the topic of glory cannot simply be eliminated from the doctrine of creation. Because the life of glory inherently exceeds creaturely capacities, it cannot be treated as the culmination of a creature's natural development (which is why in the case of human beings, e.g., "what we will be has not yet been revealed"; 1 John 3:2). Nevertheless, glory is the end God intends for creatures (Rom. 8:29–30), so even prior to the consummation, creation remains a type or figure of glorified existence, so that even now creation cannot be described adequately without reference to that end.[3] Still more to the point, it is not quite true that glory is only a future hope, for it is an established feature of Christian belief that part of creation, heaven, already experiences God's glory. And if glory is a part of creaturely experience anywhere, then it affects the whole creation as a present fact as well as a future hope. The topic of glory therefore has a place in theological reflection on the here and now of created being.

THE GLORY OF HEAVEN

Christians bear witness that glory pertains to creation's present no less than its future when they pray for God's will to be done on earth as it is in heaven (Matt. 6:10 and par.). This is not to say that heaven any more than earth has achieved its final glory, for the Christian hope includes the creation of a new heaven no less than a new earth (Rev. 21:1). According to Scripture heaven, too, will be shaken at the last day, prior to its final and definitive renewal (Matt. 24:29; Heb. 12:26; cf. Hag. 2:6, 21). Nevertheless, it is only in the future that the earthly creation will experience God's presence directly, while heaven is transparent to God now. Thus, true though it may be that for the eyes of faith the whole earth is full of God's glory in the present (Isa. 6:3), only in the future will this truth be visible to all eyes (Num. 14:21; Hab. 2:14). For the time being, God's glory is seen directly only in heaven (Acts 7:55; Rev. 15:5–8) or as coming down from heaven to a portion of the earth (Exod. 24:16; 2 Chr. 7:1–3).

---

to glory is not contingent on the fall; yet the fact that God has opened the divine life to us in the incarnation does not imply that this is the only way in which God could have done so. Even with respect to the work of reconciliation, Christians should be cautious in claiming that God could not have achieved God's intentions other than by way of the incarnation (see Thomas Aquinas, *Summa theologiae* [hereafter *ST*] 3.46.2, in Blackfriars ed., 61 vols. [London: Eyre & Spottiswood, 1964–81]; cf. p. 30 above).

3. "Creatio rerum corporalium est initium et figura et umbra redemptionis et spiritualium rerum." Martin Luther, *Dictata super Psalterium* 77 (78), in Weimarer Ausgabe (WA = *D. Martin Luthers Werke: Kritische Gesammtausgabe* [1883–2009]), 3:550.33. Luther's remarks here reflect something of the medieval practice of "anagogical" reading of Scripture, in which present realities were also interpreted as types of glory.

In all this it is necessary to reckon with ancient Near Eastern cosmology and the corresponding range of senses the word "heaven" (Hebrew šāmayîm, Greek ouranos) has in the Bible. The physical structure of the cosmos presupposed in both Testaments is three-tiered: the earth at the bottom, the heavenly ocean above, and God's throne above that. Only the last of these locations (the "third heaven" of 2 Cor. 12:2) is the place of present glory, though in the Bible the term "heaven" is also applied to the sky, conceived as a great dome holding back the heavenly ocean (Gen. 1:6–8). Taken in this sense, "heaven" is part of the realm of sensible phenomena, so that the "windows of the heavens" in the flood story (Gen. 7:11; 8:2; cf. Isa. 24:18; Mal. 3:10) are simply apertures in the dome; and Paul's talk of the glory of heavenly bodies refers to the sun, moon, and stars set in the dome (1 Cor. 15:40–41; cf. Gen. 1:14–18; Judg. 5:20). Yet though the "highest heaven" is beyond the range of our perception as earth and sky are not, Scripture is clear that it, too, was made by God and therefore is subject to God (Ps. 148:3–4). As emphasized in the first article of the Nicene Creed, God is Creator and Lord of the invisible as well as the visible. Consequently, although heaven is God's dwelling place (Deut. 26:15; 1 Kgs. 8:30, 39, 43, 49; 2 Chr. 6:21, 30, 33, 39), it is no more capable of containing God than is the earth (1 Kgs. 8:27; 2 Chr. 2:6; 6:18).

But while it is true that God transcends heaven no less than earth, heaven is distinguished from earth as God's chosen place of habitation. This claim does not vitiate the confession that God is present to all creatures, sustaining and empowering their being, because omnipresence does not mean that God is located everywhere, in the way that a mist may be diffused through or a force field extend across physical space.[4] That God's *presence* to the earthly sphere of creation is not in tension with God's *dwelling* elsewhere is reflected in the biblical identification of heaven as God's throne (Pss. 11:4; 123:1; Matt. 5:34; Rev. 7:15; cf. Isa. 14:13–14). A throne is not simply a chair, but a way of making someone present: a monarch sits on the throne in order to be present to those assembled with a particular intensity, and yet a throne is not a means of drawing physically close to the people. On the contrary, it is typical for a throne to be set apart (e.g., above the level of the floor, at one end of a room), so that the one enthroned is at a distance from everyone else in the assembly—and yet this spatial distance serves precisely to highlight the fact of her presence. So God's being in heaven is contrasted with human existence on earth (Ps. 115:16; Eccl. 5:2), without prejudice to the claim that heaven is the place from which God is present to earthly events: looking down (Deut. 26:15; Pss. 14:2; 33:13; 53:2;

---

4. "If we ask where God is, we seek in vain [in the Bible] for the banal answer that He is everywhere." Karl Barth, *Church Dogmatics* (hereafter *CD*), ed. G. W. Bromiley and T. F. Torrance (Edinburgh: T&T Clark, 1960), III/3:437. Wolfhart Pannenberg has attempted to make sense of divine omnipresence precisely by drawing an analogy with physical fields of force, but the result is a strongly spatialized understanding of God's presence that seems doomed either to qualify divine transcendence (viz., panentheism) or to limit it to the person of the Holy Spirit as that person by which "the transcendent God is himself present in his creation." See his *Systematic Theology*, trans. Geoffrey W. Bromiley (Grand Rapids: Wm. B. Eerdmans Publishing Co., 1991), 1:414; cf. 382–84.

80:14; Isa. 63:15), speaking (Exod. 20:22; Deut. 4:36; Neh. 9:13; cf. Dan. 4:31; Matt. 3:17 and pars.), and hearing (1 Chr. 21:26; 2 Chr. 6:21, 23, 25, 30, 33, 35, 39; Neh. 9:27–28). Most importantly, since God is the immediate source of all creaturely existence, "every perfect gift is from above, coming down from the Father of lights" (Jas. 1:17; cf. 3:17; John 3:27; 19:11).

In addition to the evident disagreement between the conventions of ancient Near Eastern cosmology, according to which heaven is "above" the earth, and modern, scientific understandings of the universe, the church's history of collusion with imperial power can make it hard to embrace the biblical penchant for depicting God in heaven by using the imagery of a royal court. In evaluating this language, however, we remember that its upshot is precisely to relativize the significance of all earthly powers: because God is in heaven—and from there holds the "kings of the earth . . . and the rulers . . . in derision" (Ps. 2:2, 4) and "pours contempt on princes" (Ps. 107:40)—all earthly power is relativized, and none can be equated with the divine. As the "creator of heaven and earth," God transcends the former no less than the latter; but heaven is contrasted with earth precisely as that created sphere, invisible and ungraspable to us as earthly beings, where God's will is done now, over against any earthly power's pretensions to have fulfilled it.

As a further check against the temptation to draw illicit inferences from the characterization of heaven as God's throne, it is crucial to remember that the glory of heaven is not a function of God's standing apart from creatures in splendid isolation. The character of God's own life as the mutual love of the Father, the Son, and the Holy Spirit means that even considered apart from creation, divine glory takes the form of communion rather than isolation; and because through creation, God wills to share this life with that which is not God, it is impossible for heaven, as the sphere of creation where God's will is always already done, to be conceived as a place where God draws away from creatures in order to be alone—as though that could possibly contribute to God's glory. On the contrary, as the triune Creator whose own life is one of love freely given and received, God reigns by freely sharing this life of love with creatures. Consequently, the glory of heaven is inseparable from the fact that it, like earth, is full of creatures (Jer. 33:22; Dan. 7:10).

So numerous are heaven's creaturely denizens that they are frequently described in Scripture as a vast "host" (1 Kgs. 22:19; Neh. 9:6; cf. Rev. 19:14). Indeed, fullness is so much part of heaven that in places the biblical writers all but equate heaven with the hosts of creatures that inhabit it (Ps. 33:6; Isa. 45:12; cf. Rev. 13:6), as well as identifying God as the "Lord of hosts" (e.g., 1 Sam. 1:3; 1 Kgs. 18:15; Pss. 24:10; 46:7; Isa. 54:5; Jer. 7:3; Zeph. 2:9; Jas. 5:4).[5] At the same time, nothing could be more misleading than to portray this multitude

5. Moreover, in some cases the language of the heavenly host shares the ambivalence of "heaven" more generally, so that, e.g., the "host" of Isa. 40:26 clearly refers to the heavenly bodies (since the reader is commanded to "lift up [her] eyes and see" them). By contrast, in Ps. 148 the term "hosts" is in apposition to angels (v. 2) and implicitly distinguished from sun, moon, and stars (v. 3).

as an undifferentiated mass, row after row of more or less identical humanlike beings, with or without wings, and all sporting the same white uniform. That heavenly creatures exhibit something of the differences in kinds characteristic of the earthly creation is suggested at a variety of places in Scripture. While their precise significance eludes us, the naming of heaven's denizens alternately as "seraphs" (Isa. 6:2, 6), "cherubim" (Gen. 3:24; Ezek. 10:1–20), "thrones," "dominions," "rulers," "powers" (Col. 1:16), "angels," and "authorities" (1 Pet. 3:22) seemingly refers to various types of celestial creatures. More concretely, in his vision of heaven, John the Seer identifies, in close proximity to the One seated on the throne, "twenty-four elders" with their own thrones round about (Rev. 4:4), as well as "four living creatures, . . . the first . . . like a lion, the second . . . like an ox, the third . . . with a face like a human being, and the fourth . . . like a flying eagle" (Rev. 4:6–7)—all evidently distinct from the "myriads of myriads" of angels also surrounding the throne (Rev. 5:11). And while Thomas Aquinas's claims go beyond anything that can be substantiated scripturally, there is certainly nothing inherently unbiblical about his view that the diversity of the heavenly host is such that every celestial creature constitutes its own species.[6] Such diversity is belied when the church places too great a reliance on the generic term "angels" to name the heavenly host.

And yet as much as Christians need to remember that the term "angel" is a generic designation that encompasses a diversity of types no less (and quite possibly much more) extensive than covered by the terms like "animal" or "plant," there is a genuine theological appropriateness to the place of honor "angel" enjoys in Scripture and the Christian tradition.[7] As noted in chapter 3 (above), "angel" is a transliteration of the Greek word *angelos*, which means "messenger." While *angelos* can be used for any sort of envoy (see, e.g., Luke 7:24; Jas. 2:25), in the New Testament it plays a special role in referring supernatural agents of God.[8] These references, in turn, seemingly derive from the Old Testament language of the "angel [Hebrew *mal'āk*] of the LORD" (e.g., Num. 22:22; Judg. 6:11; 1 Kgs. 19:7; Zech. 1:12), who represents God on earth with such power and immediacy that in many cases the angel's identity seems to merge with that of God.[9] While angels are depicted in Scripture as doing many different things

6. This position follows from Thomas's commitment to Aristotelian metaphysics, according to which it is difference in material composition that distinguishes individuals within a species. Since Thomas held that angels were purely spiritual beings with no material component, he inferred that it is impossible for any angelic species to have more than one member. Thomas Aquinas, *ST* 1.50.4.

7. In the Bible yet other generic terms are used for the creatures of heaven, including "holy ones" (Deut. 33:2; Ps. 89:5, 7; Zech. 14:5), "glorious ones" (2 Pet. 2:10; Jude 8), "watchers" (Dan. 4:17), "princes" (Dan. 10:13, 20), and even "gods" (Deut. 32:8, 43 NRSV; *'elohîm* in Pss. 29:1; 82:1, 6; cf. Gen. 6:2); but none of them is used anywhere nearly as frequently as "angel" (though "watcher" shares a functional meaning with "angel").

8. It is also used to refer to demonic forces in Matt. 25:41; 2 Cor. 12:7; Rev. 12:7.

9. The story of the binding of Isaac, e.g., begins with "God" telling Abraham to sacrifice his son, but when Abraham is about to do so, "the angel of the LORD" stops him, saying, "Do not lay your hand on the boy, . . . for now I know that you fear *God*, since you have not withheld your son, your only son, from *me*" (Gen. 22:1–12). See also Gen. 16:7–14; Exod. 3:2–4; Judg. 13:19–22.

(e.g., protecting Israel in Exod. 14:19 and afflicting Israel in 2 Sam. 24:17), their role is epitomized by the words Gabriel addresses to Mary in the Gospel of Luke: "I stand in the presence of God, and I have been sent to speak to you and to bring you this good news" (1:19). As heavenly beings ("I stand in the presence of God") commissioned to serve God's purposes in time and space ("I have been sent"), angels both mark and bridge the gap between heaven and earth. Like all creatures, angels are servants of the One who created them (Ps. 103:20–21; Heb. 1:6), but their service takes the particular form of manifesting the glory of heaven on earth.

Yet in this context we distinguish this task of *manifesting* heaven's glory on earth from the very different work of *effecting* earth's glorification. The latter belongs to God alone. Angels have no capacity to glorify the terrestrial sphere, because glory is not theirs to give. The angels have been glorified, but they were not created that way. Even where heaven is concerned, glory, as a participation in the (uncreated) life of God, can only be enjoyed by creatures as a gift and never held as a property, since (as we have noted at several points) uncreatedness cannot be intrinsic to that which is created.[10] Because they dwell in heaven and not on earth, angels' reception of this gift is not a matter of temporal history, but it is no less real.[11] Indeed, as creatures who have been in the presence of God's glory from the beginning, the angels are a sign of God's will for the glorification of the whole creation (so that glorified human beings will be "like angels in heaven" [Matt. 22:30; Mark 12:25]), which will be accomplished precisely by bridging the gap between heaven and earth. Scripture portrays this bridging through the image of the descent of the heavenly Jerusalem: whereas previously God's dwelling was in heaven in contrast to earth, in glory "the home of God is among mortals. He will dwell with them; they will be his peoples, and God himself will be with them" (Rev. 21:3).

---

10. "The powers of the heavens are not holy by nature; were it so there would in this respect be no difference between them and the Holy Spirit." Basil of Caesarea, *On the Holy Spirit* 16.38, in *Nicene and Post-Nicene Fathers*, 2nd ser. (hereafter *NPNF²*), ed. Philip Schaff and Henry Wace, 14 vols. (1890–1900; repr., Peabody, MA: Hendrickson Publishers, 1994–99]), 8:24. Cf. the discussion of Irenaeus of Lyons and his account of why human beings were not created perfect, on pp. 13–14 above.

11. Although Thomas Aquinas is careful to maintain that angels could not instantaneously have been either raised to glory or doomed to perdition without impugning their status as creatures who (for that reason) were created good (*ST* 1.62.1; 1.63.5), he is nevertheless reluctant to affirm a temporal interval (*mora*) between the creation of the bad angels and their fall (*ST* 1.63.6). In this context, Karl Barth's refusal to endorse the traditional doctrine of an angelic fall on the grounds that texts like Jude 6 and 2 Pet. 2:4 (one might also add Luke 10:18 and Rev. 12:7–9) are "too uncertain and obscure . . . to be expounded . . . along these lines" (*CD* III/3:530–31) fails to reckon sufficiently with the fact that angels no less than humans and other earthly beings are *creatures*. On the other hand, Jonathan Edwards's belief that angels were not confirmed in glory until Christ's ascension errs in the opposite direction, as though angels, too, were part of the visible world of time and space rather than belonging to a different created sphere. For a discussion of Edwards's views, with particular emphasis on his tendency to draw strong parallels between heavenly and earthly history, see Robert W. Caldwell III, *Communion in the Spirit: The Holy Spirit as the Bond of Union in the Theology of Jonathan Edwards* (Milton Keynes, UK: Paternoster, 2006), 174–77.

This imagery of descent, corresponding to the description of heaven "above" the earth, expresses heaven's status as a realm that, though no less created than the visible world, transcends the latter, thereby providing within the created order an analogy to God's transcendence of whole creation.[12] It is, however, important always to remember that the spatial language in which this analogy is cast is metaphorical, so that just as Christians affirm that God's distance from creation is a matter of nature rather than physical location,[13] so it is with heaven. Heaven is certainly its own place within creation: that place where God dwells in glory in the company of the holy angels; but it is not a parallel universe that moves along independently of earth. Precisely because it is the place where the God who sovereignly sustains the whole creation at every moment of its existence, heaven's transcendence is not rightly interpreted in physical terms. On the contrary, because heaven is the place where God dwells and from which God acts, it always impinges on earth. To be sure, the fact that heaven—as appropriate for the dwelling place of the invisible God (Col. 1:15; cf. 1 Tim. 1:17; Heb. 11:27)—is itself invisible (Col. 1:16) means that it is not naturally a possible object of human perception. Nevertheless, the claim that earth exists always in the presence of heaven (since it always exists in the presence of God) is consistent with the occasional appearances of heaven's host in Scripture. Perhaps most striking is one of the stories associated with the prophet Elisha:

> When an attendant of the man of God rose early in the morning and went out, an [Aramaean] army with horses and chariots was all around the city [of Samaria]. His servant said, "Alas, master! What shall we do?" He replied, "Do not be afraid, for there are more with us than there are with them." Then Elisha prayed: "O LORD, please open his eyes that he may see." So the LORD opened the eyes of the servant, and he saw; the mountain was full of horses and chariots of fire all around Elisha. (2 Kgs. 6:15–17; cf. Num. 22:22–35; 2 Sam. 5:24; 2 Kgs. 7:6)

Similarly, in the Lukan account of the nativity, "the glory of the Lord" shines about the shepherds who hear the announcement of Jesus' birth, followed by the appearance of "a multitude of the heavenly host, praising God" (Luke 2:9, 13). In both cases (the first quite explicitly), the appearance of angels seems to be a matter of their miraculous disclosure to mortal eyes—the normally invisible being made temporarily visible.[14] Be that as it may, given the stress in the Old Testament in particular on the (physical) distance between heaven above and

12. Barth honors the analogical character of heaven's transcendence: while it is true to say that "within the one cosmos God is nearer to one of the spheres, i.e., heaven, than He is to the other, i.e., earth," it is nevertheless "better not to say that heaven is nearer to God than earth," since "it is not a question of qualities proper to heaven and earth as such, but of an action and attitude of God" (*CD* III/3:422; cf. 419).

13. "All things are distant from God not by place, but by nature." John of Damascus, *On the Orthodox Faith* 1.13, in Patrologia graeca (hereafter PG), 94:853C (see p. 19 above).

14. Luke goes on to report that the angels later "went away from them into heaven" (2:15, RSV), and Acts describes Jesus' departure from the disciples in terms of his being "lifted up" (Acts 1:9–10), but there remains some ambiguity in both cases as to whether the resulting absence is the

earth beneath (Isa. 55:9), it should come as no surprise that such angelic appearances are rare; but while these appearances give us no substantive information on angelic natures or the character of heavenly existence, they do remind us that glory is a present reality for creation, albeit one that we on earth see only in the briefest of glimpses.

Although angelic appearances continue in the New Testament even beyond the nativity stories (in, e.g., Acts 5:19; 12:7–9; cf. Heb. 13:2), the fact that with the advent of Jesus "the kingdom of heaven has come near" (Matt. 3:2; 4:17) gives rise to a further way in which the glory of heaven impinges on earthly existence. Heaven's glory remains intrinsically invisible, but now that the kingdom of heaven has drawn near, it is possible for Jesus, speaking in parables, to compare it to certain natural phenomena (the growing of seed [Matt. 13:24–26, 31–32 and pars.], the fermentation of yeast [Matt. 13:33 and par.], a fishing net [Matt. 13:47–48]), as well as to particular forms of social relationship (settling accounts [Matt. 18:23–33], the hire of day laborers [Matt. 20:1–16], a marriage feast [Matt. 22:2–14 and par.]).[15] As with the vision of angels, here too the ability to see depends on being enabled to do so: to know the "secrets of the kingdom of heaven" is only given to some (Matt. 13:10–13 and pars.; cf. Mark 4:9). The point remains, however, that the kingdom's drawing near means that something of its character can be discerned through earthly analogues. Because it is nothing less than the glorification of the earthly sphere—the fulfillment of the prayer that God's will be done on earth as in heaven—the coming of the kingdom is not a natural process that grows organically out of the created order. As "a new creation" (2 Cor. 5:17; Gal. 6:15), it is every bit as much "from nothing" as the old creation was. Jesus himself makes this clear when he teaches that the kingdom is "not coming with things that can be observed," but for those with eyes to see it, "in fact, the kingdom of God is among you" (Luke 17:20–21).[16]

---

consequence of physical movement (e.g., the story of the ascension attributes the final disappearance of Jesus to the interposition of a cloud).

15. See Barth, *CD* III/3:434.

16. At first blush, Paul's claim that "since the creation of the world [God's] eternal power and nature, invisible though they are, have been understood and seen through the things that were made" (Rom. 1:20) also seems to relate to the theme of the present visibility of God's glory. Without entering into the long discussion of the extent to which this verse does or does not lend support to the task of "natural theology" (viz., the possibility of acquiring knowledge of God apart from God's self-revelation in Jesus), I simply observe that there is no reference here to any perception of heaven or its glory (when Paul does speak of these realities in 2 Cor. 12:2–4, he clearly regards human experience of them as exceptional). Thus, whatever exactly Paul may have had in mind with his claim that things invisible are seen and understood through the (visible) creation, it seemingly has nothing to do with the sphere of heaven impinging on earth, but only with recognition of God's status as Creator.

ICONS: SEEING HEAVEN'S GLORY

In Scripture visions of heavenly glory are episodic, unpredictable, and as likely cause fear as joy or comfort (see, e.g., 1 Chr. 21:16). And though Jesus proclaimed the advent of the kingdom of heaven, earthly appearances of angels remain rare even after the incarnation, and Paul gives personal testimony to having experienced heaven and earth as quite distinct spheres (2 Cor. 12:1–4); but there are later forms of Christian practice based on the assumption that Jesus' coming and, more particularly, his resurrection and ascension have established the basis for a more stable and continuous interchange between earth and heaven. The Orthodox theology of icons, for example, reflects the belief that while heaven and earth remain distinct, the fact that God has taken a human body and brought that body into heaven means that the two spheres now intersect not only (as was the case in the Old Testament) from above to below, as human beings on earth are given passing glimpses or parabolic hints of heavenly glory, but also from below to above, as earthly substances can be used to depict heavenly glory in a way that anticipates the union of earthly and heavenly spheres that is the object of Christian hope.[17]

Important qualifications need to be declared here. Although icons have assumed a central place in the devotional life of many, the Decalogue's proscription of images (Exod. 20:4; Deut. 5:8) has made such depiction an ongoing point of contention among Christians. Even within Orthodox circles the vindication of icons was achieved only after more than a century of often brutal conflict between iconoclasts (who rejected the use of icons as part of Christian worship) and iconodules (who defended it). Although the Second Council of Nicaea, which formally vindicated the iconodule position in 787, is counted as one of the seven ecumenical councils of the ancient church, its decisions were initially received with considerable misgivings by the Latin churches of the West.[18] Subsequently, churches in the Reformed tradition in particular have been known for their uncompromising rejection of devotional art of any kind, while, on the other side, the commitment of some Orthodox to a particular set of iconographic canons has given rise to cavalier dismissal of all other forms of Christian liturgical art.[19]

---

17. For the idea of heaven and earth being united from below to above, see Maximus the Confessor's claim that in his ascension Christ "clearly united heaven and earth . . . [and] by passing with his soul and body, that is, with the whole of our nature, through all the divine and unintelligible ranks of heaven, he united the sensible and the intelligible and showed the convergence of the whole creation." Maximus the Confessor, *Difficulties* 41, in Andrew Louth, *Maximus the Confessor* (New York: Routledge, 1996), 159–60.

18. Even in the East the iconodule victory in 787 was followed by more than a half century of further debate that ended only in 843, when an assembly convened by the Byzantine Empress Theodora, acting as regent for her three-year-old son, definitively affirmed the decrees of II Nicaea.

19. For a particularly egregious example of the latter, see Pavel Florensky, *Iconostasis*, trans. Donald Sheehan and Olga Andrejev (Crestwood, NY: St. Vladimir's Seminary Press, 1996), esp. 100–114.

In light of this history of controversy, it is worthwhile to explore the logic of the iconodule position in order to clarify the ways in which the theology of icons may contribute to the doctrine of creation. Interestingly (and notwithstanding its prominence in post-Reformation debates over liturgical art in the West), the Ten Commandments played a relatively small role in iconoclastic controversies of the eighth and ninth centuries.[20] Appeal to the Decalogue was a feature of early iconoclastic polemic; in the first extensive theological response to iconoclasm, John of Damascus addressed the issue by distinguishing between worship (*latreia* in Greek), which may be offered to God alone, and practices of veneration or reverence (*proskynēsis*) that are legitimate ways of honoring creatures and, as such, were practiced even by those Old Testament patriarchs who were most uncompromising in their observance of the law.[21] As the debate matured, however, arguments on both sides were conducted almost exclusively in christological terms. Here too, John of Damascus set the stage by arguing that the incarnation had fundamentally changed the context for theological reflection on matter. Because God had inhabited a human body, the veneration of creatures was no longer simply a matter of social propriety, but had acquired a specifically liturgical function:

> Of old, God the incorporeal and formless was never depicted, but now that God has been seen in the flesh and has associated with humankind, I depict what I have seen of God. I do not venerate matter, I venerate the fashioner of the matter, who became matter for my sake and accepted to dwell in matter and through matter worked my salvation, and I will not cease from reverencing matter, through which my salvation was worked.[22]

Since Jesus' body is God's body, its veneration is crucial to honoring God's condescension on our behalf. Importantly, however, because the matter of Jesus' body in inextricably connected to the rest of the material order, the liturgical implications of the incarnation are not limited to Jesus:

---

20. The extent to which Byzantine iconoclasm was influenced by the iconoclastic fervor of the Muslim armies that threatened the Byzantine Empire from the late seventh century onward remains a matter of disagreement. While stories of Muslim influence at the imperial court are almost certainly malicious propaganda, the idea that iconoclasm may have gained momentum in part as a reaction to Muslim military success (interpreted as a judgment on Christian idolatry) has more merit. Certainly both sides in the iconoclastic debate tried to interpret military victory against Arab armies as a vindication of their position, and there is no doubt that the military success and social stability provided by the iconoclastic Isaurian emperors gave considerable impetus to Byzantine iconoclasm (esp. in the army) through much of the eighth century. See Paul J. Alexander, *The Patriarch Nicephorus of Constantinople: Ecclesiastical Policy and Image Worship in the Byzantine Empire* (Oxford: Clarendon Press, 1958).

21. John of Damascus, *Three Treatises on the Divine Images* (1.8), trans. Andrew Louth (Crestwood, NY: St. Vladimir's Seminary Press, 2003), 24–25.

22. John of Damascus, *Three Treatises* (1.16), 29. John also notes that images had a liturgical role in Israel's worship (ibid. [1.16, 20], 30–31, 33–34), but he does not provide a parallel explanation for it in terms of the economy of salvation.

I reverence the rest of matter [also] and hold in respect that through which my salvation came, because it is filled with divine energy and grace. Is not . . . the wood of the cross matter? Is not the holy and august mountain, the place of the skull matter? Is not . . . the holy tomb, the source of the resurrection, matter? Are not the ink and the all-holy book of the Gospels matter? Is not the life-bearing table, which offers to us the bread of life, matter? . . . Either do away with the reverence and veneration of all these or submit to the tradition of the Church and allow veneration of images of God and friends of God, sanctified by name and therefore overshadowed by the divine Spirit.[23]

By virtue of the incarnation, the glory of heaven is no longer simply behind or above matter, because the material is now "filled with divine energy and grace." While matter has no intrinsic glory (as already noted, creatures receive glory as a gift of grace even in the heavenly sphere), God can make it glorious—and has done so by raising Jesus from the dead.

And yet if it is the resurrection that renders the earthly as glorious, then it is necessary to qualify John's attempt to justify the veneration of icons in terms of a reverence for matter as such.[24] The icon is not a celebration of the inherent glory of matter, but rather of the fact that God has glorified matter through Christ. For this reason (and as even John's own examples tend to suggest), even where Christ is not the explicit subject of depiction, icons need to maintain an implicit christological reference, since it is only in and through the person of Christ that other creatures, too, are glorified.[25] Consequently, although a wide range of figures may be represented on icons (among permissible objects of representation, the Second Council of Nicaea includes "the figures . . . of our spotless Lady, the Mother of God, of the honorable angels, of all saints, and of all pious people" in addition to Jesus), whatever is represented is to be depicted not as an earthly phenomenon, but as participating in the glory of the risen Christ.[26] Only at the consummation will heaven and earth be joined so fully as to render the glorified creation immediately visible to all. In the meanwhile, icons serve as a means of anticipating this event by giving what are effectively eschatological portraits of their subjects: when we see an icon of a saint, we see her transfigured by glory and not as though viewing an earthly portrait[27]

23. Ibid. (1.16), 29–30, trans. slightly alt.
24. See John Meyendorff, *Christ in Eastern Christian Thought* (Crestwood, NY: St. Vladimir's Seminary Press, 1975), 191.
25. The conciliar decree defines iconography as consisting in "the making of pictorial representations, agreeable to the history of the preaching of the Gospel." "The Decree of the Holy, Great, Ecumenical Synod, the Second of Nicaea," in *NPNF*[2] 14:550.
26. Ibid. Cf. John of Damascus, *Three Treatises* (1.19), 32–33: "For to make an image of Christ as glorified and yet spurn the image of the saints as without glory is to endeavor to show that the truth is false. 'For I live,' says the Lord, 'and I shall glorify those who glorify me' [cf. 1 Sam. 2:30]."
27. So "the icon . . . is an image . . . not of corruptible flesh, but of flesh transfigured, radiant with Divine light. It is Beauty and Glory, represented by material means and visible in the icon to physical eyes; . . . a temporal portrait of a saint cannot be an icon, precisely because it reflects not his transfigured but his ordinary, carnal state." Leonid Ouspensky, "The Meaning and Language of Icons," in Leonid Ouspensky and Vladimir Lossky's *The Meaning of Icons*, trans. G. E. H. Palmer

It is an important feature of icons that they are not tied to formally desig-
nated places of worship. They can be displayed in offices, shops, and homes, and
even carried about on one's person for private devotion. And yet it is arguably
in the worship space that icons have greatest symbolic impact. In Byzantine
churches like the two basilicas of Sant'Apollinare in Ravenna, the whole inner
space of the building becomes an icon of heavenly glory, with mosaics completely covering the walls and ceiling, and thereby surrounding the worshiping
community on every side. Even in more modest structures, however, the same
intention to display the irruption of heaven's glory on earth is seen in the Orthodox iconostasis: the icon-covered screen that stands between the altar and the
nave and symbolizes the way in which heaven (the altar) is united with the earth
(the nave) through the intercession of Christ and the saints. The screen itself
represents the continuing division of heaven from earth in the present age, while
the icons indicate that the two realms are nevertheless intimately connected, as
the earthly assembly is joined in worship by the great "cloud of witnesses" (Heb.
12:1) who now dwell with the risen Christ.[28]

From this perspective icons are best interpreted not as books for the illiterate
(although they may also serve that function), but rather as a form of witness to
belief in the resurrection of Christ, and (through the iconic depiction of plants
and animals alongside the saints) to the glorification of all creation to which his
resurrection points.[29] The established conventions of Orthodox icon painting
are designed to further this aim. Most obviously, the halo or nimbus surrounding the heads of the figure depicted indicates glorified status. More subtly, figures are given high foreheads to suggest wisdom, large eyes as a sign that their
whole being is oriented to the vision of God, and closed mouths to indicate
contemplative silence in the face of divine glory. Hands are invariably given
a liturgical function,[30] and all saints are portrayed either in full face or three-
quarter view to indicate their simultaneous presence both to God and to us.[31]

---

and E. Kadloubovsky (Crestwood, NY: St. Vladimir's Seminary Press, 1982), 36. As noted below,
however, this does not mean that iconic depictions entail any diminishment of the subject's personal
identity.

28. Florensky, *Iconostasis*, 62–63. Robert Jenson has rightly noted serious ecclesiological problems with the modern iconostasis, which completely blocks the view of the altar from the nave: "It
is one thing for the biblically mandated action [viz., the Eucharist] to be interpreted by intervening
icons and quite another to be compelled to behold them *instead* of the action"; in *The Works of God*,
vol. 2 of *Systematic Theology* (New York: Oxford University Press, 1999), 288. These difficulties
could be avoided by reversion to earlier forms of the iconostasis, in which icons are hung from a low
rail that sets apart the chancel area and does not screen the sight of the altar from the congregation.

29. "The earth, the vegetable and animal kingdoms are . . . depicted . . . in order to make nature
itself participate in the transfiguration of man and consequently to connect it with existence outside
time." Ouspensky, "Meaning," 40. See, e.g., the amount of space given over to depicting the nonhuman, earthly creation in the apse of the church of Sant'Apollinare in Classe in Ravenna. Particularly
striking is the way that the golden "light" that forms the background of the mosaic is used to frame
even individual rocks, shrubs, and patches of grass.

30. "People do not gesticulate. . . . They officiate, and each of their movements bears a sacramen-
tal liturgic character" (ibid., 40).

31. "They are hardly every represented in profile. . . . In a certain sense the profile breaks communion, it is already the beginning of absence. Therefore it is allowed chiefly in the case of persons

Perhaps most significant from the perspective of a doctrine of creation, however, is the way light functions in Orthodox iconography. The first thing to note in this context is that icons contain no shadows, because the light of the divine glory surrounds and permeates everything, rather than originating at a particular point in space. In fact, because icons portray creation as transfigured by glory, the whole scheme of space and time is transformed. Even when the subject represented in the icon is a biblical story, "the action is not enclosed in or limited to a particular place, just as, while being manifested in time, it is not limited to a certain time."[32] The all-pervasive and unearthly character of iconic light is secured by its role as the background of the icon as well as by the preference for using gold leaf rather than paint to depict it.[33] Once the icon's surface has been prepared, this background gilding is applied first. While this practice is partly dictated by practical considerations (it lessens the possibility of the gilding marring or mixing with the paint), it also is subject to theological interpretation: "Iconpainting considers light not as something external to objects; neither does it consider light as belonging to some primordial substance: for iconic light establishes and builds things, becoming the objective cause of their existence."[34]

Insofar as light provides the ground and space for the figures of the icon, it bears witness to the doctrine of creation from nothing, now extended to the eschatological sphere. As noted in chapter 2 (above), "light" is one of the three scriptural "definitions" of God (1 John 1:5), and in the icon this characterization takes visual form as light frames, defines, and gives rise to the reality it illumines.[35] Creatures (whether human or nonhuman) have no intrinsic capacity for glory; it is rather the relentless pressure of the divine light that causes their earthly forms to be transfigured. They are remade in glory as they were made originally: from nothing, and so by God alone.

That we are destined to be remade in this way is the content of the gospel and so explains why there could be no icons prior to Jesus, even though the worship life of Israel did not lack depictions of heavenly realities (see, e.g., Exod. 37:7–9; 1 Kgs. 6:23–35; 7:36). For the icon does not portray general truths, but individual people, so that even though icons are not signed by the iconographer, they are always *named* by having the subject of the painting inscribed on the

---

who have not yet attained sanctity. (See for instance the shepherds or the wise men in the icon of the Nativity of Christ)" (ibid., 39).

32. Ibid., 40. Cf. Michel Quenot, *The Icon: Window on the Kingdom* (Crestwood, NY: St. Vladimir's Seminary Press, 2002), 106: "The image of the new man regenerated by Christ refers to a world where dimensions no longer exist."

33. "Light" is actually the technical term for an icon's background (Ouspensky, "Meaning," 40).

34. Florensky, *Iconostasis*, 150.

35. "Until a thing is formed by light, it has no existence whatever; for a thing comes to possess concreteness not by negation but by the positive act of creation: that is, by the quick play of light. . . . Precisely upon that which the light comes to rest, there—in the measure of its illumination—is that which enters existence"; ibid., 145–46; cf. 136–37: "In the heart of this [divine] light 'we live, and move, and have our being'; it is the space of true reality."

icon itself.[36] An icon is, in short, always the icon of a particular someone (or several someones), never anonymous or generalized. As witnesses to Christ's resurrection, icons display the reality of heavenly glory now enjoyed by creatures of earth. As such, they reflect both God's glorification of creaturely existence in all its particularity and the conviction that this affirmation impacts even the sphere of creation that has yet to be glorified.[37]

This emphasis on particularity is central to the theology of icons that received dogmatic shape at Nicaea in 787. Icons portray *persons*. A person is a particular instantiation (or, in more technical theological language, a "hypostasis") of human nature. This nature is characterized by a certain physical form and a corresponding set of spiritual capacities that, as the object of God's creative work, are good; but it is not an end in itself. "Human nature," like any other created nature, is an abstraction that can neither be perceived nor depicted. To focus on the nature is to conceive of humanity in terms of a norm in relation to which the concrete variations that mark individual particular human beings are at best a distraction. But what we see—and what the iconographer paints—are persons: the particular, unsubstitutable instantiations of human nature identified not by general characteristics, but by particular features.

> When anyone is portrayed, it is not the nature but the hypostasis that is portrayed. For how could a nature be portrayed unless it were contemplated in a hypostasis? For example, Peter is not portrayed insofar as he is animate, rational, mortal, and capable of thought and understanding [i.e., his natural properties]; for this does not define Peter only, but also Paul and John, and all those of the same species. But [he is portrayed] insofar as he adds along with the common definition certain properties, such as a long or short nose, curly hair, a good complexion, bright eyes, or whatever else characterizes his particular appearance.[38]

So if, to an eye unused to the conventions of Orthodox iconography, the figures seem characterized by a certain uniformity, the aim is just the opposite: to highlight the individual hypostasis as the object of God's glorifying work.[39] In

---

36. "It is by the inscription that the icon receives a presence" (Quenot, *The Icon*, 85; cf. Florensky, *Iconostasis*, 142.

37. In the history of the church, there has been some debate as to whether those who die in faith are glorified immediately or need to await the general resurrection. Paul's words in 1 Thess. 4:15–17 seem to suggest the latter, but although the tradition has wanted to affirm that creaturely beatitude is complete only with the final resurrection, it has also been fairly consistent in rejecting the doctrine of "soul sleep": that those who have died in the faith do not experience God's presence immediately after death. In the West the claim that the saints enjoy the beatific vision was given formal status by Pope Benedict XII in the bull *Benedictus Deus* (1336).

38. Theodore the Studite, *On the Holy Icons* (3.34), trans. Catharine P. Roth (Crestwood, NY: St. Vladimir's Seminary Press, 2001), 90.

39. "The icon, in depicting the body of a man with all its peculiarities, does not eliminate anything human: it does not exclude either the psychological or the worldly element. It also transmits the feelings of a person, . . . his knowledge, his artistic creativeness and the particular external occupation, be it ecclesiastical . . . or temporal . . . which the given saint has transformed into spiritual endeavor." Ouspensky, "Meaning," 39.

this way the nature is a means for the display of the hypostasis, so that ultimately what human nature "is" will be revealed only at the end of time, when all its various hypostatic instantiations have finally appeared.[40]

The theology of the icon thus serves the theology of creation by countering any suggestion that the value of any person might simply be instrumental to the flourishing of the race. Nor can this principle be limited to human beings. If, by virtue of the fact that God took human flesh, the promise of sharing in the divine nature is limited to human beings (2 Pet. 1:4), the conviction that the glorification of human beings includes the release of all creation from bondage (Rom. 8:19–21) means that there is no biblical basis for limiting the renewal of existence, of which human glorification is one manifestation, to a single species. If the direction of movement within the divine economy is from heaven to earth, from the invisible to the visible, icons bear witness that this movement has now progressed to the point that the glory of heaven now includes creatures that have lived in time and space. In seeing this, those of us who still await glory are not only reminded of our destiny, but also taught that our destiny is a specifically *human* one, in which the validation of our particularity as objects of God's love does not sever but rather deepens our connection with other creatures in that love. The light of glory that illumines us neither puts others in our shadow nor allows us to be put in theirs, but rather catches us all up together in its brilliance.

THE EUCHARIST: TASTING HEAVEN'S GLORY

If icons offer a vision of glorified matter, they are not themselves glorified. They reflect a belief that terrestrial materials can bear witness to the glory of the kingdom, but they remain themselves objects of this world, composed of everyday, terrestrial materials like wood and gold, egg and oil. Even when they are understood to mediate the presence of the persons they depict, they remain depictions, bringing to appearance a human hypostasis through the medium of nonhuman nature.[41] By contrast, for many Christians the consecrated bread and wine of the Eucharist (or Lord's Supper) have a different status. They are not simply depictions of glory, but also actual instances of heaven's glory on the not-yet-glorified earth—a belief reflected in the practice of uttering the words "The body

40. There is a close analogy here to the way that Christian talk about the divine nature is tied to the revelation of the three divine hypostases. For example, apart from knowledge of the Trinity, an attribute like omnipotence might be interpreted in all manner of ways; but the concrete reality of the Father, Son, and Spirit shows that divine power is nothing else than the act of giving existence without condition or reserve.

41. Christ's image "is called 'Christ' because of the signification of the name, but not because it has the nature of divinity and humanity. For it has its quality from painting with colors, perhaps, or assembling variegated stones, or the sculptor's art, or gold, or silver, or some other material delineation. It shares in the name of its prototype, as it shares also the honor and veneration; but it has no part in the nature of the prototype." Theodore the Studite, *On the Holy Icons* (2.17), 52.

of Christ, the bread of heaven," when distributing the consecrated bread.[42] For if
Christ's entire humanity has been glorified in the resurrection, and if the body and
blood of the risen Christ are confessed as present in the consecrated elements of the
Eucharist, then it follows that in the Eucharist we come into direct contact with
glorified matter (viz., Christ's body and blood) in the world of time and space.

To be sure, not all Christians follow this line of reasoning; even among those
who do, there is no consensus about how Christ's presence in the Eucharist is
to be understood.[43] The Catholic doctrine of transubstantiation involves perhaps the most metaphysically precise account of Christ's presence. Making use
of ontological categories derived from Aristotle, Catholic eucharistic theology
presumes a distinction between an entity's "substance" (its fundamental identity
or "whatness") and its "accidents" (its "howness," or the totality of its sensible
properties, including color, physical structure, and chemistry). Within this conceptual framework, substance and accidents are ontologically independent of
one another, so that alteration in one does not necessitate any change in the
other. Thus the phenomena of a person's hair turning gray, or an insect meta-
morphosing from a caterpillar to a butterfly—these would be examples of a
substance staying the same while one or more of its accidents change. The doctrine of transubstantiation teaches that in the Eucharist the converse takes place:
the accidents of the bread and the wine (including their appearance, taste, and
texture) remain unchanged, but their substance is changed into Christ's body
and blood.[44] The Greek term *metousiōsis*, which is etymologically equivalent
to "transubstantiation," has a prominent place in Orthodox tradition, though
without any commitment to the Aristotelian metaphysics that underlies Catholic doctrine.[45] Lutherans agree that Christ is present in the elements, but they are

42. See, e.g., Catholic Church, *Catechism of the Catholic Church* §1355, 2nd ed. (New York:
Doubleday, 1997).

43. The Reformed tradition in particular has been consistently suspicious of the claim that the
risen Christ is locally present in the elements of the Lord's Supper. This suspicion can be seen as
parallel to Reformed uneasiness with iconography, in that both reflect a basic worry about eliding
the distinction between heaven and earth. In the case of icons (and liturgical art more generally),
this takes the form of a refusal to allow that the heavenly is subject to earthly depiction; thus in the
Reformed theology of the Lord's Supper is an insistence that Christ's ascension to heaven precludes
his bodily presence on earth prior to the Parousia. Even though I disagree with both lines of argument, there is certainly cause to recognize that the Reformed position constitutes a salutary warning
of the risks of idolatry that attend claims for the interpenetration of the heavenly and earthly spheres
prior to the eschaton.

44. "The Council of Trent summarizes the Catholic faith by declaring: 'Because Christ our
Redeemer said that it was truly his body that he was offering under the species of bread, it has always
been the conviction of the Church of God, and this holy Council now declares again, that by the
consecration of the bread and wine there takes place a change of the whole substance of the bread
into the substance of the body of Christ our Lord and of the whole substance of the wine into the
substance of his blood. This change the holy Catholic Church has fittingly and properly called transubstantiation'" (*Catechism of the Catholic Church* §1376).

45. Though Orthodox churches do not regard any church council since II Nicaea as truly ecumenical, various councils held since then have been extraordinarily influential on Orthodox life and
thought, including the Council of Jerusalem in 1672, which affirmed *metousiōsis*. See Orthodox
Eastern Church, *The Acts and Decrees of the Synod of Jerusalem* (6.17), trans. J. N. W. B. Robertson
(London: Thomas Baker), 1899.

even more suspicious of the metaphysics of transubstantiation as lacking a clear basis in Scripture and so prefer to speak instead of Christ's presence "in, with, and under" (rather than instead of) the bread and wine.[46]

While these different theologies give rise to significant variations in devotional practice (e.g., the metaphysics of transubstantiation is the basis for Catholic veneration of the consecrated host, which Lutherans reject), in no case is the confession of Christ's presence in the Eucharist understood to produce any change in the appearance of the consecrated elements. On the contrary, all view Christ's presence as a matter of faith rather than sight, so that the fact that the consecrated elements continue to look like ordinary bread and wine is integral to their respective eucharistic theologies: Catholics hold that the sensible "accidents" of the elements are completely unaffected by consecration, while Lutherans insist that they retain their integrity as earthly substances in such a way as to preclude any visible alteration following consecration.[47] Given that Christians tend to describe (and in their art to portray) glory in visually arresting terms (see Dan. 12:3; Matt. 13:43; Eph. 5:14), it may at first blush seem odd that there should be no sign that what is eaten is nothing less than the "bread of angels," but on further reflection it is perhaps not so unusual after all.[48] There are certainly places in Scripture where the earthly appearance of heavenly realities is associated with an irruption of unearthly light (e.g., Matt. 28:3; Luke 2:9), but this is by no means always the case. Hebrews speaks of the possibility of entertaining angels unawares (13:2; cf. Gen. 18:1–19:1), and according to the Gospels even the risen Jesus himself did not stand out from the ordinary—to the extent that as often as not his own friends failed to recognize him (Luke 24:15–16; John 20:14; 21:4–7).[49] In these cases, at least, it seems that the glorified creation does not differ in any visible way from that which still awaits glory.

46. Luther himself combines all three prepositions in his *Confession concerning Christ's Supper* (in *Word and Sacrament* III, vol. 37 of *Luther's Works*, ed. and trans. Robet H. Fischer, American ed. [Philadelphia: Fortress Press, 1961], 306). In the Lutheran Confessions all three prepositions are used, but not together in a single phrase, so that the Eucharist is characterized as "the true body and blood of the Lord Jesus Christ *in and under* the bread and wine" (Luther, *Large Catechism*) and that "in the Holy Supper the body and blood of Christ are truly and essentially present and are truly distributed and received *with* the bread and wine" (Formula of Concord, Epitome, art. 7). See Theodore G. Tappert, ed. and trans., *The Book of Concord: The Confessions of the Evangelical Lutheran Church* (Philadelphia: Muhlenberg, 1959), 447, 482. It may also be noted here that the frequent designation of the Lutheran position as "consubstantiation" is not accurate, insofar as it suggests either a mixture or juxtaposition of body and blood with bread and wine. See Heinrich Schmid, *Doctrinal Theology of the Evangelical Lutheran Church*, trans. Charles A. Hay and Henry E. Jacobs, 3rd ed. (Minneapolis: Augsburg Publishing House, 1899), 571.

47. On the Catholic side, Thomas Aquinas explicitly denies that the body of Christ in the sacrament is perceptible by the bodily eye even in glory (*ST* 3.76.7).

48. The phrase "bread of angels" is applied to the manna eaten by the Israelites in the wilderness in Ps. 78:25. It is applied to the Eucharist in Thomas Aquinas's hymn *Lauda Sion* (cf. John 6:48–51), and it is listed as one of many synonyms for the sacrament (alongside, e.g., "bread of heaven") in the *Catechism of the Catholic Church* §1331.

49. The risen Jesus' later appearances to Stephen and Paul (Acts 7:55–56; 9:3–6) are characterized by visible glory, but these epiphanies are also pointedly *not* of Jesus walking about on earth, but rather are meant to emphasize his having ascended to heaven. In the transfiguration, Jesus shines

This lack of distinguishing visual features will also seem less surprising if we keep in mind that the heavenly sphere of creation that is already glorified is precisely the realm of the invisible. This invisibility is not merely accidental, as though heaven were simply hidden and could be seen only if God would pull back the curtain; rather, invisibility is part of heaven's nature. Only that which is part of the sphere of space and time can be seen by physical eyes, and heaven and its creatures are not part of the spatiotemporal order.[50] Consequently, they can be made visible to human beings only indirectly, through the use of earthly elements.[51] If light is part of this appearance, then it too must be understood as an earthly phenomenon (albeit one designed to testify to the heavenly origin of the vision) and not as an indication of what heaven "really" looks like, for the simple reason that heaven, because it is invisible, doesn't *look* like anything. So for earthly creatures, being glorified cannot be identified with any particular change in the physical characteristics of the creature, because glory is not a physical property, but rather the "putting on of immortality" that transcends the realm of the physical (1 Cor. 15:53). In this context, if icons serve to give the church a vision of heavenly glory in the wake of Christ's resurrection, they should not be understood as literal depictions of how the glorified appear (as though their value depended on the degree of physical correspondence when the reality they depict is not physical), but simply as witness to the church's belief in their glorification.[52]

Through Christ's resurrection, the glory that has been heaven's from the beginning and that will be the destiny of all creation has made a decisive inroad into the earthly sphere.[53] To be sure, the earth is not yet glorified (Phil. 3:14; 2 Tim. 2:18; cf. 1 Cor. 13:12); creation continues to groan as it waits for the time when it "will be set free from its bondage to decay and will obtain the freedom of the glory of the children of God" (Rom. 8:21). But as icons bear witness that some creatures have already passed on to glory, the Eucharist reminds us what the glorification of the creature means—or better, what it does not mean. Specifically, it does not mean changing the way a creature looks. It is perfectly

with glory prior to his death and resurrection, but this event's location on a mountain probably symbolizes proximity to heaven, and the story as a whole is frequently understood to be a prefiguration of Jesus' glory as the heavenly Son of Man (cf. Matt. 17:1–2 and pars. with Matt. 26:64 and pars.).

50. Although Paul classifies his own experience of being "caught up to the third heaven" as a matter of "visions and revelations of the Lord," he focuses less on what he had *seen* than on his having "*heard* things that are not to be told" (2 Cor. 12:1–4).

51. It is on these grounds that Thomas Aquinas deduces that in order to appear to us angels must assume material bodies, "making use of sensible things as images of what is, properly speaking, only discernible by intelligence" (*ST* 1.51.2.2).

52. Thus, though Theodore the Studite insists that an icon always portrays a concrete hypostasis, he explicitly denies that its devotional value depends on the accuracy of the portrait. See *On the Holy Icons* (3.5), 104.

53. See, in this context, N. T. Wright's speculation that the reason for the seemingly rapid loss of the Jewish Sabbath in the early church was a that the Sabbath is properly understood as a sign of the eschatological promise of God's coming to dwell on earth, a sign that is no longer necessary once the promise is fulfilled in the incarnation. N. T. Wright, *Scripture and the Authority of God: How to Read the Bible Today* (New York: HarperOne, 2013), 166.

appropriate that glory should be symbolized in Christian art through icono-graphic conventions suggesting physical transfiguration, since Scripture reports that glorified creatures have appeared to human beings in physically transfigured form. But the fact that there is no necessary correlation between seeing glorified creation and special visual effects makes it important to caution against equating the reality of glory with the appearance of light or any other sensible phenom-enon. After all, Paul warns that the devil himself can take on a glorious appear-ance (2 Cor. 11:14), while the "Lord of glory" can seem worthy of contempt (1 Cor. 2:8).[54]

All this is in no way to diminish the significance of glory as a real change in the conditions of creaturely existence. The freedom from bondage to decay and the putting on of immortality, mentioned by Paul, bespeak a very clear alteration in those conditions; whether the risen Jesus appears bathed in light or not, the point remains that he has death behind him. To observe that the glorious can seem quite ordinary is not to argue that glory has no effect on earthly existence, but to clarify the nature of that effect. There is a problem with the imagery of glorification as an ascent to an imperishable realm of light: it suggests that glory is simply a negation of the earthly realm, as though salva-tion were a matter of extraction from the full range of relationships with other creatures that both constitute and threaten our existence in time and space. The very characterization of creation in terms of the dynamic of *exitus* and *reditus* can easily lend support to this vision, if the former is interpreted as a physical movement away from God and the latter as a corresponding return, as though existence in time and space were a measure of linear distance from God that is brought into being only to be negated.

In this book I have tried to counter such a way of interpreting *exitus* and *reditus* by emphasizing that the topics covered in the various chapters do not describe sequential stages in a temporal movement first away from and then back to God. They are rather as a series of snapshots of a single relation as seen from a variety of different angles, differing according to whether the focus is on creation's origination *in* God (*exitus*) or its orientation *to* God (*reditus*). At no point, however, should any of these snapshots be taken to imply a spatial distance between God and the world. To be sure, there is (as John of Damas-cus taught) a unimaginable distance in *being* between Creator and creature, but that gulf holds for the highest angel in heaven no less than for the most

---

54. This position does not necessarily contradict the Orthodox belief, most closely associated with the fourteenth-century theologian Gregory Palamas, that light is an intrinsic feature of divine glory. According to Palamas, the light of glory—precisely because it is intrinsic to God—is uncre-ated and thus not (like the light of the sun or an incandescent bulb) the product of physical pro-cesses. It follows that the light of glory is intrinsically invisible to creaturely eyes, so that if a creature suddenly appears visibly glorious to us, that is solely because God enables us to see it as such and not because of any physical alteration in the thing itself. Palamas thus avers that in the transfiguration, Jesus, while "remaining identical to what he had been before, . . . bestowed . . . a divine power upon the eyes of the apostles and enabled them to look up and see for themselves." Gregory Palamas, *The Triads* (3.1.15), ed. John Meyendorff, trans. Nicholas Gendle (New York: Paulist Press, 1983), 76; cf. 57 (2.3.8), where he calls the uncreated light "a grace invisibly seen."

inert creature of earth. But it is precisely the ontological rather than physical character of this "distance" that renders untenable the thought that God is at any time removed from any aspect of creation. In whatever respect it may be contemplated, creation exists only as God is with it. Thus it is possible to speak of an *exitus* insofar as the creature takes its origin in a movement outward (and thus "exiting") from God, as God extends divine love beyond the life of the Trinity; yet talk of *reditus* is potentially more misleading, because it suggests a process of creaturely movement toward God that is either impossible (since creation's status as created precludes any abrogation of its ontological distance from the Creator) or unnecessary (since God's status as Creator means that there is and can be no physical distance between God and creatures to be overcome). But if glorification is not a "return" to God in which the earthly is simply left behind, then what is it?

The status of the Eucharist as an instance of the glorified Christ's presence in time and space suggests that the answer to this question involves reconceiving the subject of the *exitus* and *reditus*. This terminology originated in a Neoplatonic milieu, in which the *exitus* referred to the emanation of being from the transcendent One and *reditus* to the reverse process by which the philosopher, through a process of spiritual purification and disciplined contemplation, reascends through the intermediate stages of being to union with the One. In this scheme, it is the creature who moves, since the One is by definition without parts and thus immovable. By contrast, for Christians the *exitus* of creation is a deliberate act (and in this sense a "movement") of God: there is no "natural" emanation of creatures from the Creator; instead, creatures come into existence as God determines to love beyond the bounds of God's own Trinitarian life, and so to bring creatures into existence as the object of that love. If the Eucharist is an instance of glorification of earthly creation, here too the "movement" is a matter of divine rather than creaturely activity: the *reditus* is not an act of the creature "returning" to God (for such an ascent to divinity lies beyond any creature's capacity), but, so to speak, God's "return" (which Rev. 21 describes by using the imagery of descent) to the creature. This "return" must be understood in a very specific sense. It is not the overcoming of a previous absence, as though God overcome some intervening distance separating divinity from the world; for within the context of creation from nothing, at every moment a creature's existence depends on the fact that God is there, sustaining it in existence. Instead, God's "return" is best understood as an *intensification* of divine presence. I am no nearer to a person sitting next to me before than after we are introduced, but the fact of acquaintance profoundly changes the quality of that nearness. Similarly, there is (because there can be) no augmentation of God's proximity to creation in glory, but there is an increase in intimacy. Prior to glory, the creature is absolutely dependent on God for its being at every moment that it exists, but God's presence to the creature is hidden. Under these conditions one can give a perfectly satisfactory account of the creature's existence without any reference to God's sustaining presence (which is what the natural sciences do). In glory, by contrast, God enters into a relationship with the creature that discloses God's presence as Creator. This disclosure does not necessarily entail any change in physical appearance (again, the elements of the Eucharist do not look any different after consecration), but, however it is mediated, the result is that the believer is assured not only that God is there *with* her as the Creator who sustains her in being, but also there *for* her, establishing a relationship of communion in which God invites and enables the believer to return the love that grounds her existence.

The idea that to see God's glory means to cease to be a creature and become quite literally divine has been consistently rejected within the Christian tradition. Even the most exalted accounts of the Orthodox doctrine of deification have insisted on a permanent and unbridgeable gap between Creator and creature. But it is not at all uncommon for glorification to be interpreted as a process of extraction from the earthly matrix of creation. Nor can this legacy be attributed entirely to a disdain for the material inherited from non-Christian (e.g., Platonic) sources. Biblical reference to the eschatological dissolution of the elements (2 Pet. 3:10) and to believers being "caught up in the clouds . . . to meet the Lord in the air" (1 Thess. 4:17) give some credence to the idea that the earth is just a launching pad from which the faithful soul is destined (as one popular hymn puts it) to "fly away." And yet as we have already seen, the Bible's final image of creation's destiny is quite different; not an ascent from earth to heaven, but quite the opposite—the descent of heaven to earth:

> And I saw the holy city, the new Jerusalem, coming down out of heaven from God, prepared as a bride adorned for her husband. And I heard a loud voice from the throne saying,
>> "See, the home of God is among mortals.
>>> He will dwell with them;
>> they will be his peoples,
>>> and God himself will be with them."
>
> (Rev. 21:2–3)

Together with the hope of Christ's returning to earth from heaven, this image of descent illustrates the principle that God's dealings with creation move from heaven to earth. It follows that the content of Christian hope is not to leave the earth behind, but to see it liberated and renewed, so that what is experienced now in a few, widely scattered meals of bread and wine may truly be a foretaste of the feast to come.

One particularly arresting account of how the Christian faith blends affirmation of the enduring value of the creatures we see now with the hope of deep transformation of the conditions of created existence is found in Paul:

> For we know that if the earthly tent we live in is destroyed, we have a building from God, a house not made with hands, eternal in the heavens. For in this tent we groan, longing to be clothed with our heavenly dwelling—if indeed, when we have taken it off we will not be found naked. For while

we are still in this tent, we groan under our burden, because we wish not
to be unclothed but to be further clothed, so that what is mortal may be
swallowed up by life. (2 Cor. 5:1–4)

At first it seems that Paul's hope for "a building from God . . . in the heavens"
implies just the sort of movement away from earth that justifies indifference
toward (if not disdain for) the body, but it turns out that things are not so simple. The present order is indeed one of groaning, but the hope for a "heavenly
dwelling" is explained in terms of a desire for the renewal of our present form
of existence rather than its abandonment. Paul wants to emphasize that God's
power is such that even the destruction of our bodies is no obstacle to life with
God; but he also stresses that our present groaning has nothing to do with want-
ing to be "unclothed," but reflects instead a desire to be *further* clothed." For
Paul, the Christian hope is not to have anything taken away but to have the mortal "swallowed up by life," in the form of an augmentation that Paul elsewhere
describes as the earthly body "put[ting] on" immortality and imperishability (1
Cor. 15:54–55).[55] And however different (or not) the result may *look* from the
creation we now see, the content of the Christian hope is that it will *be* as different as the Eucharist is from mere bread and wine.

As I stated at the beginning of this chapter, the topic of glory is distinct from
the doctrine of creation. Nevertheless, one's theology of glory has a direct impact
on how creation is understood. If glorification is a matter of shedding the earthly
in order to rise up to a heavenly realm, then there is little reason to regard the
matrix of relationships among creatures that governs our present life as anything
more than a series of obstacles to be negotiated on the way to a future when we
will be freed equally from the tyranny of inanimate objects and the hell of other
people. But as Paul makes clear, any such vision of the glorified state is deeply
mistaken. The point of glory is not to negate the present form of creation but to
perfect it. The earthly creation is bound by time, and for this reason it is necessary that its present form should pass away (1 Cor. 7:31); but nothing could be
less justified in this context than to confuse "form" with substance. The Christian hope is not that we should be freed from relationships with others, whether
to be reabsorbed in the One or to enjoy a purely private relationship with God.
Crucial here are the symbolism and reality of the Eucharist as the event in which
we receive, quite literally, a taste of glory in the present. For the Eucharist draws
us upward by drawing us together, binding us not only to one another but
also to the bread and wine, which in their organic connection with soil, water,
sun, and air implicate the whole web of creaturely relations that makes our life
specifically and genuinely human. In Christ, God the Creator—without for a
moment ceasing to be the Creator—has also become a creature of earth. In

---

55. In 2 Cor. 5:6–7 Paul contrasts being "at home in the body" with being "away from the
Lord," and vice versa; but the body in question is precisely that which has not been renewed in glory.
Nothing in 2 Corinthians or elsewhere in the Pauline corpus suggests that Paul envisions glory as a
disembodied state; indeed, his lengthy reflection on humanity's eschatological transformation in 1
Cor. 15 is a counter to those who deny the resurrection of the body.

eating the bread and drinking the wine that are Christ's body and blood, we confess that it is because God has become a creature of earth that we creatures of earth have become children of God, bound up in our living with the all the rest of the earthly creation, which is destined to share with us (and with the heavenly sphere that is already bathed in divine glory) the glorious liberty of God's children. "For the Word of God wills always and in all things to accomplish the mystery of his embodiment."[56]

56. Maximus the Confessor, *Ambiguum 7*, in *On the Cosmic Mystery of Jesus Christ: Selected Writings from St. Maximus the Confessor*, trans. Paul Blowers and Robert Louis Wilken (Crestwood, NY: St. Vladimir's Seminary Press, 2003), 60.

Conclusion

What is the point of the doctrine of creation? A classic answer is found in the Heidelberg Catechism: "We learn that we are to be patient in adversity, grateful in the midst of blessing, and to trust our faithful God and Father for the future, assured that no creature shall separate us from his love, since all creatures are so completely in his hand that without his will they cannot even move."[1]

There is much to admire in this summary, which provides a lapidary formulation of the chief points of Christian belief in creation from nothing. At the same time, the framing of these insights is in certain ways less than felicitous. One might begin by questioning whether patience in adversity is necessarily to be encouraged on the basis of the doctrine of creation. Certainly there are occasions where such patience is to be commended (e.g., the inevitable setbacks encountered when undertaking any challenging task), but other times when there seems to be every ground for thinking that God would rather see resistance to adversity than submission to it (e.g., when a person is suffering from a debilitating disease). But even leaving this point to one side, it surely remains open to question

---

1. *The Heidelberg Catechism*, Q. 28, in Presbyterian Church (U.S.A.), *Book of Confessions: Study Edition* (Louisville, KY: Geneva Press, 1996), 63.

whether, as the language of the Heidelberg Catechism implies, the main point of the doctrine of creation is to instill particular feelings or attitudes. Gratitude and trust (along with genuine patience, as opposed to resignation) just cannot be summoned up at will, however good the reasons one may have for feeling them. That we often do not feel grateful to or trust in God is certainly cause for regret and repentance. But the reason is not necessarily that we lack adequate understanding of creation, as though the cure for our hardness of heart were a lesson in doctrine. Patience, thanksgiving, and trust are gifts of grace for which we must pray, not deductions from dogmatic premises.

This is certainly not to suggest that the reverse is the case, and that theologians' claims about creation are merely ways of communicating the patience, gratitude, and trust that Christians already feel toward God, but it is to argue that the point of the doctrine of creation is not to elicit certain feelings. Indeed, given the infrequency with which any honest Christian can credit herself with an appropriate sense of thankfulness toward and trust in God, attempts to use the doctrine in this way are arguably far more likely to give rise to feelings of frustration, resentment, or despair than love of God. What then is the point of Christian teaching about creation? It was once common to argue that the Israelite belief in God as Creator was a deduction from the experience of the exodus, so that belief in creation emerged as a corollary of soteriology rather than as a topic of interest in its own right.[2] Present-day biblical scholars no longer feel that the evidence supports this genealogy of biblical teaching on creation, but there is a good case to be made that the logic of creation from nothing is closely bound up with how Christians think about salvation. During the second century, a Christian preacher admonished his audience as follows: "Brothers and sisters, we ought to think of Jesus Christ as of God, as the judge of the living and the dead; and we ought not to belittle our salvation. For when we belittle him, we hope to get but little."[3] The line of inference here seems clear enough: if we are to trust Jesus' capacity to save, we cannot think of him as any less than God. But this conclusion begs a further question: Why should we trust God? Surely God is worthy of ultimate trust only if it is indeed true (as authors of the Heidelberg Catechism rightly recognized) that nothing can separate us from God's love (Rom. 8:39). From this perspective, it's not that the doctrine of creation motivates us to trust God, but that it provides an explanation of why it makes sense for us to trust God in the way that the gospel says we should.

As noted in chapter 1 (above), this reasoning apparently contributed to the relatively rapid triumph of the doctrine of creation from nothing in the church. As received and developed over the centuries, however, the doctrine retained a strongly anthropocentric and even ecclesiocentric focus on God's providential

---

2. For the classic formulation of this position, see Gerhard von Rad, *Old Testament Theology*, trans. D. M. G. Stalker, 2 vols. (New York: Harper & Row, 1962–65), 1:136–39; he concedes that the Wisdom literature is an exception to this pattern.

3. See *2 Clement* 1.1–2, in *Early Christian Fathers*, trans. and ed. Cyril C. Richardson (New York: Macmillan, 1970), 193, trans. slightly alt.

care for human beings (and Christians in particular) to the virtual exclusion of other creatures. But the implications of creation from nothing are not consistent with the kind of hierarchical vision of the created order that would justify narrow focus on the church, or even on humanity considered more broadly. Most obviously, where all creatures are equally dependent on God for their existence, there can be no sense in which any creature is ontologically closer to God than any other: the most unimpressive lump of rock is no more distant from God than the most glorious of the seraphim. To be sure, human beings may reflect more of the divine image than other creatures (by virtue of possessing the capacity to think and to love, e.g., that a rock lacks),[4] but that is not grounds for viewing other creatures as simply instrumental to our glorification. There are two reasons for this. First, since God, as primary cause, is directly responsible for every created effect, even when a creature functions as a secondary cause of some such effect, its purpose in the created order cannot be reduced to that role. Because God does not need any creaturely cause to bring about a given created effect, if God brings a creature into existence, then that creature must have value in God's sight beyond its instrumentality in giving rise to such effects.[5] Second, where glorification is concerned, no creature can function instrumentally in relation to another: the relationships of secondary causation that obtain among creatures may sustain them in time and space as potential objects of glorification, but these relationships do not in themselves advance any creature toward glory; for glorification is entirely and exclusively a work of divine grace. So here too, there can be no question of any creature being no more than a means to the flourishing of another.

In short, creation from nothing dictates that *everything* is of immediate (i.e., noninstrumental) concern to God insofar as it exists at all, and what is of concern to God cannot be a matter of indifference to us who are called to life in communion with God. Of course, most of what exists is beyond our purview. The life of angels is not our concern (they flourish quite independently of what we do or fail to do), and absent currently unimaginable technological developments, we are unable to affect or to be affected by life that may exist beyond the solar system.[6] Within our terrestrial environment, by contrast, there is no shortage of nonhuman creatures for our consideration. It is frequently difficult for us to see *how*

4. For an excellent discussion of this point, see Kathryn Tanner, *Christ the Key* (Cambridge: Cambridge University Press, 2010), 10–28.
5. So the fact that the heavenly bodies serve to mark the passing of time (Gen. 1:14–15) does not exhaust their significance (see Job 38:7), any more than the purpose of my mother's existence is reducible to her having given birth to me.
6. It is possible that humans could recover a space probe sent by some extraterrestrial civilization, even as some distant society might conceivably find the Pioneer and Voyager spacecraft launched into interstellar space from the earth, but (even leaving aside the infinitesimal odds of a probe from one advanced civilization drifting anywhere near another) the gap between the launching of such vehicles and any possible recovery would span many millions of years. Radio contact with distant civilizations seems less fanciful, but unless such beings inhabited the very nearest stellar systems, genuine conversation would be impossible, given the length of time needed for messages to travel back and forth.

other creatures are of concern to God, especially when their flourishing seems to come at our expense; but insofar as it is our vocation as servants of God to honor God's will for the flourishing of the whole creation, that does not relieve us of the obligation to try. Particularly in our present global context, where the evidence is overwhelming that our existing patterns of interaction with the creation are systematically undermining the viability of ecosystems around the globe, this obligation is augmented by basic considerations of self-interest.

Because it teaches that God is the sole antecedent condition of the existence of every creature, creation from nothing is certainly an affirmation of divine power: every creature exists solely because God wants it to exist. In light of the enormous diversity of creation even within the astronomically miniscule confines of earth, however, the chief significance of the doctrine arguably lies less in its implications for divine power than in what it says about God's generosity. In bestowing existence on all that is, God wills that it should be. Insofar as we have been given the capacity to recognize this fact and, indeed, to help sustain it (Gen. 2:15), we have the responsibility of figuring out how best to honor God's willing the existence of other creatures alongside ourselves. In certain respects this challenge is no different from our obligation to acknowledge other people whose differences from us can make their status as fellow members of the body of Christ appear puzzling or even offensive to us at first glance. But where other people are concerned, we have at least the ability to speak with them to work out together what our joint participation in Christ's body might mean. We have no such possibility where nonhuman creatures are concerned. They cannot tell us directly what understanding—if any—they have of their place in creation, so we need to proceed indirectly, through (e.g.) scientific investigation of the conditions under which individual species flourish, and of the effects of our behavior on the ecosystems that are the matrix for their flourishing. As is the case in our engagement with other human beings, the conclusions we draw will be contestable, but again, that does not release us from the responsibility to proceed as best we can, trusting—on the basis of the belief that God created the whole world from nothing—that other creatures have a rightful place in the world and that we are called to honor it.

Sometimes the claim is made that a sustained commitment to the flourishing of nonhuman creatures will lead us to feel a more intimate connection with them. It is certainly possible that acknowledging other creatures' place before God will have this effect, but it is not necessary. It is equally possible, and in its own way perhaps no less desirable, that in developing a genuine appreciation for the integrity of other creatures as objects of God's love, we will acquire a healthy feeling of distance from them, in the recognition that they have their own forms of goodness, which may be quite alien to the possibilities of human experience. Once again, however, the point of doctrine is not to promote feelings, whether of intimacy or of awe. It is rather to discipline our speech and action in the hope that the habits thereby acquired will promote forms of behavior that enhance the church's witness to the gospel.

Recognizing how some have contended that creation from nothing is detrimental to this witness, I ended chapter 1 by suggesting that a plausible defense of the doctrine must address two questions: How does God's power to create depend on God's identity? How does this dependence help to address the charge that an omnipotent God is arbitrary? The basic contours of my answers have long since been worked out. The doctrine of the Trinity clarifies the relationship between God's power to create and God's identity. God's own life takes the form of a sharing of existence, as the Father eternally begets the Son in the power of the Holy Spirit; and in creation this same threefold structure is reflected in God's external action, as the Father brings the world into being through the Son (John 1:1–4) and sustains it through the Spirit (Ps. 104:29–30). In this respect, there is nothing arbitrary about creation: because God is internally productive as Trinity, it is entirely "natural" (i.e., appropriate, though neither logically nor ontologically necessary) that God should also be productive externally, granting that other entities should also exist sharing by grace the existence that God enjoys by nature.

So far, so good—but only so far. When critics worry that creation from nothing implies an arbitrary deity, they are not speaking about the idea of creation in the abstract. Granted that it seems appropriate for the Trinity, whose own life is love (1 John 4:8), to seek in love to extend the gift of existence beyond the Godhead, the question remains of why creation should take the form it does, with its disconcerting mix of life, beauty, and joy on the one hand, and apparently unavoidable suffering, violence, and destruction on the other. In other words, isn't God's decision to create *this particular world* inherently arbitrary? Some have been tempted to answer this question by arguing that the cosmos we have is the best of all possible worlds,[7] but proponents of this strategy share with critics of creation from nothing the same failure to appreciate what the doctrine actually implies. Here again, to avoid misunderstanding, it is vital to recognize the limits of creaturely analogies to God's work of creating. The creation of the world from nothing is not a matter of God actualizing one possibility out of many, in the way that I might choose to make chocolate rather than carrot or lemon cake (let alone apple pie or baked custard) for dessert tonight. It is not that God is incapable of having made the world differently (which amounts to another form of the "best of all possible worlds" argument), but that conceiving creation from nothing as choosing among possible worlds constitutes a logical mistake. In creating from nothing, God does not actualize one possibility among others; rather, God makes it that there can be such a thing as the actualization of possibilities. There is just no proper creaturely analogue to this relation, because the very concepts and categories we are tempted to deploy in order to illustrate creation from nothing are already features of the created order and

---

7. The most famous attempt is that of Gottfried Leibniz in his *Essais de Théodicée sur la bonté de Dieu, la liberté de l'homme et l'origine du mal* (Amsterdam, 1710), but it is also implicit in, e.g., the use of the "free will defense" to explain why a good God would permit evil.

thus invariably false to the unconditioned and unmediated character of God's activity as Creator.

From this perspective, the worry that creation from nothing makes God arbitrary is misplaced because it presupposes a relationship between Creator and creature that is inconsistent with divine transcendence. But even if the form in which it is often raised entails a confusion of categories, the charge of divine arbitrariness does reflect a serious theological question, namely, whether creation (including our own existence as creatures) is something that we can and should regard as an entirely good gift, or whether some reservation is in order. Ultimately, this reduces to the question of whether God can be trusted unreservedly; the doctrine of creation from nothing is of no help in answering this question because (as noted above) it presupposes that the question has already been answered, since creation from nothing is at bottom an account of *why* God can be trusted unreservedly: because whatever exists, exists only because God wants it to exist. If the world is judged to be inherently tragic and cruel, it will not be something for which anyone will be thankful, and therefore the world would be no sort of reality that could be ascribed to God's sole agency. From such a perspective, it makes no sense to teach creation from nothing.[8]

Why should Christians affirm creation from nothing? The doctrine does not seem to be internally inconsistent, nor is it fatally at odds either with other dimensions of Christian belief (e.g., creaturely freedom) or with the best empirical accounts of how the world works (e.g., natural selection); but such considerations merely remove possible objections to the doctrine and do not provide positive reasons for belief in it. In order to address this latter problem, I have tried to make the case that the doctrine is scriptural, even though it is not explicitly taught in the Bible, and that its deep roots in the Christian tradition reflect a broad consensus that a doctrine of creation from nothing is finally unavoidable, given the conviction that nothing can separate us from the love of God shown forth in Christ Jesus our Lord.

And yet I suspect that when asked to make sense of creation from nothing, it may be more illuminating in the first instance to identify its dogmatic function than its grounding in Scripture or tradition. Here there is every reason to concur with the Heidelberg Catechism that the confession that God created "all that is, seen and unseen" from nothing is at bottom a claim that it makes sense to trust God—even if, as a matter of fact, our feelings of trust are often wavering and uncertain. More precisely, in teaching creation from nothing, Christians affirm that in all things God is acting for creatures' good. This does *not* entail the belief that everything that happens is good, but rather that if "God so loved the

---

8. Could one imagine that God created a thoroughly evil world from nothing simply to make creatures miserable? I do not think so, because that scenario presupposes that the misery creatures experience is a genuine evil, and that in turn implies that their being is in itself good (otherwise their misery would not be anything to regret). The hypothesis therefore fails because its enabling assumption—that the world is evil in its entirety—is incoherent. It is certainly possible to imagine a malevolent deity, but not one who creates from nothing.

world that he gave his only Son" (John 3:16), then we may be confident that in all things God is working to overcome evil. In the face of the myriad threats to creaturely well-being, there is nothing self-evident about this belief, and Christians therefore have no grounds for looking down on those who do not share it. If they wish to persuade others of its truth, they need to act in ways that display their trust in God's creative work, striving to honor the integrity of all creatures in the conviction that no creature exists except as God gives it being: sustaining, empowering, and guiding it to the end that God intends for it. And if asked why God does this, their answer must be clear: it is simply and solely because God sees every creature as good. There is no other reason, no other motive, no other factor in play. Nothing.

Bibliography

Alexander, Paul J. *The Patriarch Nicephorus of Constantinople: Ecclesiastical Policy and Image Worship in the Byzantine Empire*. Oxford: Clarendon Press, 1958.

Anderson, Bernhard W. *From Creation to New Creation: Old Testament Perspectives*. Minneapolis: Fortress Press, 1994.

Anselm. *Monologion and Proslogion with the Replies of Gaunilo and Anselm*. Translated by Thomas Williams. Indianapolis: Hackett Publishing Co., 1995.

———. *Proslogion*. In *S. Anselmi cantuariensis archiepiscopi Opera omnia*, edited by Franciscus Salesius Schmitt, 1:89–140. Edinburgh: Thomas Nelson & Son, 1946.

Athanasius. *Defence of the Nicene Definition*. In *Athanasius: Select Works and Letters*, vol. 4 of *Nicene and Post-Nicene Fathers*, 2nd ser., edited by Philip Schaff and Henry Wace. 1892. Repr., Peabody, MA: Hendrickson Publishers, 1995.

Augustine. *The City of God against the Pagans*. Edited and translated by R. W. Dyson. Cambridge: Cambridge University Press, 1998.

———. *Confessions and Enchiridion*. Edited and translated by Albert Cook Outler. Philadelphia: Westminster Press, 1955.

———. *Of True Religion*. In *Augustine: Earlier Writings*, edited and translated by J. H. S. Burleigh. Philadelphia: Westminster Press, 1953.

———. *On Genesis*. Translated by Edmund Hill, OP. Edited by John E. Rotelle, OSA. Hyde Park, NY: New City Press, 2002.

———. *The Trinity*. Edited by John E. Rotelle. Translated by Edmund Hill. Hyde Park, NY: New City Press, 1991.

Balthasar, Hans Urs von. *Seeing the Form*. Vol. 1 of *The Glory of the Lord: A Theological Aesthetics*, edited by Joseph Fessio, SJ, and John Riches, translated by Erasmo Leiva-Merikakis. San Francisco: Ignatius Press, 1982.

Barth, Karl. *Church Dogmatics*. 13 vols. Edited by G. W. Bromiley and T. F. Torrance. Edinburgh: T&T Clark, 1956–75.

———. *Dogmatics in Outline*. Translated by G. T. Thompson. New York: Harper & Row, 1959.

Basil of Caesarea. *Basil: Letters and Select Works*. Vol. 8 of *Nicene and Post-Nicene Fathers*, 2nd ser., edited by Philip Schaff and Henry Wace. 1895. Repr., Peabody, MA: Hendrickson Publishers, 1995.

Beely, Christopher A. "Divine Causality and the Monarchy of God the Father in Gregory of Nazianzus." *Harvard Theological Review* 100 (April 2007): 199–214.

Blowers, Paul M. *Drama of the Divine Economy: Creator and Creation in Early Christian Theology and Piety*. Oxford: Oxford University Press, 2012.

Bonhoeffer, Dietrich. *Act and Being: Transcendental Philosophy and Ontology in Systematic Theology*. Vol. 2 of *Dietrich Bonhoeffer Works*, translated by H. Martin Rumscheidt. 1931. Repr., Minneapolis: Fortress Press, 1996.

Briggman, Anthony. "Dating Irenaeus' Acquisition of Theophilus' Correspondence *To Autolycus*: A Pneumatological Perspective." *Studia patristica* 45 (2010): 397–402

Brown, Raymond E., SS. *The Gospel According to John (i–xii)*. Anchor Bible 29. Garden City, NY: Doubleday, 1966.

Brunner, Emil. *Revelation and Reason: The Christian Doctrine of Faith and Knowledge*, translated by Olive Wyon. Philadelphia: Westminster Press, 1946.

Bulgakov, Sergius. *The Lamb of God*. Russian ed., 1933. Translated by Boris Jakim. Grand Rapids: Wm. B. Eerdmans Publishing Co, 2008.

Burrell, David B. *Faith and Freedom: An Interfaith Perspective*. Oxford: Blackwell, 2004.

———. *Towards a Jewish-Christian-Muslim Theology*. Oxford: Wiley-Blackwell, 2011.

Burrell, David B., Carlo Cogliati, Janet Martin Soskice, and William R Stoeger, eds. *Creation and the God of Abraham*. Cambridge: Cambridge University Press, 2010.

Burrell, David B., and Bernard McGinn, eds. *God and Creation: An Ecumenical Symposium*. Notre Dame, IN: University of Notre Dame Press, 1990.

Byrne, Peter. *Natural Religion and the Nature of Religion: The Legacy of Deism*. London: Routledge, 1989.

Caldwell, Robert W., III. *Communion in the Spirit: The Holy Spirit as the Bond of Union in the Theology of Jonathan Edwards*. Milton Keynes, UK: Paternoster, 2006.

Calvin, John. *Calvin's Bible Commentaries: Genesis, Part I*. Translated by John King. 1847. Repr., Charleston, SC: Forgotten Books, 2007.

———. *Institutes of the Christian Religion*. Translated by Ford Lewis Battles. Philadelphia: Westminster Press, 1960.

Catholic Church. *Catechism of the Catholic Church*. 2nd ed. New York: Doubleday, 1997.

Crenshaw, James L. *Old Testament Wisdom: An Introduction*. 1981. 3rd ed. Louisville, KY: Westminster John Knox Press, 2010.

Childs, Brevard. *Myth and Reality in the Old Testament*. London: SCM Press, 1960.

The Christian Faith in the Doctrinal Documents of the Catholic Church. Edited by Josef Neuner and Jacques Dupuis. Rev. ed. New York: Alba House, 1982.

Clark, Stephen. *How to Think about the Earth: Philosophical and Theological Models for Ecology*. London: Mowbray, 1993.

Coakley, Sarah. *Powers and Submissions: Spirituality, Philosophy and Gender*. Oxford: Blackwell Publishing, 2002.

Cobb, John B., Jr. and David Ray Griffin. *Process Theology: An Introductory Exposition*. Louisville, KY: Westminster John Knox Press, 1976.

Cohen, Arthur A. *The Tremendum: A Theological Interpretation of the Holocaust*. New York: Crossroad, 1981.

Crenshaw, James L. *Old Testament Wisdom: An Introduction*. 1981. 3rd ed. Louisville, KY: Westminster John Knox Press, 2010.

———. *Urgent Advice and Probing Questions: Collected Writings on Old Testament Wisdom*. Macon, GA: Mercer University Press, 1995.

Cunningham, David S. "What Do We Mean by 'God'?" In *Essentials of Christian Theology*, edited by William C. Placher, 76–92. Louisville, KY: Westminster John Knox Press, 2003.

Darwin, Charles. *Natural Selection: Being the Second Part of His Big Species Book Written from 1856 to 1858*. Edited by R. C. Stauffer. 1856–58. Repr., Cambridge: Cambridge University Press, 1975.

———. *On the Origin of Species*. London: Murray, 1859.

Dawkins, Richard. *The Selfish Gene*. New York: Oxford University Press, 1976.

Derrida, Jacques. *Given Time: I. Counterfeit Money*. Translated by Peggy Kamuf. Chicago: University of Chicago Press, 1992.

Dionysius the Areopagite. *Pseudo-Dionysius: The Complete Works*. Translated by Colm Luibheid. New York: Paulist Press, 1987.

Einstein, Albert, and Max Born. *The Born-Einstein Letters*. Translated by Irene Born. New York: Macmillan, 1971.

Eusebius of Caesarea. *Ecclesiastical History*. In *Eusebius*, vol. 1 of *Nicene and Post-Nicene Fathers*, 2nd ser., edited by Philip Schaff and Henry Wace. 1890. Repr., Peabody, MA: Hendrickson Publishers, 1995.

Evans, Donald D. *The Logic of Self-Involvement: A Philosophical Study of Everyday Language with Special Reference to the Christian Use of Language about God as Creator*. London: SCM Press, 1963.

Farrer, Austin. *Faith and Speculation: An Essay in Philosophical Theology*. London: Adam & Charls Black, 1967.

Finite and Infinite: A Philosophical Essay. 1943. 2nd ed., 1959. Repr., New York: Seabury Press, 1979.

The Freedom of the Will. New York: Charles Scribner's Sons, 1958.

———.*Love Almighty and Ills Unlimited: An Essay on Providence and Evil*. London: Collins, 1962.

Florensky, Pavel. *Iconostasis*. Translated by Donald Sheehan and Olga Andrejev. Crestwood, NY: St. Vladimir's Seminary Press, 1996.

Fretheim, Terence E. *God and the World in the Old Testament: A Relational Theology of Creation*. Nashville: Abingdon Press, 2005.

Galloway, Allan D. *The Cosmic Christ*. New York: Harper & Brothers, 1951.

Geertz, Clifford. "Thick Description: Toward an Interpretive Theory of Culture." In *The Interpretation of Culture: Selected Essays*. New York: Basic Books, 1973.

Glei, Reinhold . "*Et invidus et inbecillus*: Das angebliche Epikurfragment bei Laktanz, *De ira Dei* 13,20–21." *Vigiliae christianae* 42 (1988): 47–58.

Gould, Stephen Jay. *Full House: The Spread of Excellence from Plato to Darwin*. New York: Three Rivers Press, 1997.

———. *The Structure of Evolutionary Theory*. Cambridge, MA: Belknap Press, 2002.

Gregersen, Niels Henrik. "Three Types of Indeterminacy: On the Distinction between God's Action as Creator and as Providence." In *The Concept of Nature in Science and Theology*, edited by Niels H. Gregersen, pt. 1:165–84. Studies in Science and Theology 3. European Conference on Science and Theology. Geneva: Labor & Fides, 1997.

Gregory of Nazianzus. *Oration 29: The Third Theological Oration—On the Son*. In *Cyril of Jerusalem, Gregory Nazianzen*, translated by Charles Gordon Browne and James

Edward Swallow, vol. 7 of *Nicene and Post-Nicene Fathers*, 2nd ser., edited by Philip Schaff and Henry Wace, 301–9. 1894. Repr., Peabody, MA: Hendrickson Publishers, 1995.

————. *Oration 30: The Fourth Theological Oration, Which Is the Second concerning the Son*. In *Cyril of Jerusalem, Gregory Nazianzen*, translated by Charles Gordon Browne and James Edward Swallow, vol. 7 of *Nicene and Post-Nicene Fathers*, 2nd ser., edited by Philip Schaff and Henry Wace, 309–18. 1894. Repr., Peabody, MA: Hendrickson Publishers, 1995.

————. *Oration 31: The Fifth Theological Oration—On the Holy Spirit*. In *Cyril of Jerusalem, Gregory Nazianzen*, translated by Charles Gordon Browne and James Edward Swallow, vol. 7 of *Nicene and Post-Nicene Fathers*, 2nd ser., edited by Philip Schaff and Henry Wace, 318–28. 1894. Repr., Peabody, MA: Hendrickson Publishers, 1995.

Gregory of Nyssa. *An Answer to Ablabius: That We Should Not Think of Saying There Are Three Gods*. Edited and translated by Cyril C. Richardson. In *Christology of the Later Fathers*, edited by Edward R. Hardy, 256–67. Philadelphia: Westminster Press, 1954.

————. *On the Making of Man*. In *Gregory of Nyssa: Dogmatic Treatises, etc.* Translated by William Moore and Henry Austin Wilson. In vol. 5 of *Nicene and Post-Nicene Fathers*, 2nd ser., edited by Philip Schaff and Henry Wace, 387–427. 1893. Repr., Peabody, MA: Hendrickson Publishers, 1995.

————. *Opera*. 2 vols. Edited by Werner Jaeger. Leiden: E. J. Brill, 1960.

Gregory Palamas. *Hagioriticus tomus de quietistis*. In *Gregorii Palamae Opera omnia*, in vol. 150 of Patrologiae cursus completus: Series graeca [PG], edited by J.-P. Migne, cols. 1225–36. Paris, 1865.

————. *The Triads*. Edited by John Meyendorff. Translated by Nicholas Gendle. New York: Paulist Press, 1983.

Griffin, David Ray. "Creation out of Nothing, Creation out of Chaos, and the Problem of Evil." In *Encountering Evil: Live Options in Theodicy*, edited by Stephen T. Davis, 108–25. Louisville, KY: Westminster John Knox Press, 2001.

————. *God, Power, and Evil: A Process Theodicy*. 1976. Repr., Louisville, KY: Westminster John Knox Press, 2004.

Gunton, Colin E. *The Triune Creator: A Historical and Systematic Survey*. Edinburgh: Edinburgh University Press, 1998.

Hartshorne, Charles. *The Divine Relativity: A Social Conception of God*. 1948; repr., New Haven, CT: Yale University Press, 1964.

Hector, Kevin W. *Theology without Metaphysics: God, Language, and the Spirit of Recognition*. Cambridge: Cambridge University Press, 2011.

Hefelbower, Samuel Gring. *The Relation of John Locke to English Deism*. Chicago: University of Chicago Press, 1918.

Hick, John. *Evil and the God of Love*. 1966. 2nd ed. New York: Palgrave Macmillan, 2007.

Hippolytus. *Refutatio omnium haeresium*. Edited by Miroslav Marcovich. Vol. 25 of *Patristische Texte und Studien*, edited by K. Aland and E. Mühlenberg. Berlin: Walter de Gruyter, 1986.

Hunsinger, George. "A Response to William Werpehowski." *Theology Today*, 43 (October 1986): 354–60.

Irenaeus of Lyons. *Against Heresies*. In *The Apostolic Fathers with Justin Martyr and Irenaeus*, vol. 1 of *The Ante-Nicene Fathers*, edited by Alexander Roberts and James Donaldson. 1885. Grand Rapids: Wm. B. Eerdmans Publishing Co., 1985.

Jenson, Robert W. *Systematic Theology*. 2 vols. New York: Oxford University Press, 1997–99.

———. *The Triune Identity: God according to the Gospel.* Philadelphia: Fortress Press, 1982.

John of Damascus. *On the Orthodox Faith.* Translated by S. D. F. Salmond. In *Hilary of Poitiers, John of Damascus,* vol. 9 of *Nicene and Post-Nicene Fathers,* 2nd ser., edited by Philip Schaff and Henry Wace. 1899. Repr., Peabody, MA: Hendrickson Publishers, 1995.

———. *Three Treatises on the Divine Images.* Translated by Andrew Louth. Crestwood, NY: St. Vladimir's Seminary Press, 2003.

Julian of Norwich. *Showings.* Translated by Edmund Colledge, OSA, and James Walsh, SJ. New York: Paulist Press, 1978.

Jüngel, Eberhard. *The Doctrine of the Trinity: God's Being Is Becoming.* Translated by Horton Harris. Edinburgh: Scottish Academic Press, 1976.

Justin Martyr. *Dialogue with Trypho, a Jew.* In *The Apostolic Fathers with Justin Martyr and Irenaeus,* vol. 1 of *The Ante-Nicene Fathers,* edited by Alexander Roberts and James Donaldson. 1885. Repr., Grand Rapids: Wm. B. Eerdmans Publishing Co., 1985.

———. *First Apology.* In *Early Christian Fathers,* translated and edited by Cyril C. Richardson. New York: Collier, 1970.

Käsemann, Ernst. *Commentary on Romans.* Translated and edited by Geoffrey W. Bromiley. Grand Rapids: Wm. B. Eerdmans Publishing Co., 1980.

Kasper, Walter. *The God of Jesus Christ.* Translated by Matthew J. O'Connell. New York: Crossroad, 1991.

Keller, Catherine. *Face of the Deep: A Theology of Becoming.* New York: Routledge, 2003.

Kelly, J. N. D. *Early Christian Creeds.* 1960. 3rd ed. London: Continuum, 2006.

Kelsey, David H. "The Doctrine of Creation from Nothing." In *Evolution and Creation,* edited by Ernan McMullin, 176–96. Notre Dame, IN: University of Notre Dame Press, 1985.

———. *Eccentric Existence: A Theological Anthropology.* 2 vols. Louisville, KY: Westminster John Knox Press, 2009.

King, Robert H. *The Meaning of God.* Philadelphia: Fortress Press, 1973.

Lindbeck, George A. *The Nature of Doctrine: Religion and Theology in a Postliberal Age.* Philadelphia: Westminster Press, 1984.

Lossky, Vladimir. *In the Image and Likeness of God.* Edited by John H. Erickson and Thomas E. Bird. Crestwood, NY: St. Vladimir's Seminary Press, 1985.

Louth, Andrew. *Maximus the Confessor.* New York: Routledge, 1996.

Lovelock, James. *Gaia: A New Look at Life on Earth.* New York: Oxford University Press, 2000.

Luther, Martin. *Confession concerning Christ's Supper.* In *Word and Sacrament* III. Vol. 37 of *Luther's Works.* Edited and translated by Robet H. Fischer. American ed. Philadelphia: Fortress Press, 1961.

———. *Large Catechism.* In *The Book of Concord: The Confessions of the Evangelical Lutheran Church.* Translated and edited by Theodore G. Tappert. Philadelphia: Muhlenberg Press, 1959.

Marshall, Bruce D. "Christ and the Cultures: The Jewish people and Christian Theology." In *The Cambridge Companion to Christian Doctrine,* edited by Colin E. Gunton, 81–100. Cambridge: Cambridge University Press, 1997.

Maximus the Confessor. *The Ascetic Life; The Four Centuries on Charity.* Translated by Polycarp Sherwood. New York: Newman Press, 1955.

———. *Disputatio cum Pyrrho.* In *Maximi Confessoris Opera omnia,* in vol. 91 of Patrologiae cursus completus: Series graeca [PG], edited by J.-P. Migne, cols. 287–360. Paris, 1863.

———. *On the Cosmic Mystery of Jesus Christ: Selected Writings from St. Maximus the Confessor.* Translated by Paul Blowers and Robert Louis Wilken. Crestwood, NY: St. Vladimir's Seminary Press, 2003.

———. *Maximus Confessor: Selected Writings.* Translated by George C. Berthold. New York: Paulist Press, 1985.

May, Gerhard. *Creatio ex Nihilo: The Doctrine of "Creation out of Nothing" in Early Christian Thought.* Translated by A. S. Worrall. Edinburgh: T&T Clark, 1994.

McCabe, Herbert. "Aquinas on the Trinity." In *Silence and the Word: Negative Theology and Incarnation,* edited by Oliver Davies and Denys Turner, 76–93. Cambridge: Cambridge University Press, 2002.

McFarland, Ian A. "Christ, Spirit and Atonement." *International Journal of Systematic Theology* 3 (March 2001): 83–93.

Meyendorff, John. *Christ in Eastern Christian Thought.* Crestwood, NY: St. Vladimir's Seminary Press, 1975.

Milbank, John. "Can a Gift Be Given? Prolegomena to a Future Trinitarian Metaphysic." *Modern Theology* 11 (January 1995): 119–61.

———. "The Second Difference: For a Trinitarianism without Reserve." *Modern Theology* 2 (April 1986): 213–34.

Moltmann, Jürgen. *The Crucified God: The Cross of Christ as the Foundation and Criticism of Christian Theology.* 1974. Repr., Minneapolis: Fortress Press, 1993.

———. *God in Creation: A New Theology of Creation and the Spirit of God.* Translated by Margaret Kohl. 1985. Repr., New York: Harper & Row, 1991.

Nellas, Panayiotis. *Deification in Christ: The Nature of the Human Person.* Translated by Norman Russell. Crestwood, NY: St. Vladimir's Seminary Press, 1997.

Neusner, Jacob. *Genesis Rabbah: The Judaic Commentary to the Book of Genesis; A New American Translation.* Vol. 1. Atlanta: Scholars Press, 1985.

Newsom, Carol A. *The Book of Job: A Contest of Moral Imagination.* New York: Oxford University Press, 2003.

———. "Job." In *Women's Bible Commentary.* Edited by Carol A. Newsom and Sharon H. Ringe. Louisville, KY: Westminster John Knox Press, 1998.

Nicholas of Cusa. *Nicholas of Cusa on God as Not-Other: A Translation and Appraisal of "De li non aliud."* 2nd ed. Translated by Jasper Hopkins. Minneapolis: Arthur J. Banning Press, 1983.

Norris, Richard A., Jr. *God and World in Early Christian Theology.* New York: Seabury Press, 1965.

O'Donovan, Oliver. *Resurrection and the Moral Order: An Outline for Evangelical Ethics.* Grand Rapids: Wm. B. Eerdmans Publishing Co., 1986.

Origen. *Contra Celsum.* Translated by Henry Chadwick. Cambridge: Cambridge University Press, 1965.

Orthodox Eastern Church. *The Acts and Decrees of the Synod of Jerusalem.* Translated by J. N. W. B. Robertson. London: Thomas Baker, 1899.

Ouspensky, Leonid, and Vladimir Lossky. *The Meaning of Icons.* Translated by G. E. H. Palmer and E. Kadloubovsky. Crestwood, NY: St. Vladimir's Seminary Press, 1982.

Page, Ruth. *God and the Web of Creation.* London: SCM Press, 1996.

Pannenberg, Wolfhart. *Systematic Theology.* 3 vols. Translated by Geoffrey W. Bromiley. 1988–93. Repr., Grand Rapids: Wm. B. Eerdmans Publishing Co., 1991–98.

Placher, William C. *The Domestication of Transcendence: How Modern Thinking about God Went Wrong.* Louisville, KY: Westminster John Knox Press, 1996.

Plantinga, Alvin. *The Nature of Necessity.* Oxford: Oxford University Press, 1974.

Plato. *Plato's Cosmology: The "Timaeus" of Plato.* Translated by Francis MacDonald Cornford. 1937. Repr., Indianapolis: Bobbs-Merrill Co., 1959.

Polkinghorne, John. *Quarks, Chaos, and Christianity.* London: Triangle, 1994. 2nd ed. London: SPCK, 2005.

———. *Science and Providence: God's Interaction with the World.* 1989. Templeton ed. Philadelphia: Templeton Foundation Press, 2005.

Preller, Victor. *Divine Science and the Science of God: A Reformulation of Thomas Aquinas.* Princeton, NJ: Princeton University Press, 1967.

Prenter, Regin. *Creation and Redemption.* Philadelphia: Fortress Press, 1967.

Presbyterian Church (U.S.A.). *Book of Confessions: Study Edition.* Louisville, KY: Geneva Press, 1996.

Quenot, Michel. *The Icon: Window on the Kingdom.* Crestwood, NY: St. Vladimir's Seminary Press, 2002.

Rad, Gerhard von. *Old Testament Theology.* 2 vols. Translated by D. M. G. Stalker. New York: Harper & Row, 1962–65.

Rahner, Karl. *The Trinity.* Translated by J. Donceel. New York: Herder & Herder, 1970.

Ratzinger, Joseph [Pope Benedict XVI]. *Introduction to Christianity.* London: Burns & Oates, 1969.

Raup, David, and Steven M. Stanley. *Principles of Paleontology.* 2nd ed. New York: W. H. Freeman, 1978.

Reumann, John. *Creation and New Creation: The Past, Present, and Future of God's Creative Activity.* Minneapolis: Augsburg Publishing House, 1973.

Richardson, Cyril C., trans. and ed. *Early Christian Fathers.* New York: Macmillan, 1970.

Rogers, Eugene F., Jr. *After the Spirit: A Constructive Pneumatology from Resources outside the Modern West.* Grand Rapids: Wm. B. Eerdmans Publishing Co., 2005.

Rubenstein, Richard L. *After Auschwitz: History, Theology, and Contemporary Judaism.* Baltimore: Johns Hopkins University Press, 1992.

Ryle, Gilbert. *Collected Essays, 1929–1968.* Vol. 2 of *Collected Papers.* London: Hutchinson, 1971. Repr., London: Routledge, 2009.

Samuelson, Norbert M. *Judaism and the Doctrine of Creation.* Cambridge: Cambridge University Press, 1994.

Saunders, Jason L., ed. *Greek and Roman Philosophy after Aristotle.* New York: The Free Press, 1966.

Saunders, Nicholas. *Divine Action and Modern Science.* Cambridge: Cambridge University Press, 2002.

Schmid, Heinrich. *Doctrinal Theology of the Evangelical Lutheran Church.* Translated by Charles A. Hay and Henry E. Jacobs. 3rd ed. Minneapolis: Augsburg Publishing House, 1899.

The Seven Ecumenical Councils. Vol. 14 of *Nicene and Post-Nicene Fathers,* 2nd ser., edited by Philip Schaff and Henry Wace. 1900. Repr., Peabody, MA: Hendrickson Publishers, 1995.

Sittler, Joseph. *Evocations of Grace: Writings on Ecology, Theology, and Ethics.* Edited by Steven Bouma-Prediger and Peter Bakken. Grand Rapids: Wm. B. Eerdmans Publishing Co., 2000.

Speiser, Ephraim Avigdor. *Genesis: Introduction, Translation, and Notes.* Garden City, NY: Doubleday, 1964.

Stăniloae, Dumitru. *Theology and the Church.* Translated by Robert Barringer. Crestwood, NY: St. Vladimir's Seminary Press, 1980.

Tanner, Kathryn. *Christ the Key.* Cambridge: Cambridge University Press, 2010.

———. *Economy of Grace.* Minneapolis: Fortress Press, 2005.

———. *God and Creation in Christian Theology: Tyranny or Empowerment?* Oxford: Basil Blackwell, 1988.

———. "Is God in Charge?" In *Essentials of Christian Theology,* edited by William C. Placher, 116–31. Louisville, KY: Westminster John Knox Press, 2003.

Tappert, Theodore G., ed. and trans. *The Book of Concord: The Confessions of the Evangelical Lutheran Church*. Philadelphia: Muhlenberg Press, 1959.

Teilhard de Chardin, Pierre. *The Phenomenon of Man*. Translated by Bernard Wall. 1955. Repr., New York: Harper Colophon, 1975.

Tertullian. *Against Hermogenes*. In *Latin Christianity: Its Founder, Tertullian*, edited by Allan Menzies, vol. 3 of *The Ante-Nicene Fathers*, edited by Alexander Roberts and James Donaldson. 1885. Repr., Peabody, MA: Hendrickson Publishers, 1999.

Theodore the Studite. *On the Holy Icons*. Translated by Catharine P. Roth. Crestwood, NY: St. Vladimir's Seminary Press, 2001.

Theophilus of Antioch. *To Autolycus*. Translated by Marcus Dods. In *Fathers of the Second Century*, vol. 2 of *The Ante-Nicene Fathers*, edited by Alexander Roberts and James Donaldson. 1885. Repr., Peabody, MA: Hendrickson Publishers, 1999.

Thomas Aquinas. *Compendium of Theology*. Translated by Cyril Vollert. St. Louis: B. Herder, 1952.

———. *On Creation*. Translated by S. C. Selner-Wright. Washington, DC: Catholic University of America Press, 2011.

———. *On Evil*. Edited by Richard Regan. Translated by Brian Davies. New York: Oxford University Press, 2003.

———. *Summa theologiae*. 61 vols. Blackfriars ed. London: Eyre & Spottiswood, 1964–81.

Thunberg, Lars. *Microcosm and Mediator: The Theological Anthropology of Maximus the Confessor*. 2nd ed. LaSalle, IL: Open Court, 1995.

Watson, Francis. *Text and Truth: Redefining Biblical Theology*. Edinburgh: T&T Clark, 1997.

Welker, Michael. *Creation and Reality*. Translated by John F. Hoffmyer. Minneapolis: Fortress Press, 1999.

Westermann, Claus. *Genesis 1–11: A Commentary*. Translated by John J. Scullion, SJ. 1974. Repr., Minneapolis: Augsburg Publishing House, 1984.

———. *God's Angels Need No Wings*. Translated by D. L. Scheidt. Philadelphia: Fortress Press, 1979.

Whitehead, Alfred North. *Process and Reality: An Essay in Cosmology*. New York: Macmillan, 1929.

Willard, Dallas. *The Divine Conspiracy: Rediscovering Our Hidden Life in God*. San Francisco: HarperSanFrancisco, 1998.

Williams, Rowan. *On Christian Theology*. Oxford: Blackwell, 2000.

Wolter, Allan B. *The Philosophical Theology of John Duns Scotus*. Edited by Marilyn McCord Adams. Ithaca, NY: Cornell University Press, 1990.

Wood, Charles M. *The Question of Providence*. Louisville, KY: Westminster John Knox Press, 2008.

Wright, N. T. *Scripture and the Authority of God: How to Read the Bible Today*. New York: HarperOne, 2013.

Scripture Index

199

Subject Index

CPSIA information can be obtained
at www.ICGtesting.com
Printed in the USA
LVOW03s1922300817
546963LV00021B/1654/P